Mastering Arabic 1

Third edition

Jane Wightwick &
Mahmoud Gaafar

HIPPOCRENE BOOKS, INC.
New York

Hippocrene Books, Inc. edition, 2015.

First published in English by Palgrave Macmillan, a division of Macmillan Publishers Limited under the title *Mastering Arabic 1 Book, 3rd edition* by Jane Wightwick and Mahmoud Gaafar. This edition has been published under license from Palgrave Macmillan. The authors have asserted their right to be identified as the author of this Work.
For copyright reasons this edition is not for sale outside of the United States, Canada, and dependencies.

ISBN 13: 978-0-7818-1338-9
ISBN 10: 0-7818-1338-7

First edition 1990
Second edition 2007
Third edition 2015

Cataloging-in-Publication data available from the Library of Congress.

For more information, contact:
HIPPOCRENE BOOKS, INC.
171 Madison Avenue
New York, NY 10016
www.hippocrenebooks.com

Printed by CPI Group (UK) Ltd, Croydon CR0 4YY

to Leila

Contents

Preface

In developing the *Mastering Arabic* series we have always been concerned to make the course as approachable and enjoyable as possible. In preparing this third edition of *Mastering Arabic 1* we have again looked closely at how we might improve the experience of learning Arabic and hope that our innovations in this edition will build on the success of earlier editions. For example, the introduction of colour has allowed us to signal important language points, to enhance the visual accessibility, and to use photos that put the Arabic language in its cultural context from the very beginning.

At the same time we have enhanced the accompanying website, in particular by adding new video material which is integrated into the text with questions and photos. Also on the website are interactive flashcards, further activities, and additional reference both for the individual learner and for the classroom teacher.

We now have a very long list of teachers, learners and academics who have kindly contributed to and reviewed *Mastering Arabic 1* since its inception. There is no longer room to name them all, but special mention for this edition goes to Souad Baameur, Lecturer for Arabic Language and Culture at Richmond, the American International University in London; Taoufiq Cherkaoui, Lead Practitioner of Arabic, French and Assessment for Learning, and Education Consultant for Cambridge International Examinations; and Dr Abul Kalam Azad, Principal at Briton College, London. The course is immeasurably better for the input from all of our contributors.

We are grateful to everyone at Palgrave for their continued enthusiasm for *Mastering Arabic*, and specifically to Dominic Knight, Helen Bugler, Isobel Munday and Phillipa Davidson-Blake. For this edition, we would also like to thank Andrew Nash for his impeccable copyediting and helpful suggestions. They, together with an extraordinary number of other staff busying away in the background, have supported us all the way and helped to mould *Mastering Arabic* into what has proved to be a gratifyingly successful language-learning programme.

Jane Wightwick and *Mahmoud Gaafar*

Introduction

Overview of the Arabic language

Arabic is spoken in over twenty countries, from North-West Africa to the Arabian Gulf. This makes it one of the most widely-used languages in the world, and yet it is frequently regarded as obscure and mysterious. This perception is more often based on an over-emphasis on the difficulty of the Arabic script and the traditional nature of some of the learning material than it is on the complexity of the language itself. There is certainly no reason why the non-specialist should not be able to acquire a general, all-round knowledge of Arabic, and enjoy doing so.

Mastering Arabic 1 will provide anyone working alone or within a group with a lively, clear and enjoyable introduction to Arabic. When you have mastered the basics of the language, then you can go on to study a particular area in more detail if you want.

Before we go on to explain how to use this book, you should be introduced to the different kinds of Arabic that are written and spoken. These fall into three main categories:

Modern Standard Arabic

Modern Standard Arabic (MSA) is the universal language of the Arab World, understood by all Arabic-speakers. Almost all written material is in Modern Standard, as are formal and pan-Arab TV programmes, talks, etc.

Classical Arabic

This is the language of the Qur'an and classical literature. Its structure is similar to Modern Standard Arabic, but the style and much of the vocabulary are archaic. It is easier to begin by studying Modern Standard and then progress to classical texts, if that is what you wish to do.

Colloquial dialects

These are the spoken languages of the different regions of the Arab World. They are all more or less similar to the Modern Standard language. The colloquial dialects vary the most in everyday words and expressions, such as 'bread' or 'How are you?'

We have chosen to teach the Modern Standard in *Mastering Arabic 1* as it is a good starting point for beginners. Modern Standard is universally understood and is the best medium through which to master the Arabic script. However, whenever there are dialogues or situations where the colloquial language would naturally be used, we have tried to choose vocabulary and structures that are as close as possible to the spoken form. In this way, you will find that *Mastering Arabic* 1 enables you to understand Arabic in a variety of different situations and provides an excellent base from which to expand your knowledge of the written and spoken language.

How to use *Mastering Arabic 1*

This course has over two hours of accompanying audio and being able to access this recording is essential, unless you are studying in a group where the tutor has the audio. Those parts of the book which are on the recording are marked with this symbol: . The CD track number is referenced under the audio symbol for easy access.

The *Mastering Arabic* series also includes a free companion website offering a wealth of support for both learners and teachers (see page xiii). Links to the website are marked with symbols similar to this: web web web PPT.

We are assuming that when you start this course you know absolutely no Arabic at all and may be working by yourself. The individual units vary in how they present the material, but the most important thing to remember is to try not to skip anything (except perhaps the 'Structure notes' – see below). There are over two hundred exercises in the book, carefully designed to help you practise what you have learnt and to prepare you for what is coming. Work your way through these as they appear in the course, with the optional support of the companion website, and you will find that the language starts to fall into place and that words and phrases are revised. Above all, be patient and do not be tempted to cut corners.

Conversation sections
These sections are designed to introduce you to basic conversational Arabic in social and everyday situations so that you can get talking right from the start. They appear in all the units in the first half of the course, and then as appropriate in the later units.

Structure notes
These occur at the end of some units and contain useful additional information about Arabic grammar. They are not essential to your understanding of basic Arabic but will help you to recognise some of the finer points when you read or hear them.

Review units
These occur at three points in the course. They will be very useful to you in assessing how well you remember what you have learnt. If you find you have problems with a particular exercise, go back and review the section or sections of the book that cover that area.

Reference material
This section is found at the end of the book and includes alphabet and verb tables, lists of plurals and months of the year, a vocabulary glossary and an index for easy reference, plus answers to all the exercises in *Mastering Arabic 1.*

You'll find a brief audio introduction on the first track of CD1.

CD1: 01

Companion books

Alongside *Mastering Arabic 1* are three companion books: *Mastering Arabic 1: Activity Book*; *Mastering Arabic Grammar* (published in the US as *Easy Arabic Grammar*); and *Mastering Arabic Script* (published in the US as *Easy Arabic Script*). These complement the main course, providing extra practice and additional information.

So now you're ready to start learning with *Mastering Arabic 1*. We hope you enjoy the journey.

Acknowledgements and photo credits

The authors and publishers wish to thank the following who have kindly given permission for the use of copyright material: Oxford University Press for material from *The Oxford Arabic Dictionary*, 2014; Otto Harrassowitz Verlag for material from Hans Wehr, *A Dictionary of Modern Arabic*, ed. J. Milton Cowan, 1991.

The authors and publishers wish also to thank Amani Zitouni, Cyrine El Oued and Mahmoud Abdou for the use of their images and recorded video material.

Music for the audio was composed by Leila Gaafar.

The authors and publishers wish to acknowledge the following for permission to reproduce photographs:
123RF: Philip Lange p87; Robyn Mackenzie p125; Rostislav Glinsky p127; **Ahmed Rabea** p170; **Corbis** p198; **DIGITALVISION** p105; **Fotalia**: Rafael Ben-Ari p3, p211; Lucky elephant p8; al62 p13; Mahmoud Rahall p27; Jasmin Merdan p35, p37, p108; arturnyk p51; NCAimages p55; sunsinger p67; boyoz p71; philipus p91; somartin p104, p145; Ray p111, 115, 208 (*flags*); Richard Oechsner p119; jscalev p130; alekosa p137; Natika p146, 208 (*pens*); Sean p146 (*shoes*); Dmitry Vereshchagin p146 (*shirt*); Berna Safoglu p146 (*cap*); cristi180884 (*yellow bag*); Sergey Kravchenko p146 (*green bag*); Jonnystockphoto p146 (*trousers*); vvoe p157; Sophie James p162 (*Museum of Islamic Art*); luisapuccini p181; TravelPhotography p185; Byelikova Oksana p186; Photoerick p208 (*cars*); Mytho p208 (*plates*); Nico p214; Africa Studio p215 (*bell alarm clocks/English wall clock*); PepinoCZ p215 (*alarm clock bottom right*); jasckal p215 (*Arabic wall clock*); sergemi p229; Rubi Halfon p233; Marc Johnson p241; shazman p266; philipus p276; pseudopixels p284; **Getty Images** p197, 258; **istock**: Ileximage p208 (*chair*); arsenik p208 (*table*); frenchmen77 p208 (*door*); **Macmillan Australia** p28; **PIXTAL** p80, p83; **Shutterstock**: WitR p10; sowar online p17; Dmitry Kalinovsky p40; Jose Ignacio Soto p93; Maxim Tarasyugin p195

Free online companion website

www.palgrave.com/masteringarabic

The *Mastering Arabic* companion website is packed with a wealth of resources for both self-study and teaching. Take a look at some of the features:

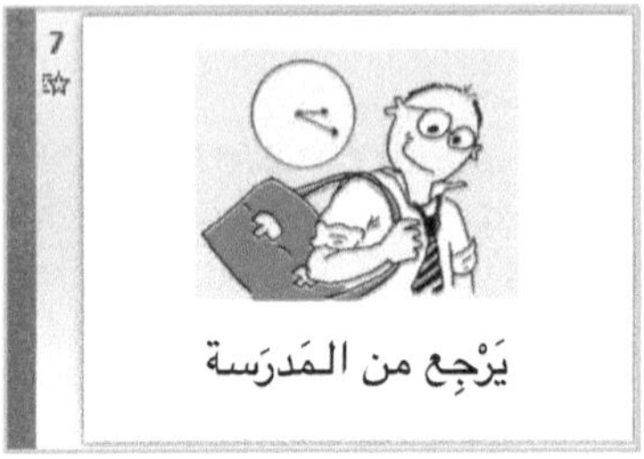

Lively PowerPoint® presentations are ideal for introducing or revising new language.

Engaging videos, featuring native speakers from different parts of the Arabic-speaking world, enhance listening skills.

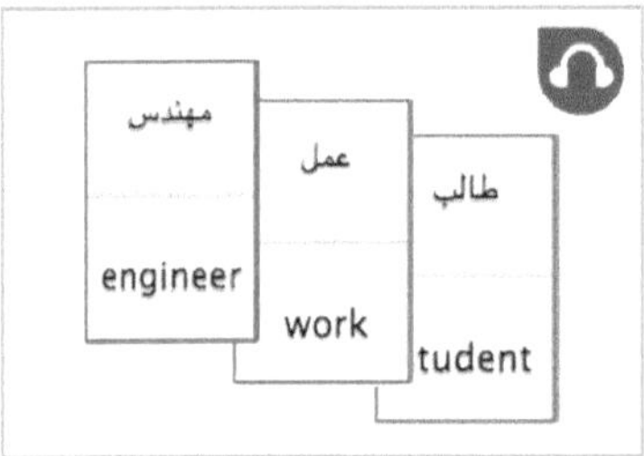

Audio flashcards teach you the spelling and pronunciation of essential words.

Printable transcripts allow you to check your understanding of the listening activities.

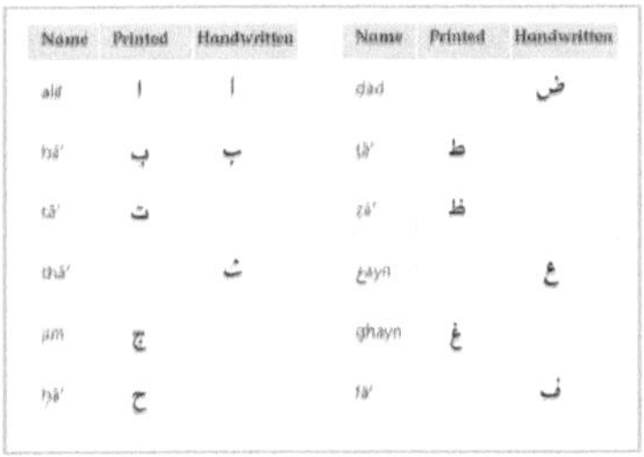

Enlarged, printable activities let you repeat selected exercises as many times as you want.

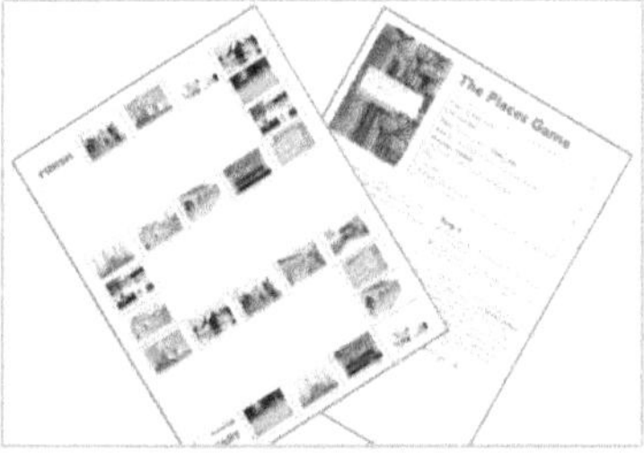

Stimulating classroom games boost skills in both spoken and written Arabic.

Language units

1 Getting started

Letters of the alphabet: group 1

Many Arabic letters can be grouped together according to their shapes. Some letters share exactly the same shape but have a different number of dots above or below; other shapes vary slightly.

Look at this group of letters and listen to the audio:

CD1: 02

	Name of letter	*Pronounced*
ب	bā'	'b' as in 'bat'
ت	tā'	't' as in 'tap'
ث	thā'	'th' as in 'thin'
ن	nūn	'n' as in 'nab'
ي	yā'	'y' as in 'yet'

You can see that bā', tā' and thā' share the same shape, but the position and the number of dots are different; whereas nūn has a slightly different shape, more circular and falling below the line, and yā' has a much curlier shape (but is connected with the other letters, as you will see later in Unit 1).

When Arabic is written by hand, the dots often become 'joined' for the sake of speed. Compare the printed and the handwritten letters opposite. It is useful to be able to recognise and write Arabic handwritten script from the beginning, but be aware that individual styles vary. Concentrate at first on the basic diferrences between printed and handwritten letters.

أهلاً وَسَهلاً! ahlan wa sahlan!
Hello and welcome! (Arab culture is famous for hospitality)

Printed letter	*Handwritten letter*
ب	ب
ت	ت
ث	ث
ن	ن
ي	ي

Exercise 1

Look at the letters below and decide which each is. Follow the exercise numbers right to left to accustom your eyes to moving in that direction.

Handwriting practice

(When practising handwriting, first trace the letters following the direction of the arrows, and then try writing them on lined paper.)

The Arabic script is written from *right* to *left*, so the letters should be formed starting from the *right*:

bā', tā', thā'

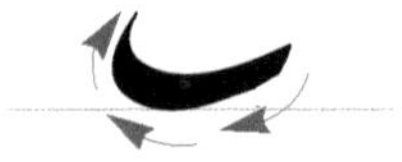

nūn

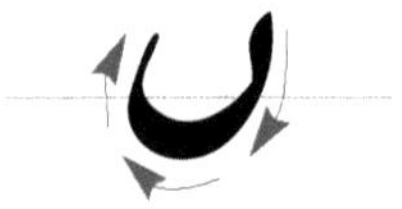

yā'

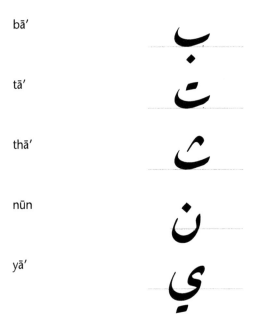

Finish the main shape of the letter first and then add the dots:

bā' ب

tā' ت

thā' ث

nūn ن

yā' ي

Tip: There are *no* capital letters in Arabic.

On the companion website (www.palgrave.com/masteringarabic) you can find a printable worksheet that will help you practise writing these letters.

Vowels

Arabic script is a form of shorthand. Not all the vowel sounds are included. The short vowels in Arabic (a, i, u) are written above and below the main script. If you read an Arabic newspaper, novel or website you will rarely see these vowels, as they are not usually written. Imagine the English sentence 'They can find the key.' as 'thy cn fnd th ky'. The Arabic reader is expected to deduce the meaning of words from experience and context.

Mastering Arabic 1 will begin by showing all the short vowels and will gradually drop them as you become more proficient.

CD1: 03

Look at these letters and listen to the audio:

بَ (ba) بِ (bi) بُ (bu)

From this you can see:

- A dash *above* the letter (ـَ) is pronounced as a short 'a' following the letter. This vowel is called fatḥa.
- A dash *below* the letter (ـِ) is pronounced as a short 'i' following the letter. This vowel is called kasra.
- A comma shape above the letter (ـُ) is pronounced as a short 'u' following the letter. This vowel is called ḍamma.

Exercise 2

CD1: 04

Listen to the audio and write the correct vowels on these letters:

7 ب	4 ث	1 ب
8 ث	5 ي	2 ن
	6 ت	3 ت

Exercise 3

Now practise saying these letters with their vowels; then check your pronunciation in the answer section at the back of the book.

7 نُ	4 تُ	1 بِ
8 ثُ	5 بَ	2 نَ
	6 تِ	3 يَ

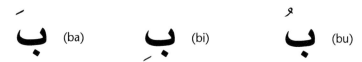

أبت Joining letters: group 1

Written Arabic is 'joined up'. When letters come at the end of a word they look very much as they do when standing alone. However, when they come at the beginning or in the middle of a word they get 'shortened'.

Look at how these letters combine:

←

(read *from right to left*)

ب + ث = بث

ت + ب = تب

ث + ب + ت = ثبت

Notice how the letter gets 'chopped' and loses its final flourish, or 'tail', when at the beginning or in the middle of a word, but still keeps its dots for recognition.

The letters nūn and yā' have exactly the same shape as the other letters in this group when they come at the beginning or in the middle of a word, but they retain their differences when at the end:

←

ب + ن = بن

ن + ي = ني

ب + ي + ت = بيت

ب + ن + ي = بني

ي + ب + ث = يبث

web On the *Mastering Arabic* website you can find a teaching grid with a unit-by-unit overview of how the *Mastering Arabic* companion books can support your learning, including handwriting practice and additional activities to reinforce your learning.

Handwriting practice

Notice how these letters are joined when written by hand:

ب + ث = بث

ب + ن = بن

ث + ب + ت = ثبت

ب + ن + ي = بني

It's easiest if you complete the main shape of the word and then go back to the right-hand side and add all the dots from right to left.

On the *Mastering Arabic* website you can find a printable worksheet that will help you practise handwriting these combinations.

Exercise 4

Look at the newspaper headline below. Two examples of the letters in group 1 are circled. How many others can you find?

Tip: When yā' is by itself or at the end of a word, you may see it without the two dots.

اتصالات ناجحة أعادت الأمور إلى
طبيعتها بين السعودية ولبنان

Exercise 5

Handwrite these combinations of letters.
The first is an example:

1 ت + ي + ن = تين

2 ن + ي = ______

3 ت + ب + ن = ______

4 ن + ب + ت = ______

5 ي + ب + ن + ي = ______

6 ب + ي + ت + ي = ______

تين tīn *Figs*

Adding vowels to words

We can now add vowels to the combinations of letters to make words:

تُ (tu) + ب (b) = تُب (tub)

بِ (bi) + ن (n) = بِن (bin)

بِ (bi) + ن (n) + ت (t) = بِنْت (bint)

بَ (ba) + ي (y) + نَ (na) =بَيْنَ (bayna)

Sukūn

A small circle (sukūn) above a letter (ـْ) indicates that there is *no* vowel sound after that letter – see bint and bayna above. Notice that the sukūn is not usually put above the *last* letter of a word.

Exercise 6

CD1: 05

Listen to the audio and write the vowels on these words. Each word will be said twice.

1 بيت	4 ثبت
2 ثبتت	5 يثب
3 تبن	6 ثبن

Shadda

In addition to the three short vowels and the sukūn, there is another symbol: the shadda. This is a small *w* shape (ـّ) written above the letter to indicate that the sound is doubled. For example:

بَ (ba) + ث (th) + ث (th) = بَثّ (bathth)

بُ (bu) + ن (n) + ن (n) = بُنّ (bunn)

The sound of a letter is doubled when there is a shadda. Take care to pronounce this by lingering on the doubled sound, otherwise you may change the meaning of the word.

CD1: 06

Listen to these examples and repeat them with the audio. Each example is given twice. Notice that kasra is often written below the shadda (ـِّ) rather than below the letter itself – see example 5:

1 بَثَّ	4 بُنّ
*2 ثَبَّتَ	5 بَيِّن
*3 ثَبَتَ	6 يَبُثُّ

* *To hear the* shadda *compare the pronunciation of examples 2 and 3.*

Exercise 7

CD1: 07

Write these letter combinations and then try to pronounce them. Check your pronunciation with the audio or answer section.

1 بَ + ت + ت = ________

2 بَ + ي + يِ + ن = ________

3 تُ + ن + ن = ________

4 نَ + ي + ي = ________

Exercise 8

Look at these words and try to remember the meanings:

C بِنْت

B بَيْت

A تِبْن

E بَيْن

D بُنّ

Handwrite the Arabic words on a separate piece of paper and cover the pictures. Then match the Arabic words you have written with this English:

1 girl/daughter **2** coffee beans **3** house **4** hay **5** between

Conversation sections

The Conversation panels are designed to introduce you to basic conversational Arabic in social and everyday situations. They appear in all the units in the first half of the course, and then as appropriate in the later units.

You'll find the expressions in these panels on the audio, and you'll also be given the opportunity to take part in short dialogues with native speakers. Concentrate on speaking and listening in these sections. At first you may not be able to read all the Arabic script, but you will be able to recognise some of the letters and words.

صباح الخير ṣabāḥ al-khayr

Good morning (Sunrise over Luxor)

CD1: 08

 Conversation

Greetings and leave-taking

One of the most important conversational skills initially in any language is to know how to greet people. Arabic greetings can be elaborate and prolonged, but some all-purpose expressions will get you by:

أَهلاً	(ahlan)	Hello
أَهلاً وَسَهلاً	(ahlan wa sahlan)	Hello and welcome
أَهلاً بِك/بِكِ	(ahlan bik/biki)	Hello to you *(talking to a male/female)*
صَبَاح الخَير	(ṣabāḥ al-khayr)	Good morning
صَبَاح النُّور	(ṣabāḥ an-nūr)	Good morning *(reply)*
مَسَاء الخَير	(masā' al-khayr)	Good evening
مَسَاء النُّور	(masā' an-nūr)	Good evening *(reply)*
مَعَ السَّلامة	(maɛa s-salāma)	Goodbye

Tip: The reply to a greeting often varies from the original, although it is also acceptable simply to repeat the original phrase in reply.

 Vocabulary in Unit 1

بِنْت	(bint) girl/daughter	بُنّ	(bunn) coffee beans
بَيْت	(bayt) house	بَيْنَ	(bayna) between
تِبن	(tibn) hay	تِين	(tīn) figs

أَهلاً (ahlan) Hello

أَهلاً وَسَهلاً (ahlan wa sahlan) Hello and welcome

أَهلاً بِك/بِكِ (ahlan bik/biki) Hello to you

صَبَاح الخَير (ṣabāḥ al-khayr) Good morning

صَبَاح النُّور (ṣabāḥ an-nūr) Good morning *(reply)*

مَسَاء الخَير (masā' al-khayr) Good evening/afternoon

مَسَاء النُّور (masā' an-nūr) Good evening/afternoon *(reply)*

مَعَ السَّلامة (maɛa s-salāma) Goodbye

 You'll find a PowerPoint presentation on the companion website to help you remember the key words in every unit.

Vocabulary learning

Arabic presents some challenges to the beginner trying to learn vocabulary, as both the words *and* the script are unfamiliar. However, you can use strategies to help yourself. One method recommended for learning vocabulary in new scripts is the use of flashcards, similar to the method used to teach young children how to read.

Try the following method to learn your vocabulary:

- Make a set of small cards, blank on both sides.
- Get five envelopes and mark them 'Day 1', 'Day 2', etc.
- Write each Arabic word, with vowels in pencil, on one side of a card and the English on the other:

  This is good handwriting practice and will help you remember the word.
- Put each card Arabic side up and say the Arabic aloud. Try to remember what it means. When you've finished, shuffle the cards and put them *English* side up, this time trying to remember the Arabic.
- If you remember a word, move that card to the 'Day 2' envelope; if you forget, put it in the 'Day 1' envelope.
- Each day, take the cards out of each envelope in turn starting with the highest-numbered envelope and working down to 'Day 1'. (After you have completed five days you'll have cards in each envelope.)
- If you forget a card at any point it returns to the 'Day 1' envelope.

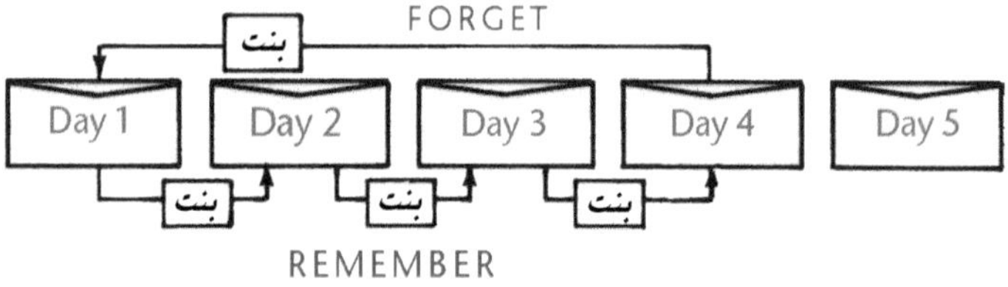

- If you can remember a word five days running you can throw the card away. (Or you could erase the pencil vowel marks and put it back in the 'Day 1' envelope.)
- You can add up to 15 words a day to the 'Day 1' envelope. How many you add will depend on the progress of the other cards up the sequence of envelopes.

You can adapt the method above for electronic flashcards. The *Mastering Arabic* companion website has some ready-made online flashcards. In addition, there are various flashcard websites and downloadable apps that will allow you to make and sort your own Arabic flashcards.

2 Putting words together

Letters of the alphabet: group 2

Look at the next group of letters and listen to the audio:

CD1: 09

	Name of letter	*Pronounced*
ا	alif	(see pages 17 and 20)
د	dāl	'd' as in 'dad'
ذ	dhāl	'th' as in 'that'
ر	rā'	rolled 'r' as in Spanish 'arriva'
ز	zāy	'z' as in 'zone'
و	wāw	'w' as in 'wet'

بيتزا وزَيتون bītzā wa zaytūn

Pizza and olives

You can see that the dāl and dhāl have the same basic shape, as do rā' and zāy. The only difference is that dhāl and zāy have the dot over the basic shape. Pay special attention to the position and shape of these four letters – dāl and dhāl sit *on* the line while rā' and zāy fall *under* the line.

Wāw and alif have very distinctive shapes, but their connection with the other letters in this group will become clear later in this unit.

As there are no dots to 'join up' in this group of letters, the handwritten versions tend to look very similar to the printed versions.

Exercise 1

Draw a line between the printed letters, their handwritten versions and the names of the letters, as in the example:

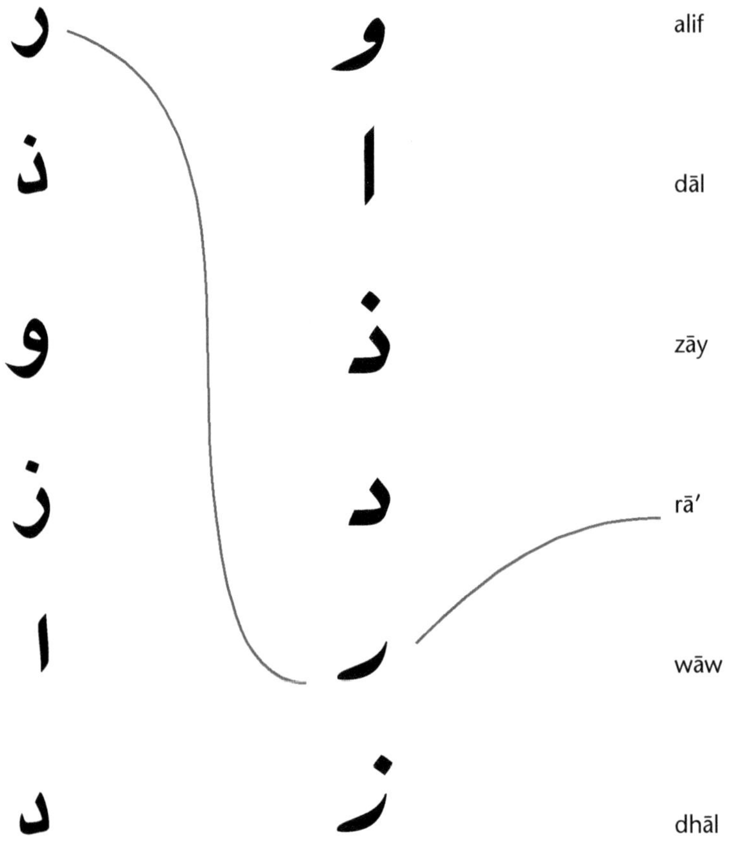

Handwriting practice

dāl, dhāl

rā', zāy

wāw

alif

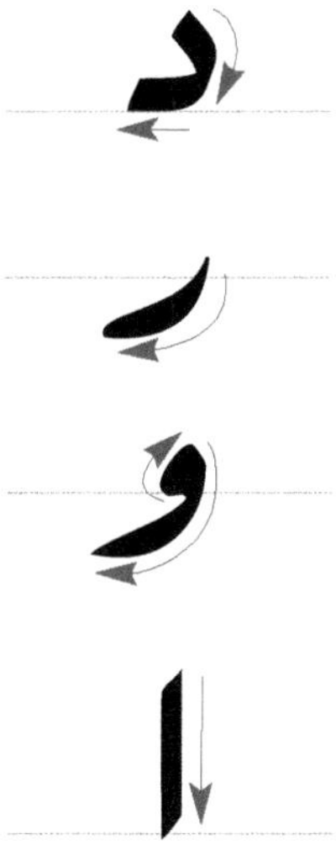

Remember, finish the shape first and then add any dots:

ا د ذ ر ز و

On the website you can find a worksheet to practise handwriting these letters.

Joining letters: group 2

The similarity between the letters in group 2 becomes clear when we look at how they are joined to other letters. All of the six letters in this group are joined to the letter *before* but cannot be joined to the letter *after*. Look at how alif joins in these combinations:

ب + ا = با

ا + ب = اب

ب + ا + ب = باب

The letters in group 2 have the same basic shape wherever they appear in a word, and *always* have a space after because they do not join to the next letter.

←

ن + ا + ر = نار

ب + ر + د = برد

ز + ي + ن = زين

ا + ب + د + ا = ابدا

ذ + و + ب = ذوب

و + ز + ي + ر = وزير

The letters in group 2 are the only letters which cannot be joined to the letter following in a word. All other letters can be joined on either side.

Exercise 2

Fill in the missing letters and pronunciation as in the example:

(bard) بَرْد	=	(d) د	+	(r) ر	+	(ba) بَ	1
وَرْد	=		+		+		2
رَبْو	=		+		+		3
	=	ر	+	ذ	+	بَ	4
بِرّ	=		+		+		5
	=	بُ	+	ثِ	+	يَ	6
ثَوْب	=		+		+		7
	=	زَ	+	رَ	+	دَ	8

Long vowels

In Unit 1 you met the three Arabic vowel signs: fatḥa (a), kasra (i) and ḍamma (u). These are all pronounced as short vowels. They can be made long by adding the three letters alif (ا), yā' (ي) and wāw (و).

CD1: 10

Look at the following and listen to the audio:

با (bā)	←	بَ (ba)
بي (bī)	←	بِ (bi)
بو (bū)	←	بُ (bu)

From this you should be able to see that long vowels are made like this:

letter + alif = ā (long 'a' as in h*ai*r or as in f*a*r)

letter + yā' = ī (long 'i' as in m*ee*t)

letter + wāw = ū (long 'u' as in b*oo*t)

Tip: The pronunciation of the long ā varies, depending on the sounds before and after it. For example, the ā in the word باب bāb (door/gate) is pronounced as in 'hair'; but in the word نار nār (fire) the ā is pronounced as in 'far'.

بَاب زُوَيلة bāb zuwayla

Zuweila Gate (Old Cairo)

Handwriting practice

Practise copying these words. Remember to write the whole word and then add the dots.

ابن ود دار ثوب نزور يبرد

On the website you can find a worksheet to help you practise handwriting these combinations.

Now listen to the pairs of words on the audio and then repeat them. Listen carefully for the difference in the short and long vowels. Each pair is given twice:

CD1: 11

1 نُذُر	2 بَرَّد	3 يَزِد
نُذور	بَرّاد	يَزيد

It may have occurred to you that if the vowel signs are not usually included at all in written Arabic, then pronunciation requires interpretation. For example, if you come across this word ...

زور

it could be pronounced:

زور (zūr) or ...

زَوْر (zawr) or ...

زَوَر (zawar) or even ...

زَوَّرَ (zawwara) or ...

زُوِّرَ (zuwwira).

(All of these words exist!) The answer is that you do not know *automatically*. However, when you have learned more about the structure and vocabulary patterns in Arabic, you will usually be able to tell from the context.

Exercise 3

Listen to the audio and write the short vowels on these words as appropriate. Each word will be given twice.

CD1: 12

1 وزير
2 دين
3 دين
4 بيت
5 يريد
6 بريد
7 بين
8 بين
9 زين
10 وارد

Exercise 4

Now try and write the eight words you hear, with their short vowels. Each word will be given twice.

CD1: 13

Alif

Alif is unique amongst Arabic letters because it does not have a definite sound. There are two main ways an alif is used:

1 To form the long vowel ā (see page 17).

2 To 'carry' a short vowel. If a word begins with a short vowel, the vowel sign cannot simply hang in the air before the next letter. So the vowel sign is placed above or under an alif, as in these examples:

أَب (ab)   أُريد (urīd)   إِن (in)

The small 'c' shape (ء) that accompanies the vowel sign is known as hamza. (For more details about hamza, see Unit 6, page 77.)

Don't forget: you'll find more details of the *Mastering Arabic* companion books on the series website. These include additional activities to help you practise reading and writing the Arabic script.

Listen carefully to these words, each of which begins with a vowel carried by an alif.

CD1: 14

1	إِذْن	4	أَنَا
2	أُذْن	5	أَنْتَ
3	إِيران	6	أَنْتِ

Putting words together

Look at the pictures and listen to the audio.

CD1: 15

أَنْوَر

نور

أَنوَر وَنور

Tip: وَ (wa, 'and') is written joined to the word that follows:

أَنوَر وَنور (anwar wa-nūr, 'Anwar and Nour').

Exercise 5

Look at these pictures and read the names. Check your pronunciation with the audio or in the answer section.

CD1: 16

Now choose the correct description for each picture:

A

1 زيد وبدر
2 دينا ونادر
3 زينب وزيد
4 زينب وبدر

B

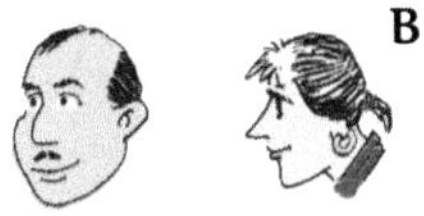

1 بدر وزين
2 نادر وبدر
3 زين ونادر
4 زينب ودينا

C

1 دينا وزينب
2 زيد وزينب
3 زيد وزين
4 دينا ونادر

D

1 دينا وزين
2 بدر ونادر
3 زيد ودينا
4 زين وزيد

Tip: Watch out for the difference in pronunciation between yā' representing the long vowel ī (e.g. the name dīnā) and yā' with a fatḥa over the letter before, when the combination is pronounced ay (zayd). Without the short vowels these look the same in Arabic script, so you need to remember the individual pronunciation. The same is true of wāw representing the long vowel ū (nūr) and with a fatḥa over the letter before, when it is pronounced aw as in 'how' (fawzī).

web PPT

You'll find a downloadable PowerPoint presentation on the website to help you read and pronounce these Arabic names.

Simple sentences

CD1: 17

Look at the picture and listen to the audio.

Many Arabic sentences do not need the verb 'to be' in the present tense (am, is, are). This means that you can have a sentence with no verb at all. (These sentences are called *nominal sentences*.)

أنا زيد. — I (am) Zaid.

أنت نادر. — You (are) Nadir.

Handwriting practice

Practise writing these sentences, firstly with the vowels and then without.

أَنا نادِر. أنا نادر.

أَنتِ دينا. أنت دينا.

Exercise 6

Look at the pictures and make sentences for each bubble:

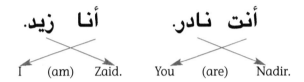

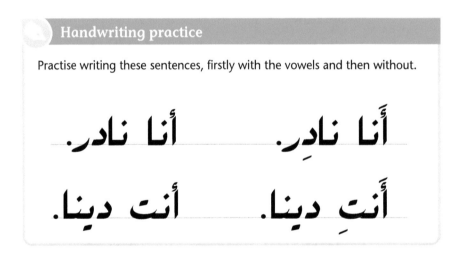

CD1: 18

Conversation

Introducing yourself

The simplest way to introduce yourself is to use ānā ... (I'm ...) or ānā ismī ... (My name's ...). Listen and repeat these expressions.

أنا نادر. (ānā nādir.)/أنا اسمي نادر. (ānā ismī nādir.)
I'm Nadir./My name's Nadir.

أنا دينا. (ānā dīnā.)/أنا اسمي دينا. (ānā ismī dīnā.)
I'm Dina./My name's Dina.

صباح الخير. أنا نادر زيدان. (ṣabāḥ al-khayr. ānā nādir zīdān.)
Good morning. I'm Nadir Zidane.

صباح النور. أنا اسمي دينا بدران. (ṣabāḥ an-nūr. ānā ismī dīnā badrān.)
Good morning. My name's Dina Badran.

For formal identification, Arabs may add the first name of their father. Western-style middle names are not common.

أنا اسمي نادر بدر زيدان. (ānā ismī nādir badr zīdān.)
My name's Nadir Badr Zidane.

أنا اسمي دينا أنور بدران. (ānā ismī dīnā anwar badrān.)
My name's Dina Anwar Badran.

Male and female

Listen to this conversation:

CD1: 19

(read *from right to left*) ←

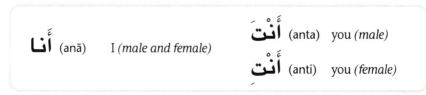

Look at the question (notice the reversed question mark):

وأَنْتِ؟ (wa-anti?), and you?

أَنْتِ (anti) is used only to refer to a female. Arabic makes a difference between male and female people and objects. It has two *genders*. So we have:

أَنا	(anā)	I *(male and female)*	أَنْتَ	(anta)	you *(male)*
			أَنْتِ	(anti)	you *(female)*

Exercise 7

Fill in the missing words in these conversations:

1

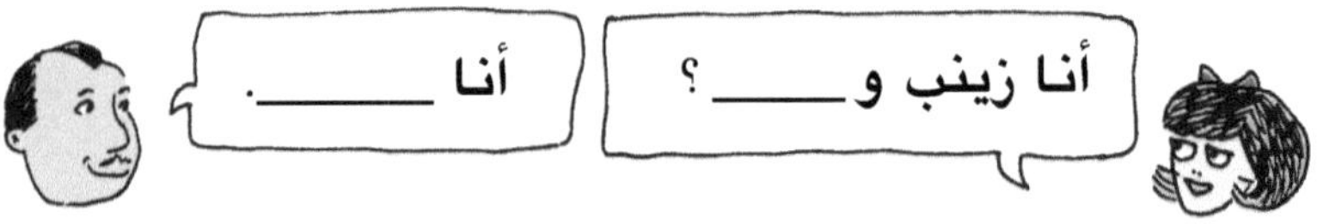

2

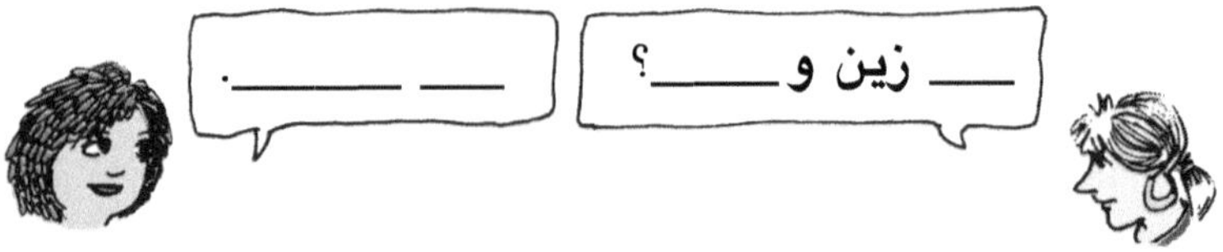

CD1: 20

Conversation

Meeting someone for the first time

You've learnt a few greetings and how to introduce yourself, so now you're ready to meet someone. After the introductions you could ask how someone is, or say you're pleased to meet him or her.

Listen to these conversations and then have a go at introducing yourself.

أهلاً. أنا توم، وأنتِ؟ (ahlan, anā Tom w-anti?) Hello, I'm Tom. And you?

أنا دينا. (anā dīnā) I'm Dina.

تشرّفنا يا دينا. (tasharrafnā yā dīnā) Pleased to meet you, Dina.

مَساء الخَير. أنا مدام لويس. (masā' al-khayr. anā madām lūwis) Good evening. I'm Mrs Lewis.

مَساء النور يا مدام لويس. كَيف الحال؟ (masā' an-nūr yā madām lūwis. kayf al-ḥāl?) Good evening, Mrs Lewis. How are you?

الحمدُ للّه. (al-ḥamdu lillāh) Fine, thanks ('thanks be to God').

Notice the use of يا (yā) when addressing someone by name. This is common in many parts of the Arab world.

You'll find a transcript of the conversation sections on the companion website.

Vocabulary in Unit 2

أَنا (anā) I

أنا إِسمي ... (ānā ismī ...) my name's ...

أَنْتَ (anta) you *(male)*

تَشَرَّفْنا (tasharrafnā) pleased to meet you

أَنْتِ (anti) you *(female)*

كَيْف الحال؟ (kayf al-ḥāl) how are you?

وَ (wa-) and

الحَمدُ للّه (al-ḥamdu lillāh) fine, thanks

3 The family

Letters of the alphabet: group 3

Look at the third group of letters and listen to the audio:

CD1: 21

	Name of letter	*Pronounced*
ج	jīm	'j' as in French 'je'
ح	ḥā'	Breathy, strong 'h'
خ	khā'	'ch' as in Scottish 'loch'
ه	hā'	'h' as in 'house'
م	mīm	'm' as in 'mastering'

Tip: jīm is commonly pronounced 'g' as in 'gate' by Egyptian Arabic-speakers.

There is an obvious similarity between the first three letters – jīm, khā' and ḥā'. The main letter has exactly the same basic shape: only the position of the dots will tell you which one it is.

The hā' and the mīm do not share their shapes with any other letters, but are included here for pronunciation and vocabulary reasons.

The pronunciation of ḥā' and khā' may be unfamiliar sounds to your ear. khā' is a sound similar to that made when clearing your throat. ḥā' is a breathy 'h' sometimes confused with hā' by beginners, so we will take extra care in showing you how to distinguish the two sounds.

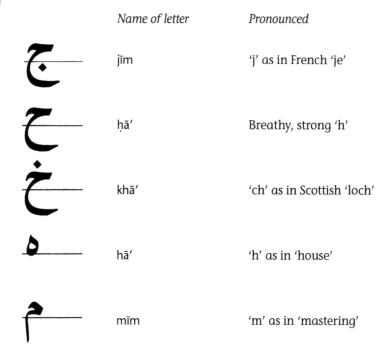

Exercise 1

CD1: 22

Listen to the audio and decide which is the first letter of each word. The first is an example. Each word is given twice.

1 خ (ح) ه
2 خ ح ه
3 خ ح ه
4 خ ح ه
5 خ ح ه
6 خ ح ه
7 خ ح ه
8 خ ح ه
9 خ ح ه
10 خ ح ه

Now replay the exercise, repeating the words after the audio.

Handwriting letters: group 3

Look at the handwritten versions of the letters in group 3:

Printed letter	*Handwritten letter*
ج	ج
ح	ح
خ	خ
ه	ه
م	م

Notice how jīm, hā' and khā' have an additional upwards stroke in the handwritten version, producing an enclosed loop at the top of the letter.

The 'head' of the mīm is produced by turning your pen in a tight circle on the same spot.

Handwriting practice

jīm, ḥā', khā'

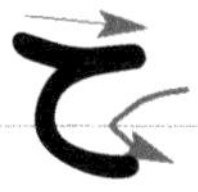

mīm

hā'

ج ح خ م ه

On the website you can find a worksheet to practise handwriting these letters.

Joining letters: jīm, ḥā', khā' and mīm

When these four letters are at the beginning or in the middle of a word, the part of the letter which falls below the line (the 'tail') gets 'chopped'. Only when they occur at the end of a word do they keep their tails.

ج + ر + ب = جرب

ح + ر + م = حرم

أ + خ + ت = أخت

أخ وأخت akh wa-ukht
Brother and sister

د + م + ج = دمج

م + ي + ز = ميز

أ + م = أم

Tip: Sometimes you can see the mīm positioned over the following letter and/or tucked in under the previous one (including another mīm). For example:

م + ح + ا = محا   م + م + ا = مما

Exercise 2

Join the words with the correct combinations of letters, as in the example:

1	أَ + ح + م + د	A	مِدْحَت
2	نَ + ج + ج + ا + ر	B	أَخ
3	ب + ح + ح + ا + ر	C	مَوْج
4	م + و + ج	D	نَجّار
5	م + د + ح + ت	E	نَجاح
6	أُ + خ + ت	F	بَحّار
7	أَ + خ	G	أَحْمَد
8	نَ + ج + ا + ح	H	أُخْت

CD1: 23 Now try to pronounce the words. Check your answer and pronunciation against the audio or in the answer section. (See page 19 for an explanation of words that start with alif.)

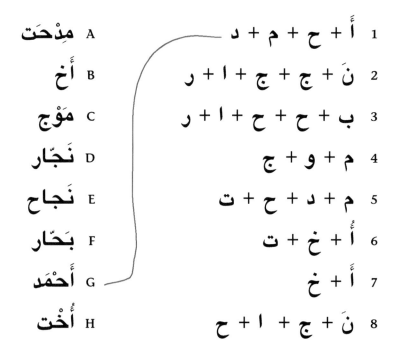

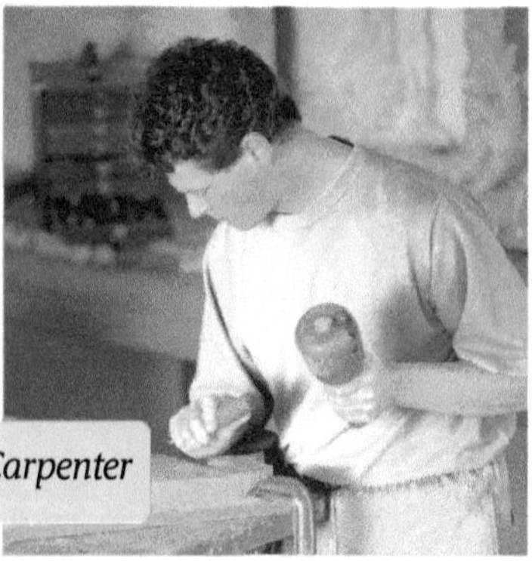

نَجّار najjār *Carpenter*

Joining hā'

Hā' changes its shape depending on how and where it is joined, so take extra care.

- If it is *not joined* to any other letter, it looks like this: ه
- If it is joined only to the letter *after* it, it looks like this: هـ
- If it is joined only to the letter *before* it, it looks like this: ـه
- If it is joined to letters on *both sides*, it looks like this: ـهـ or this: ـهـ
  (The second shape is more common in handwriting.)

Handwriting practice

Practise writing hā' in the different positions.

start here

ه ...هـ ـه... ...ـهـ...

Two of the most common words in the Arabic language start with the letter hā:

هُوَ (huwa) he　　هِيَ (hiya) she

Exercise 3

Handwrite these combinations of letters. When you've finished, check your answers and correct any mistakes you made. After that, copy out the words several more times until you can write them all fluently.

1 ن + ح + ت ________

2 ب + ه + ي ________

3 ج + م + د ________

4 ي + ت + ي + ه ________

5 ب + ح + ر ________

6 أ + م + ه ________

7 ه + ا + م + د ________

8 ن + ج + ز ________

web On the website you can find a worksheet for further practice joining jīm, ḥā', khā', hā' and mīm, and handwriting common words such as 'he' and 'she'.

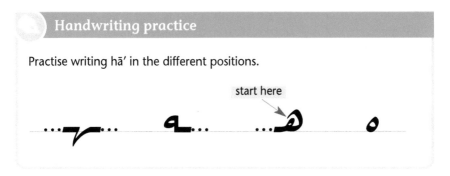

Feminine words

You have already seen that there are two genders in Arabic. All nouns (people, objects, ideas, etc.) are either *masculine* (male) or *feminine* (female). Luckily it is fairly easy to tell which gender a particular word is.

There is a special feminine ending that is a 'tied up' tā' (ت): ة . This is called tā' marbūṭa (marbūṭa literally means 'tied up'). When the word is said by itself, the tā' marbūṭa is usually pronounced as -a, without the sound of the tā':

مَدينَة (madīna) city   زَوْجَة (zawja) wife

There are two main categories of words which are feminine:

1 Female people – women, girls, and other words for females (mother, daughter, etc.). Most countries are also considered female.
2 Singular words that end in tā' marbūṭa. (There are a few exceptions to this, but they are rare.)

A word could fall into both categories, e.g. زَوْجَة (zawja) wife.

There are a small number of feminine words that do not fall into either of these categories, often words connected with the natural world (wind, fire, etc.) or parts of the body (hand, leg, etc.). However, in general you can presume a word is masculine unless it falls into one of the two categories above.

Exercise 4

CD1: 24

Listen to these words and decide whether they are masculine or feminine.

1 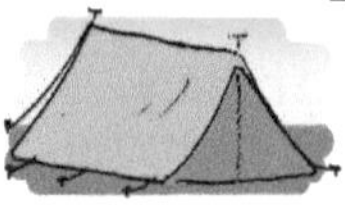
خَيْمَة

2 
بِنْت

3 
بَيْت

4 
دَجاجَة

5 
جَرِيدَة

6 
زُجاجَة

7 
حِمار

8 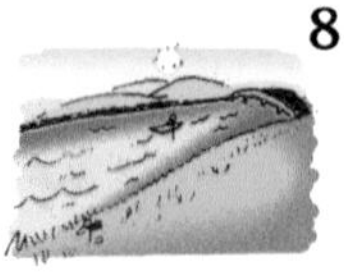
نَهْر

web PPT

You'll find a downloadable PowerPoint presentation on the website to help you remember the masculine and feminine words.

What's this? ما هذا؟

Listen to the audio and repeat the sentences:

CD1: 25

1

2

Tip: In a few common words such as هذا (hādhā) and هذه (hādhihi), you hear a long ā but this is not written as an alif in the spelling. Watch out for this and learn the spelling and pronunciation of these words by heart.

Masculine	*Feminine*
هذا بيت.	هذه جريدة.
This (is a) house.	This (is a) newspaper.

There is no need for the verb 'is' in this kind of sentence. Notice that there is also no direct equivalent of the English 'a' as in 'a house'.

Exercise 5

Make a sentence for each picture and then try writing it.

1

هذا _____ .

2

هذه _____ .

3

_____ _____ .

4

_____ _____ .

5

_____ _____ .

6

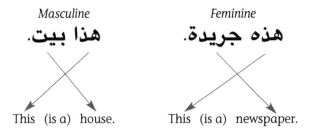

_____ _____ .

The family

Look at this family tree and read the names.

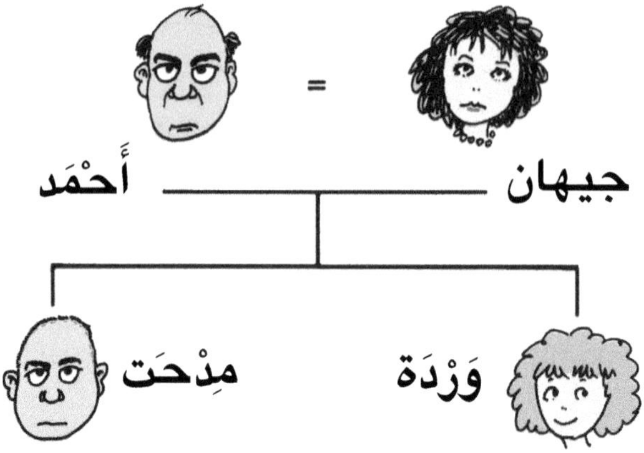
جيهان
أَحْمَد
وَرْدَة
مِدْحَت

Listen to the audio, looking at the pictures and following the words:

CD1: 26

1
أنا أحمد وهذا مدحت. هُوَ اِبْني.
2
وأنا جيهان... وهذا زَوْجي أحمد.
3
وهذه زَوْجَتي جيهان.
4
أنا وردة. وهذا أَخي مدحت.
5
وأنا مدحت وهذه أُمّي جيهان.

وَهذا أَبِي أَحمد.

وَهذه وردة. هِيَ أُخْتِي.

وَأَنا؟ أَنا جيهان وَأَنا أُمّ وردة.

If we take a noun (e.g. ابن ibn, son) and add '-ī' to the end, it then refers to 'my ...' (e.g. ابني ibnī, *my* son):

$$\text{اِبن} + \text{ي} = \text{اِبنـي}$$

noun   +   -ī   =   my son

We could also put the noun directly in front of a name. Putting two nouns together like this with a possessive meaning is known as إضافة iḍāfa, which literally means 'addition'.

$$\text{اِبن} + \text{أَحمد} = \text{اِبن أَحمد}$$

noun   +   name   =   son *of* Ahmed, or Ahmed's son

When the *first* noun in iḍāfa ends in tā' marbūṭa (ة), or when an ending such as -ī (my) is added, you should 'untie' the tā' and pronounce it as -at. In addition, when an ending is added, the spelling reverts to a regular tā'.

زوجة أحمد (zawjat aḥmad) wife of Ahmed/Ahmed's wife

مدينة بيروت (madīnat bayrūt) the city of Beirut

زوجتي (zawjatī) my wife

مدينتي (madīnatī) my city/town

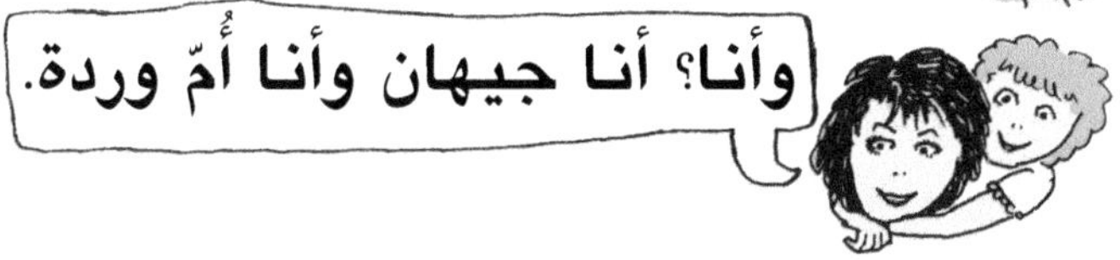

Exercise 6

Now look back at the sentences on pages 32–3 and try to match the Arabic words with their translations:

mother	أُخت
father	بِنْت
son	أُمّ
daughter	زَوْج
wife	أَخ
husband	زَوْجَة
sister	اِبْن
brother	أَب

Tip: The word بنت (bint) means 'girl' and is also informally used to mean 'daughter'. The more formal alternative for 'daughter' is ابنة (ibna).

CD1: 27

Conversation

Talking about where you live and who you live with

You can use the expression ānā askun fī ... (I live in ...) to talk about where you live:

أنا أسكن في بيروت. (ānā askun fī bayrūt.) I live in Beirut.

أنا أسكن في مدينة داربي. (ānā askun fī madīnat dārbī.)
I live in the city of Derby.

You could also add information about who you live with, using the word maʿa (with):

أنا أسكن مع زوجتي وابني. (ānā askun maʿa zawjatī wa ibnī.)
I live with my wife and [my] son.

أنا أسكن في بيروت مع أبي وأمّي. (ānā askun fī bayrūt maʿa abī wa ummī.)
I live in Beirut with my father and [my] mother.

Listen to the examples, and then have a go at talking about yourself.

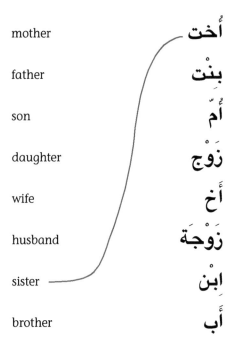

Exercise 7

Look at the family tree on page 32 and fill in the gaps in the sentences, as in the example.

1 مدحت هو __ابن__ أحمد.

2 وردة هي ______ مدحت.

3 أحمد هو ______ جيهان.

4 وردة هي ______ جيهان.

5 جيهان هي ______ وردة.

6 جيهان هي ______ أحمد.

Exercise 8

Now make eight sentences about this family, as in the example:

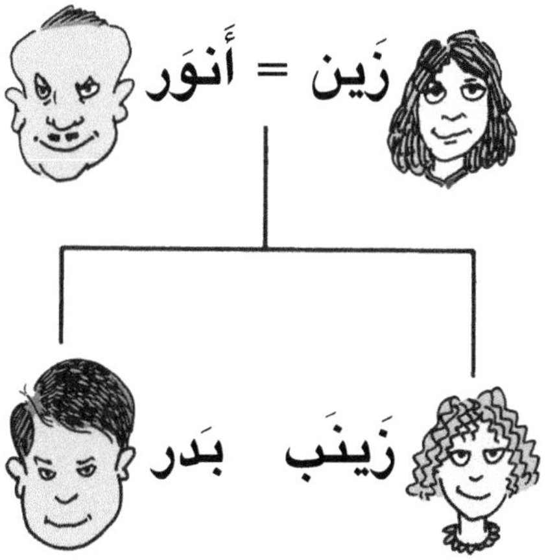

بدر هو ابن أنور.

هذه بنتي hādhihi bintī

This is my daughter

CD1: 28

Conversation

Introducing your family

You can practise the words you've learnt in this unit to introduce *your* family. Just use the expression 'this is ...': hādhā ... for a male or hādhihi ... for a female, followed by the family member and name:

مَن هذا؟ (man hādhā?) Who's this?

هذا زوجي جاك. (hādhā zawjī jāk) This is my husband, Jack.

تشرّفنا يا جاك. (tasharrafnā yā jāk) Pleased to meet you, Jack.

مَن هذه؟ (man hādhihi?) Who's this?

هذه بنتي لوسي. (hādhihi bintī lūsī) This is my daughter, Lucy.

تشرّفنا يا لوسي. (tasharrafnā yā lūsī) Pleased to meet you, Lucy.

Listen to these two conversations on the audio, then try to introduce members of *your* family. The audio will help you.

You'll find a transcript of the conversation sections on the companion website.

Vocabulary in Unit 3

أُمّ (umm) mother

أَب (ab) father

اِبْن (ibn) son

بِنْت (bint) girl/daughter *(informal)*

اِبْنَة (ibna) daughter *(formal)*

أَخ (akh) brother

أُخت (ukht) sister

زَوْج (zawj) husband

زَوْجَة (zawja) wife

هُوَ (huwa) he (and it, *masc.*)

هِيَ (hiya) she (and it, *fem.*)

أنا أَسْكُن في (ānā askun fī) I live in

هذا (hādhā) this *(masc.)*

هذِهِ (hādhihi) this *(fem.)*

زُجاجَة (zujāja) bottle

جَرِيدَة (jarīda) newspaper

خَيْمَة (khayma) tent

نَهْر (nahr) river

حِمار (ḥimār) donkey

دَجاجَة (dajāja) hen/chicken

مَدِينَة (madīna) city

مَن (man) who?

مَعَ (maع‎a) with

4 Jobs

أبت Letters of the alphabet: group 4

Listen to the audio, paying special attention to the pronunciation of the second pair of letters:

CD1: 29

	Name of letter	*Pronounced*
س	sīn	's' as in 'sea'
ش	shīn	'sh' as in 'sheet'
ص	ṣād	strong, emphatic 's'
ض	ḍād	strong, emphatic 'd'

You can see that the letters sīn and shīn have the same basic shape, but shīn has three dots above. shīn and thā' are the only two letters in the Arabic alphabet that have three dots.

ṣād and ḍād have the same basic shape, but ḍād has one dot above. All the letters in group 4 have a similarly shaped tail.

Notice that when Arabic is written in our Roman alphabet (*transliterated*), a dot is put under such letters as ṣād, ḍād and ḥā' to distinguish them from their more familiar equivalents, sīn, dāl and hā'.

ما عملك؟ mā ʿamalak?
What's your job?

Handwriting letters: group 4

Look at the handwritten versions of the letters in group 4:

Printed letter	*Handwritten letter*
س	س
ش	ش
ص	ص
ض	ض

You can see that the handwritten letters in this group look similar to the printed versions except that the three dots on shīn have become joined, as they did with thā' (ث).

Tip: the 'w' shape at the beginning of sīn and shīn can become 'smoothed out' in handwriting, like this: س . It's worth recognising that this happens. However, as a beginner, it's easier to stick to the more standard versions.

Handwriting practice

sīn, shīn

ṣād, ḍād

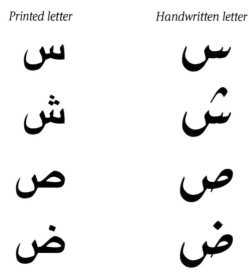

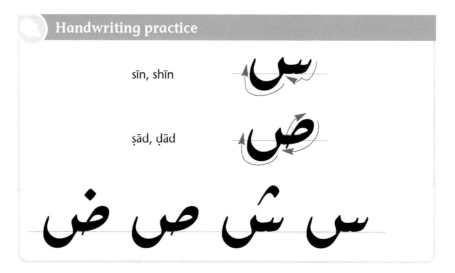

ض ص ش س

On the website you can find a worksheet to practise handwriting these letters.

أبت

Joining letters: group 4

All of the letters in group 4 work on the same principle as the other letters which have tails (e.g., ح and م). The tail falling below the line gets 'chopped' when the letters are joined to another following. Only when they are standing by themselves or at the end of a word do they keep their tails.

1 ض + ر + ب = ضرب

2 م + ص + ر = مصر

3 ب + ي + ض = بيض

4 س + ي + د = سيد

5 ح + ش + م = حشم

6 ح + ر + س = حرس

Handwriting practice

ṣād, ḍād	• joined only to the letter after:	صـ...
	• joined on both sides	...ـصـ...
	• joined only to the letter before:	...ـص
sīn, shīn	• joined only to the letter after:	سـ...
	• joined on both sides:	...ـسـ...
	• joined only to the letter before:	...ـس

web

On the website you can find a worksheet to practise handwriting these letters.

ṣād and ḍād are emphatic letters and have no direct equivalent in English. The difference in the pronunciation of sīn and ṣād is similar to the difference between the initial sounds of the English words 'silly' and 'sorry'; and that between dāl and ḍād is similar to the difference between 'din' and 'dot'.

It is important to try to distinguish between emphatic and non-emphatic letters, and also between hā' (ه) and ḥā' (ح). Listen to these pairs of words and repeat them after the audio. Each pair is given twice.

CD1: 30

1 ضَرْب
دَرْب

2 حَزَمَ
هَزَمَ

3 صَدَّ
سَدَّ

4 حَرَمَ
هَرَمَ

5 صَارَ
سَارَ

6 ضَرَسَ
دَرَسَ

Exercise 1

Listen to the words on the audio and decide which is the first letter of each. The words are given twice. The first answer is an example.

CD1: 31

1 س ص (س circled)
2 د ض
3 ه ح
4 د ض
5 س ص
6 ه ح
7 د ض
8 د ض
9 س ص
10 س ص
11 ه ح
12 س ص

Now check your answers and repeat the words after the audio.

مطعم بيتزا maṭعam bītzā
Pizza restaurant

Exercise 2

All these Arabic words are similar to English words. Can you match them to the pictures?

1 باص

2 بيتْزَا

3 شورْت

4 تِنِس

5 بورجَر

6 سينِما

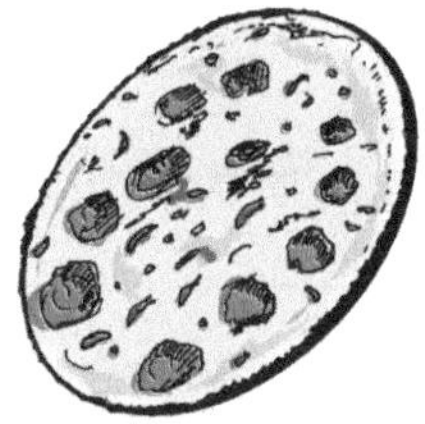

A

B

C

D

E

F

Handwriting practice

Practise writing these words from Exercise 2:

باص شورت سينما تنس بيتزا

Jobs

CD1: 32

Listen to the audio and look at the pictures:

1

2

3

4

A word referring to a single male (*masculine singular*) can be made to refer to a single female (*feminine singular*) by adding a fatḥa (ـَ) and a tā' marbūṭa (ة): مدرّس (mudarris) male teacher, مدرّسة (mudarrisa) female teacher; مصوّر (muṣawwir) male photographer, مصوّرة (muṣawwira) female photographer.

Exercise 3

CD1: 33

Here are some more jobs. Look at the list and listen to the audio.

خَبَّاز	baker
مُحاسِب	accountant
مُمَرِّضَة	nurse *(fem.)*
مُهَنْدِس	engineer
نَجَّار	carpenter

Now make one sentence for each picture. The first is an example:

1

هي مُمَرِّضَة.

2

3

4

5

6

Download a PowerPoint presentation to help you remember the jobs.

Family occupations

CD1: 34

You can combine the vocabulary you learnt in Unit 3 and the occupations to talk about what your family does for a living. Listen to these examples:

أَبي مهندس. (abī muhandis) My father is an engineer.

أُمّي مصوّرة. (ummī muṣawwira) My mother is a photographer.

أَخي محاسب. (akhī muḥāsib) My brother is an accountant.

أُختي ممرّضة. (uktī mumarriḍa) My sister is a nurse.

وزَوجَتي ممرّضة كَذلِك. (wa zawjatī mumarriḍa kadhālik) And my wife is a nurse as well.

Exercise 4

Anwar has written a short passage about himself and his family. Read the text and fill in the missing information in the table below.

أنا اِسمي أَنوَر. أنا مُصَوِّر وزَوجَتي نور
مُهَندِسة. أَبي اِسمه حَسَن وهو نَجّار. أُمّي
شادِيَة مُحاسِبة وأَخي بَدر مُحاسِب كَذلِك.

Family member	Name	Occupation
me	Anwar	
wife		
father		
mother		
brother		

If you are learning in a group, play 'Happy Families' with an Arabic twist.

CD1: 35

Conversation

Talking about what you do

If you want to know what someone does for a living, you can ask:

ما عملك؟ (mā ع‍amalak/ع‍amalik?) What's your job? (*to a man/woman*)

أنا مدرّس/ممرّضة. (anā mudarris/mumarriḍa) I'm a teacher/a nurse.

ع‍amal means 'work' or 'job' and the ending -ak or -ik means 'your' (-ka and -ki in more formal Arabic). You could also ask where someone works:

أين عملك؟ (ayna ع‍amalak/ع‍amalik?) Where's your job?

في لندن/في بيروت. (fī lundun/fī bayrūt) In London/In Beirut.

If you're studying at university or school you may want to say:

أنا طالب/طالبة. (anā ṭālib/ṭāliba) I'm a student (*male/female*).

أنا تلميذ/تلميذة. (anā tilmīdh/tilmīdha) I'm a pupil (*male/female*).

A good phrase to express interest or admiration is:

ما شاء الله! (mā shā'a allāh) Wonderful!

Listen and then try to say what your job is and where you work or study.

You'll find a full transcript of the conversation on the website.

Making words plural

CD1: 36

Look at the pictures and listen to the audio.

هُمْ مُدَرِّسُون.

هُنَّ مُدَرِّسَات.

هُمْ مُحاسِبون.

هُنَّ مُحاسِبات.

مدرّسون

masculine singular + ūn = *masculine plural*

مدرّسات

masculine singular + āt = *feminine plural*

These plurals are known as the *sound masculine plural* and the *sound feminine plural* ('sound' here means 'complete' and does not refer to the pronunciation). All the jobs in this unit can be made plural by adding the endings shown above.

Notice that although there is only one word for 'we', نحن (naḥnu), the word for 'they' is هم (hum) for the masculine plural and هنّ (hunna) for the feminine plural:

هم مدرّسون. (hum mudarrisūn) They are *(male)* teachers.

هنّ مدرّسات. (hunna mudarrisāt) They are *(female)* teachers.

If the group is mixed, the masculine plural is used. For this reason, the feminine plural is not as common. (Spoken dialects often use the masculine plural only, whatever the gender of the group.)

Exercise 5

Look again at the words listed in Exercise 3. Write the masculine and feminine plurals for these words.

Exercise 6

Now write the words in the speech bubbles and underneath the pictures, as in the example.

1 هنّ

2 ____________

3 ____________

4 ____________

5 ____________

6 ____________

CD1: 37

Conversation

Talking about where you work or study

It's useful to be able to talk about your place of work or study.
You can use the phrase 'I work in ...' followed by your workplace:

أنا أعمل في ...	(anā aعmal fī)	I work in ...
مكتب	(maktab)	an office
مستشفى	(mustashfā)	a hospital
مطعم	(maṭعam)	a restaurant
مصنع	(maṣnaع)	a factory

Or you can say 'I study in ...' and add some more detail:

أنا أدرس في ...	(anā adrus fī)	I study in ...
مدرسة في لندن	(madrasa fī lundun)	a school in London
جامعة تونس	(jāmiعat tūnis)	the University of Tunis

Listen to those expressions and practise the ones that apply to you. Then have a go at talking about what you and your family do. Try to include the following information:

- a greeting
- your name
- what you do and where you work or study
- the occupation of a male family member
- the occupation of a female family member

If you don't know the Arabic for your occupation and don't have access to a native speaker, try using an internet translation site (with audio so that you can hear the Arabic). Why not record yourself? You can send it to an Arabic friend or teacher, or post it on a forum for learners of Arabic.

web

You'll find a full transcript of the conversation on the website.

web

Video: *Amani talks about her family*

Go to www.palgrave.com/masteringarabic to play the video of Amani talking about her family. See if you can answer these questions:

1 What does Amani do?
2 Where is she based?
3 What are the occupations of her parents?
4 Who else does Amani mention?

Don't worry if you don't understand everything. Just listen for the key information. You'll find a transcript, a translation and an extension activity on the website.

Structure notes

These notes are intended to give more details about the grammar of the Arabic language. They will be useful mainly for recognition purposes – you needn't learn them slavishly. If you only require a more general understanding of Arabic, you can quickly skim through these sections or even skip them altogether.

Case endings

Arabic nouns and adjectives have case endings – grammatical endings that can be added to the end of words. However, unlike many languages, for example German, these endings are rarely pronounced and only exist in spoken dialects in set expressions. So learners of Arabic (and native speakers) can get by without a detailed knowledge of these endings.

You may meet the full endings in readings of classical literature, the Qur'ān, poetry, and in more formal radio and TV broadcasts, especially if the speaker wishes to speak perfectly inflected, 'high-end' Arabic. You will rarely find them written in newspapers or magazines. However, there are some occasions in Modern Standard Arabic when the endings affect the spelling and pronunciation, so a basic knowledge of how they work is desirable.

The nominative case (الرفع ar-rafع)

There are three cases. The first is the *nominative*. (We'll come to the other two later.) The easiest way to identify this case is to say that you can assume a noun is nominative unless there is a reason for it *not* to be. Almost all of the nouns you have met in the book so far have been in the nominative case.

If we take the noun بنت (bint), girl/daughter, and add the full ending for the nominative case, we have:

بنتٌ (pronounced 'bint<u>un</u>')

The ending (ـٌ) is written above the final letter, and is pronounced '-un'. So the sentence هذا بَيت (hādhā bayt, This is a house), would be هذا بَيتٌ (hādhā baytun) if fully pronounced. Look at these other nouns with their case endings:

نَجّارٌ	(najjārun)	carpenter
زُجاجَةٌ	(zujājatun*)	bottle
مُمَرِّضاتٌ	(mumarriḍātun)	nurses

* The tā' marbūta is pronounced '-at' when a case ending is added to the noun, as it is in iḍāfa (see page 33).

The sound masculine plural, for example مُدَرِّسون (mudarrisūn), works in a different way. More details of this will be given in later units.

Optional exercise

Go back to Exercise 3 and say the sentences again, this time pronouncing the full endings on the words.

Vocabulary in Unit 4

نَحْنُ (naḥnu) we

هُمْ (hum) they *(masc.)*

هُنَّ (hunna) they *(fem.)*

مُدَرِّس (mudarris) teacher

مُحَاسِب (muḥāsib) accountant

خَبَّاز (khabbāz) baker

مُمَرِّضَة (mumarriḍa) nurse

مُهَنْدِس (muhandis) engineer

نَجَّار (najjār) carpenter

مُصَوِّر (muṣawwir) photographer

طَالِب (ṭālib) student

تِلْمِيذ (tilmīdh) pupil

تَنِس (tanis) tennis

بَاص (bāṣ) bus

سِينِما (sīnimā) cinema

بِيتزا (bītzā) pizza

شورت (shūrt) shorts

بورجَر (būrgar) burger

ما عَمَلَك؟ (mā ɛamalak/ɛamalik?) What's your job? *(to a man/woman)*

أَيْنَ عَمَلَك؟ (ayna ɛamalak/ɛamalik?) Where's your job? *(to a man/woman)*

أنا أَعْمَل في ... (anā aɛmal fī) I work in ...

مَكْتَب (maktab) an office

مُسْتَشْفى (mustashfā) a hospital

مَطْعَم (maṭɛam) a restaurant

مَصْنَع (maṣnaɛ) a factory

أَنا أَدْرُس في ... (anā adrus fī) I study in ...

جامِعة ... (jāmiɛ at) the University of ...

مَدْرَسة في ... (madrasa fī) a school in ...

كَذلك (kadhālik) as well

ما شاءَ الله! (mā shā'a allāh) Wonderful!

On the website you can find links to interactive audio flashcards to review the key vocabulary in *Mastering Arabic* Units 1–4.

5 Describing things

Letters of the alphabet: group 5

Listen to the audio and look at the letters:

CD1: 38

	Name of letter	*Pronounced*
ف	fā'	'f' as in 'foot'
ق	qāf	*see page 52*
ك	kāf	'k' as in 'kettle'
ل	lām	'l' as in 'lamb'

The fā' and qāf have similar shapes, but the tail of the qāf is rounder and falls below the line (a little like the difference between ب and ن).

The tail of the lām must also fall below the line and not sit on it like our Latin-script 'l'. Both lām and kāf have distinctive shapes which are not shared with any other letter.

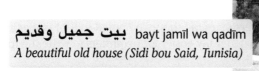

بيت جميل وقديم bayt jamīl wa qadīm

A beautiful old house (Sidi bou Said, Tunisia)

Pronunciation of qāf

It takes practice to pronounce qāf properly. You should say a 'q' from the back of your throat. In Modern Standard Arabic, care must be taken to distinguish the pronunciation of kāf and qāf (listen again to the audio).

However, spoken dialects tend to pronounce the qāf either as a 'g' as in 'gate' or as a *glottal stop*. (A glottal stop is the sort of sound produced when you pronounce 'bottle' with a Cockney accent, or in 'Estuary English', dropping the 'tt'.) This course will pronounce the qāf in the classical way, but be prepared to hear the same words pronounced with a 'g' or a glottal stop by native speakers.

Exercise 1

CD1: 39

Listen to these pairs of words. All the words begin with either qāf or kāf. Decide whether each pair of words begins with the same or different letters. Each pair is given twice. The first answer is an example.

1	(same)	different	5	same	different
2	same	different	6	same	different
3	same	different	7	same	different
4	same	different	8	same	different

Handwriting letters: group 5

Look at the letters in group 5 handwritten:

Printed letter	*Handwritten letter*
ف	
ق	
ك	
ل	

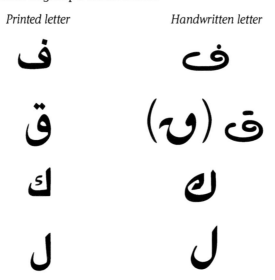

Notice how in the handwritten version the 'hamza' shape in the middle of the kāf becomes 'joined' to the rest of the letter for the sake of speed. The alternative handwritten version of qāf should be noted so that you will recognise it, although it is generally easier for beginners to write the more standard version.

Handwriting practice

fā’ 

qāf 

kāf 

lām 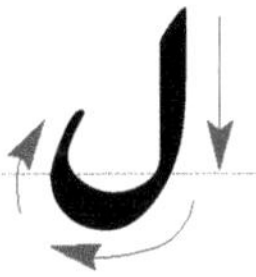

On the website you can find a worksheet to practise handwriting these letters.

Joining letters: group 5

fā’, qāf and lām all lose their tails when they are joined to a following letter. This leaves fā’ and qāf with the same shape when at the beginning or in the middle of a word. The only difference is that fā’ has one dot above and qāf has two:

ف + ر + ق = فرق

ق + ر + ن = قرن

ق + ف + ل = قفل

ل + ف + ق = لفق

م + ل + ل = ملل

It is important to remember that lām can be joined on *both sides*. Beginners often confuse this letter with alif, which can be joined only to the letter before:

ج + ا + ب = جاب

ج + ل + ب = جلب

kāf, like hā' (ه), changes its shape depending on how it is joined:

- If it stands on its own or is at the end of a word, it looks like this: ك
- If it stands at the beginning or in the middle of a word, it looks like this: كـ

Exercise 2

Look at this newspaper headline. It contains 2 kāfs and 6 qāfs. Can you find and circle them?

كلمات أمير قطر الصادقة

تعكس عمق علاقات الشعبين الشقيقين

Handwriting practice

When a kāf is written at the beginning or in the middle of a word, the main shape of the word is often completed first without the downwards stroke of the kāf, which is added with the dots:

Stage 1: ىلـ

Stage 2: كلب

Compare this with the way most people would write the English word 'tin':

Stage 1: lın

Stage 2: tin

Now practise copying these words:

كلب كتاب كسكس بنتك مكسور

On the website you can find a worksheet to practise joining kāf.

كسكس بالدجاج kuskus bid-dajāj

Couscous with chicken

Everyday objects

Look at these pictures and listen to the audio:

CD1: 40

1

كِتاب

2

مِفْتاح

3

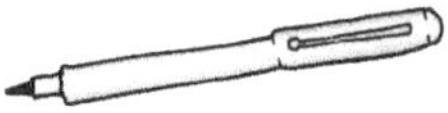

قَلَم

4

حَقيبَة

5

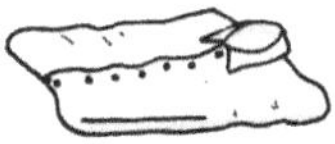

قَميص

6

كَلْب

7

دَرّاجَة

8

سَيّارَة

9

خاتِم

web

On the website you can find an activity to help you with spelling these words.

Exercise 3

Now make a sentence for each picture on page 55, as in the example:

1 هذا كِتاب.

Signs and crosswords

If an English word is written vertically instead of horizontally, as in a crossword or a shop sign, then the same letters are used. However, because of the way Arabic letters are joined, vertical words have to be written using the separate, isolated letters:

Horizontal:	accountant	محاسب
Vertical:	a c c o u n t a n t	م ح ا س ب

Arabic crosswords are compiled entirely in separate letters.

Exercise 4

Look at the picture clues and complete the crossword.
One clue is completed for you.

رَأْسِيّ ↓

1

2

3

أُفْقِيّ ←

1

2

4

Describing things

CD1: 41

Look at these pairs of descriptive words *(adjectives)* and listen to the audio.

1

جَديد

2

قَديم

3

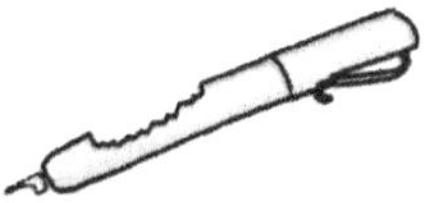

مَكْسور

4

سَليم

5

خَفيف

6

ثَقيل

7

قَبيح

8

جَميل

9

أَسْوَد

10

أَبْيَض

Tip: قديم (qadīm, old) is normally used with objects, not people.

web PPT

Download a PowerPoint presentation to help you remember the adjectives.

CD1: 42

Now listen to these sentences:

القَلَم سلَيم. 

الحَقيبة خَفيفة. 

هذا القلم مَكسور. 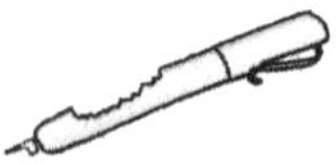

هذه الحقيبة ثقَيلة. 

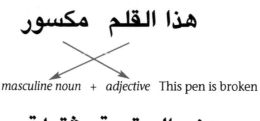

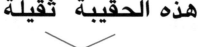

Using الـ (al, the)

القلم

الـ (al) the + قلم (qalam) pen = القلم (al-qalam) the pen

الـ (al) is the same for all nouns, whether masculine, feminine or plural, and is written as part of the word that follows. Adding hādha or hādhihi directly in front of al changes the meaning from 'the' to 'this', for example from القلم (al-qalam), the pen, to هذا القلم (hādha l-qalam), this pen.

هذا القلم مكسور

masculine noun + *adjective* This pen is broken

هذه الحقيبة ثقيلة

feminine noun + *adjective with* ة This bag is heavy

Tip: In spoken dialects الـ can be pronounced al, il or el.

An adjective must have the feminine ending (ة, a) if the noun it is describing is feminine. In other words, the adjective 'agrees with' the noun.

When the word before ال (al) ends with a vowel, the 'a' of 'al' is dropped and the sound is elided:

اَلْحَقيبة (al-ḥaqība) the bag

هذه الْحَقيبة (hādhihi l-ḥaqība) this bag (*not* hādhihi al-ḥaqība)

Be careful about distinguishing these:

هذا قلم. (hādha qalam) This is a pen.

هذا القلم (hādha l-qalam) this pen

Exercise 5

Match the opposite pairs of adjectives:

جميل	سليم
ثقيل	قديم
أبيض	قبيح
مكسور	خفيف
جديد	أسود

Now pronounce the adjectives out loud.

Exercise 6

Fill in the gaps in these descriptions to match the English in brackets. Remember to add the feminine ending ة a to the adjective if necessary.

1 هذا القميص ________ . (This shirt is white.)

2 وهذا ________ أسود. (And this shirt is black.)

3 ________ المدينة جميلة. (This town is beautiful.)

4 ________ المدينة ________ . (And this town is ugly.)

5 ________ السيّارة ________ . (This car is old.)

6 ________ ________ ________ . (And this car is new.)

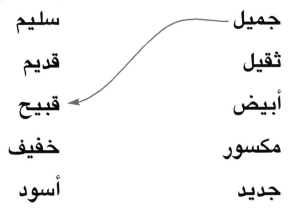

Possessive endings (attached pronouns)

Look at these endings, which describe possession:

my	-ī	كتابي	(kitābī)	my book
your *(talking to a male)*	-(u)ka*	كتابُكَ	(kitābuka)	your book
your *(talking to a female)*	-(u)ki*	كتابُكِ	(kitābuki)	your book
his	-(u)hu*	كتابُهُ	(kitābuhu)	his book
her	-(u)hā	كتابُها	(kitābuhā)	her book

**Tip:* In informal Arabic these endings are often simplified to -ak, -ik and -uh: kitāb<u>ak</u>, kitāb<u>ik</u>, kitāb<u>uh</u>.

These endings are known as *attached pronouns* since they are 'attached' to the end of the word. Remember that when you add an ending to a word which finishes in tā' marbūṭa, the tā' unties and is pronounced:

حقيبة (ḥaqība, bag) حقيبتكَ (ḥaqībatuka, *informal* ḥaqībatak)

CD1: 43

Conversation

Asking about names

You can use the informal attached pronouns to ask someone's name, or to talk about the names of family members. For example:

ما اسمك؟ (mā ismak?) What's your name? *(to a male)*
أنا اسمي محمّد. (āna ismī muḥammad) My name's Mohammed.

ما اسم زوجتك؟ (mā ism zawjatak?) What's your wife's name?
اسمها فاطمة. (ismuhā fāṭima) Her name's Fatima.

ما اسمِك؟ (mā ismik?) What's your name? *(to a female)*
أنا اسمي كريمة. (āna ismī karīma) My name's Karima.

وابنِك؟ ما اسمه؟ (w-ibnik? mā ismuh?) And your son? What's his name?
اسمه قاسم. (ismuh qāsim) His name's Qasim.

Listen to the example conversations, and then have a go at talking about the names of your family members.

web

You'll find a full transcript of the conversations on the website.

Whose is it?

CD1: 44

Listen to these two exchanges and read the descriptions below:

1

2

Tip: Two fatḥas above alif (اً) at the end of a word is pronounced -an: شكراً (shukran), thank you; أهلاً (ahlan), hello.

هذا كِتاب البِنت وكِتابُها جَديد وأَبيَض.

هذا كِتاب الوَلَد وكِتابُهُ قَديم وأَسوَد.

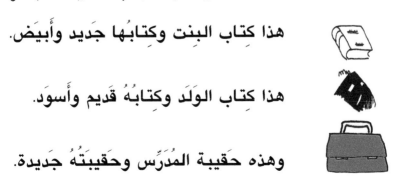

وهذه حَقيبة المُدَرِّس وحَقيبَتُهُ جَديدة.

Exercise 7

Read the description of Jihan's dog. Then look at the pictures of Jihan and her friend Mohammed, together with some of their possessions.

هذا كَلب جيهان وهو أَبيَض.

كَلبها قَبيح وثَقيل.

جيهان | مُحَمَّد

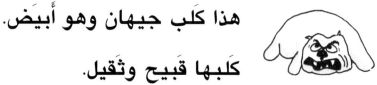

Now make similar descriptions of Jihan's and Mohammed's other possessions.

Tip: The adjectives أبيض (abyaḍ, white) and أسود (aswad, black) have a special feminine form which you will learn later in the course. For the moment, stick to using these colours with masculine objects.

Exercise 8

Try to describe some of your own possessions, using the sentences you produced in Exercise 7 as models.

CD1: 45

Conversation

Polite requests

It is useful at an early stage of learning a language to master a few phrases so that you can ask politely for what you want. These can come in handy in stores or when you want someone to pass you something.

ممكن ...؟ (mumkin ...?) May I have ...? (literally 'possible?')

ممكن كتابي من فضلك؟ (mumkin kitābī min faḍlak?)

May I have my book, please? *(said to a male)*

ممكن القميص الأبيض من فضلك؟ (mumkin al-qamīṣ al-abyaḍ min faḍlik?)

May I have the white shirt, please? *(said to a female)*

أريد ... (urīd ...) I'd like ...

أريد حقيبة جديدة. (urīd ḥaqība jadīda) I'd like a new bag.

أريد بيتزا من فضلك. (urīd pītzā min faḍlak) I'd like pizza, please.

When the item is handed over, you may hear:

تفضّل (tafaḍḍal) Here you are. *(said to a male)*

تفضّلي (tafaḍḍalī) Here you are. *(said to a female)*

And don't forget to say 'thanks': شكراً (shukran).

Listen to the request phrases on the audio with some examples, and then try asking for the following items:

هذه الزجاجة (hādhihi z-zujāja) this bottle

قلمك (qalamak) your pen

القميص الأسود (al-qamīṣ al-aswad) the black shirt

مفتاحي (miftāḥī) my key

web

You'll find a full transcript of the conversation on the website.

web

If you're learning in a group, play the 'May I have' game. You'll find instructions on the website.

Structure notes

Definite and indefinite

When you add الـ (al, the) to an indefinite noun, you make it definite. The case ending you met in Unit 4 changes slightly:

بنتٌ	(bintun)	a girl/daughter *(indefinite)*
البنتُ	(al-bintu)	the girl/daughter *(definite)*

The indefinite case ending -un becomes -u when the noun is definite.

Nouns which have possessive endings are also definite, and this accounts for the 'u' which appears before the attached pronouns:

بنتُكَ	(bintuka)	your daughter *(talking to a male)*
بنتُكِ	(bintuki)	your daughter *(talking to a female)*
بنتُهُ	(bintuhu)	his daughter
بنتُها	(bintuhā)	her daughter

But notice that when you add ي (ī, my), the case ending is not included.

Look at these sentences, which you have already met in this unit, with the full case endings added. Notice that the adjectives as well as the nouns carry the case endings.

اَلسَّيارةُ جَديدةٌ.	(as-sayyāratu jadīdatun)	The car is new.
بِنْتُكَ جَميلةٌ.	(bintuka jamīlatun)	Your daughter is beautiful.
اَلكِتابُ قَديمٌ	(al-kitābu qadīmun)	The book is old.

Vocabulary in Unit 5

قَلَم (qalam) pen

دَرّاجة (darrāja) bicycle

مِفْتاح (miftāḥ) key

سَيّارة (sayyāra) car

كِتاب (kitāb) book

خاتِم (khātim) ring

قَميص (qamīṣ) shirt

حَقيبة (ḥaqība) bag

كَلْب (kalb) dog

وَلَد (walad) boy

خَفيف (khafīf) light (weight)

ثَقيل (thaqīl) heavy

قَبيح (qabīh) ugly

جَميل (jamīl) beautiful

جَديد (jadīd) new

قَديم (qadīm) old

مَكْسور (maksūr) broken

سَليم (salīm) whole/unbroken

أَسْوَد (aswad) black

أَبْيَض (abyaḍ) white

...ـي (-ī) my

...ـكَ (-ka, *informal* -ak) your *(masc.)*

...ـكِ (-ki, *informal* -ik) your *(fem.)*

...ـهُ (-hu, *informal* -uh) his

...ـها (-hā) her

ما اِسمك؟ (mā ismak/mā ismik) what's your name? *(to a male/female)*

مُمكِن ...؟ (mumkin) may I have ...?

أُريد ... (urīd) I'd like ...

كُسْكُس (kuskus) couscous

دَجاج (dajāj) chicken

مِن فَضْلك (min faḍlak/min faḍlik) please *(to a male/female)*

شُكْراً (shukran) thank you

تَفَضَّل/تَفَضَّلي (tafaḍḍal/tafaḍḍalī) here you are *(to a male/female)*

6 Where is it?

Letters of the alphabet: group 6

This is the final group of letters. All of these sounds are less familiar to a non-Arab ear, so listen carefully to the audio:

CD1: 46

	Name of letter	*Pronounced*
ط	ṭā'	Strong, emphatic 't'
ظ	ẓā'	Strong, emphatic 'z'
ع	ʿayn	Guttural 'ah' (see below)
غ	ghayn	a gargling sound similar to a French 'r'

You can see that the ṭā' and ẓā' share the same basic shape, and that ʿayn and ghayn also share the same basic shape. A single dot distinguishes each pair of letters.

Emphatic letters

The letters ṭā' and ẓā', together with ṣād and ḍād you met in Unit 4, are 'emphatic' sounds. You should take care to distinguish the sound from their non-emphatic equivalents. The emphatic letters are pronounced further back in the mouth, a little like the difference between the English words 'silly' and 'sorry' or 'tin' and 'ton'.

When Arabic is written in English letters (transliterated), a dot is put under the emphatic letter to distinguish it from its non-emphatic equivalent.

مدينة صنعاء في اليمن
madīnat ṣanεā' fil-yaman
The city of Sanaa in Yemen

Listen to the audio and repeat the letters below.

CD1: 47

Emphatic letter	*Non-emphatic letter*
ط ṭā'	ت tā'
ظ ẓā'	ذ dhāl
ص ṣād	س sīn
ض ḍād	د dāl

Exercise 1

Listen to the words on the audio and decide which of the letters above each word begins with. The first is an example. Each word will be given twice.

CD1: 48

5	ط 1
6	2
7	3
8	4

Now check your answers and repeat the words after the audio.

ʿayn and ghayn

These two letters, especially ʿayn, represent unfamiliar sounds and take practice to pronounce. However, you will develop a feel for them and will gradually find them easier to say and to recognise.

- ghayn (غ) is pronounced like the French 'gr' as in 'gratin', and is similar to the noise you make when you gargle.
- ʿayn (ع) is produced by tightening your throat and making an 'ah' sound by pushing out air from your lungs – easier said than done! Imagine you are at the dentist and the drill touches a nerve. Beginners often fail to hear ʿayn as a letter at all, but to native speakers it is a letter like any other and leaving it out when you speak could lead to blank looks. ʿayn does not have a near equivalent in English, so the Arabic letter itself is used in the transliteration.

CD1: 49

Repeat the six words that you hear on the audio. They all contain the letter ghayn. Then repeat the next six words, which all contain the letter ʿayn.

Exercise 2

CD1: 50

Listen to the eight words on the audio. Decide whether or not the word begins with ʿayn. The first is an example. Each word is repeated.

1 ✔	3	5	7
2	4	6	8

Handwriting practice

ṭā', ẓā'

ʿayn, ghayn

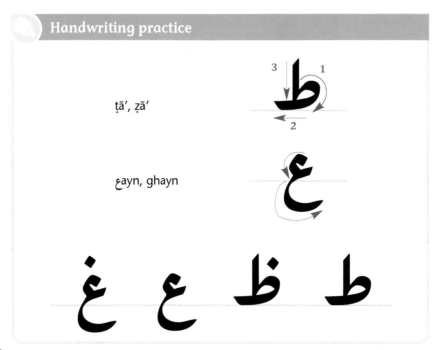

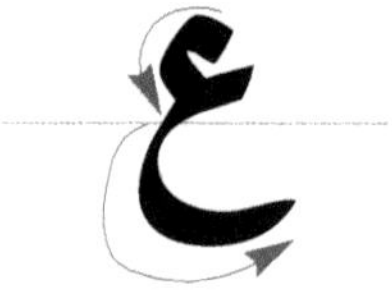

غ ع ظ ط

On the website you can find a worksheet to practise handwriting these letters.

Exercise 3

You have now met all 28 Arabic letters. Look at the following table of all the letters in *alphabetical order*. Fill in the missing letters in either their printed or handwritten versions.

(The alphabet starts in the left-hand column.)

Name	Printed	Handwritten	Name	Printed	Handwritten
alif	ا	ا	ḍād		ض
bā’	ب	ب	ṭā’	ط	
tā’	ت		ẓā’	ظ	
thā’		ث	ʿayn		ع
jīm	ج		ghayn	غ	
ḥā’	ح		fā’		ف
khā’		خ	qāf	ق	
dāl	د		kāf	ك	
dhāl		ذ	lām		ل
rā’		ر	mīm	م	
zāy	ز		nūn	ن	
sīn		س	hā’		ه
shīn	ش		wāw	و	
ṣād	ص		yā’		ي

web

On the website you can find a large printable version of this activity.

أبت Joining letters: group 6

ṭā’ and ẓā’

These two letters have the same basic shape, wherever they appear in a word:

و + س + ط = وسط

ط + ي + ر = طير

ن + ظ + ر = نظر

ظ + ب + ي = ظبي

ر + ب + ا + ط = رباط

Handwriting practice

ṭā’ and ẓā’ are formed a bit like ṣād and ḍād, except that there is no ‘dink’ after the loop:

- joined only to the letter after: ط...
- joined on both sides: ...ط...
- joined only to the letter before: ...ط

The downwards stroke and dot are usually added after the whole shape of the word is complete:

Stage 1: ٮصر

Stage 2: نظر

Practise copying these words:

وسط طير نظر ظبي رباط

You’ll find a printable worksheet on the website to practise handwriting.

ɛayn and ghayn

Like hā' (ه), these two letters change their shapes depending on where they appear in a word.

- Joined only to the following letter they look like this: ...عـ (like the isolated version without its tail)
- Joined on both sides they look like this: ...ـعـ...
- Joined only to the letter before they look like this: ـع...

Look carefully at how ɛayn and ghayn combine:

غ + ي + ر = غير

م + و + ع + د = موعد

ص + غ + ي + ر = صغير

ش + ا + ر + ع = شارع

م + ص + ن + ع = مصنع

م + غ + ر + ب = مغرب

Notice especially that ɛayn and ghayn each look very different at the end of a word, depending on whether or not they are joined to the previous letter (see the fourth and fifth examples above).

في مدينة الرباط، المغرب
fī madīnat al-rabāṭ, al-maghrib
In the city of Rabat, Morocco

Handwriting practice

- Joined only to the letter after: عـ...
- Joined on both sides: 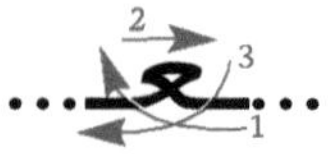
- Joined only to the letter before: ...ـع

Practise copying these words:

غير عاطف صغير بالغ جامع

On the website you can find a worksheet to practise joining these letters.

Exercise 4

Each of these twelve cities in the Arab world contains one of the four new letters: ṭā', ẓā', ɛayn or ghayn. Can you match the Arabic spelling to the English equivalent?

1 أَبو ظَبي

2 بَغداد

3 مَسقَط

4 صَنعاء

5 عَدَن

6 الخَرطوم

7 بَنغازي

8 طَنجة

9 عَمّان

10 بور سَعيد

11 غَزّة

12 الرِّباط

a Baghdad **b** Amman **c** Port Said **d** Abu Dhabi **e** Khartoum **f** Gaza
g Tangiers **h** Muscat **i** Benghazi **j** Rabat **k** Sanaa **l** Aden

Exercise 5

Handwrite these combinations of letters, as in the example :

1. ع + ل + ي = علي ______
2. ج + م + ع = ______
3. غ + ط + س = ______
4. ظ + ل + م = ______
5. ط + ي + ن = ______
6. ن + ع + م = ______
7. ب + غ + د + ا + د = ______
8. م + س + ق + ط = ______

Sun letters

Listen to these two sentences:

CD1: 51

القميص أبيض. (al-qamīṣ abyaḍ) The shirt is white.

السيّارة جديدة. (as-sayyāra jadīda) The car is new.

القميص is pronounced al-qamīṣ, but السيّارة is pronounced as-sayyāra. When الـ (al-, the) is added to words beginning with particular letters, the lām is pronounced like the first letter of that word and not as a lām. The first letter of the word sounds as though it is pronounced twice: as-sayyāra.

Letters like sīn, which take over the sound of the lām, are known as 'sun letters'. The others are 'moon letters'. All sun letters are pronounced with your tongue at the top of your mouth, just behind your teeth. This is the same position as lām. Half the letters of the alphabet are sun letters. All of the letters in group 4 (sīn, shīn, ṣād and ḍād) are sun letters, and none of the letters in group 3 (jīm, ḥā',khā', mīm and hā').

You will gradually become used to hearing the the sun letters and mimicking what you hear.

Exercise 6

CD1: 52

Listen to these words, identify the initial letter and decide which of them is a sun letter. The first is an example. Each word will be given twice.

Sun letter?	Initial letter	Word
✗	ب	البنت
		التبن
		الثوب
		النهر
		الياسمين
		الدجاجة
		الذباب
		الراديو
		الزجاجة
		الولد
		الفيلم
		القميص
		الكتاب
		الليمون
		الطين
		الظاهر
		العرب
		الغرب

Asking questions

CD1: 53

Look at these objects and listen to the audio:

1 

مائِدَة

2 

كُرْسيّ

3 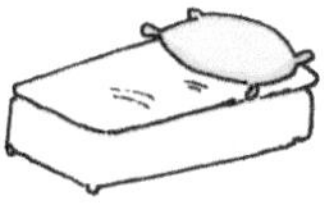

سَرير

4 

باب

5 

تِليفِزْيون

6 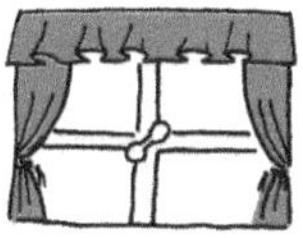

شُبّاك

7 

صورَة

8 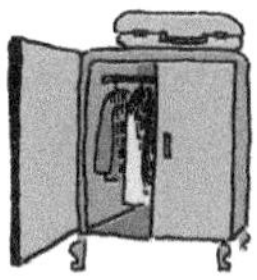

خَزانَة

Exercise 7

Fill in the missing words in the sentences and match them to the correct pictures, as in the example. (To review هذا hādhā and هذه hādhihi, see page 31.)

a 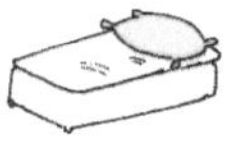

b 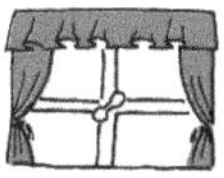

c 

d 

e 

f 

g 

h 

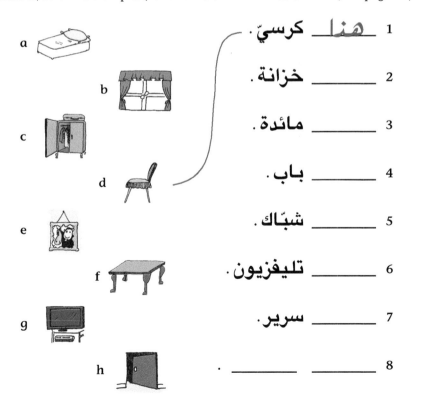

1 هذا كرسي .

2 ______ خزانة .

3 ______ مائدة .

4 ______ باب .

5 ______ شبّاك .

6 ______ تليفزيون .

7 ______ سرير .

8 ______ ______ .

Yes/no questions

You can form a question in Arabic to which the answer is either 'yes' (نعم, naɛam) or 'no' (لا, lā) by adding the question marker هل (hal) in front of a sentence:

هذا نهر. (hādhā nahr) This is a river.
هل هذا نهر؟ (hal hādhā nahr) Is this a river?

هذه جريدة. (hādhihi bjar) This is a newspaper.
هل هذه جريدة؟ (hal hādhihi bint) Is this a newspaper?

Exercise 8

CD1: 54

Listen to these two exchanges:

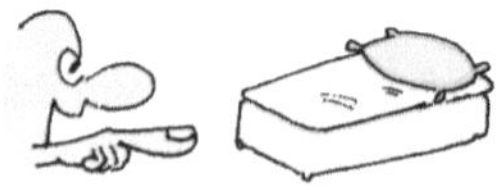

هل هذا كرسي؟ (hal hādhā kursī?)
✗ لا، هو سرير. (lā, huwa sarīr.)

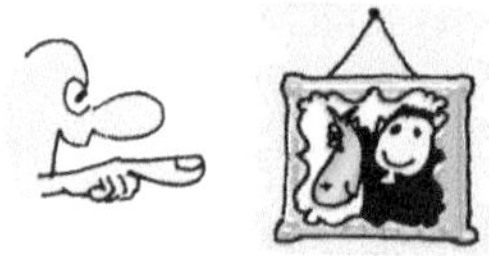

هل هذه صورة؟ (hal hādhihi ṣūra?)
✓ نعم، هي صورة. (naɛam, hiya ṣūra.)

Tip: Note the reversed shape of the Arabic question mark (؟) and comma (،). The comma is also raised to sit on the line rather than below it.

Now say and write exchanges for each of these pictures, following the examples.

1 خزانة؟

2 كتاب؟

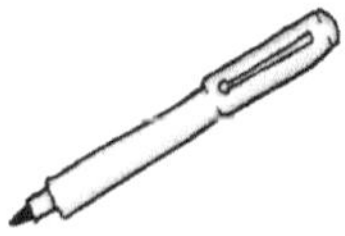

3 مفتاح؟

4 كلب؟

5 درّاجة؟

6 شبّاك؟

Practise *yes/no* questions with the 'Mystery object' game on the website.

Hamza (ء)

The hamza shape (ء) that you have seen sitting on an alif in words such as أمّ (umm, mother) or أب (ab, father) can also be found written in other ways. One of these is on a yā' letter shape with no dots, as in مائدة (mā'ida, table). When it falls in the middle of a word, hamza is pronounced as a short pause or sigh. There are detailed rules concerning how to write hamza, but it is best at first to learn each word as it appears.

Where? أَيْنَ؟

Listen to the audio and look at the pictures:

CD1: 55

1 أَيْنَ الكلب؟

هو تَحْتَ المائدة.

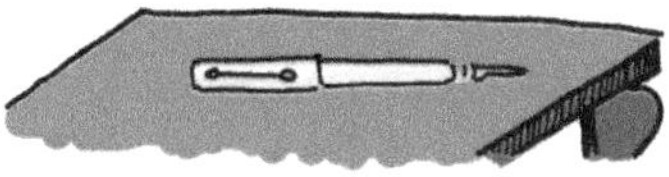

2 أَيْنَ القلم؟

هو عَلَى المائدة.

3 أَيْنَ الولد؟

هو بين الكرسي والمائدة.

4 أَيْنَ البنت؟

هي في الخزانة.

5 أَيْنَ الصورة؟

هي فَوْقَ المائدة.

6 أَيْنَ الكلب؟

هو بِجانِب الكرسي.

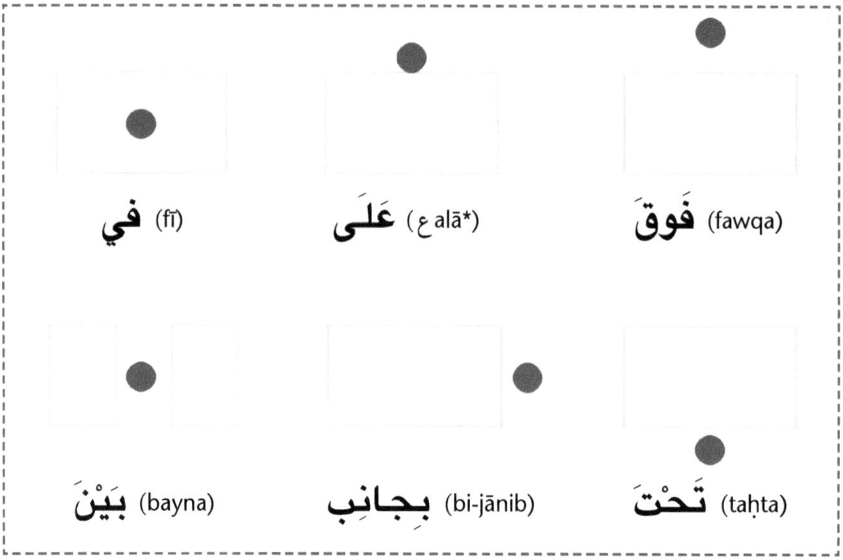
فَوقَ (fawqa)
عَلَى (ع alā*)
في (fī)
تَحْتَ (taḥta)
بِجانِب (bi-jānib)
بَيْنَ (bayna)

* *Note:* على (ع alā, on) finishes with a yā' with no dots and yet is pronounced ā. Some words that end in ā are written with a yā' instead of an alif. This makes no difference to the pronunciation and is only ever found at the end of a word. This yā' is known as alif maqṣūra.

web PPT On the companion website you can find a PowerPoint presentation to help you remember the objects and positional words in Unit 6.

Exercise 9

Fill in the gaps in these sentences:

1

الزجاجة ___ المائدة.

2

الجريدة ___ الكرسيّ.

3

___ ___ الخيمة و___.

4

الصورة ___ ___.

5

___ ___ ___.

6

___ ___ ___.

Exercise 10

Now look at this bedroom and answer the questions, as in the example.

1 هل الكرسيّ بجانب المائدة؟

نعم، هو بجانب المائدة.

2 أيْن التليفزيون؟

3 أيْن المائدة؟

4 هل الصورة بجانب الشبّاك؟

5 أين الخزانة؟

6 هل التليفزيون تحت الشبّاك؟

7 أين السرير؟

8 هل الباب بجانب المائدة؟

9 أين الحقيبة؟

10 هل المائدة بين الكرسيّ والخزانة؟

If you are learning in a group, play 'Describe my room'. Instructions are on the companion website.

Arabic and computers

Keying Arabic is simpler than writing by hand as the computer automatically joins the letters. An Arabic keyboard will show mainly separate letters (ج م ل , etc.). All you need to do is key the individual letters in a word. For example, the word جميل, beautiful, is four keystrokes. As you key each letter, you will see the one *before* alter to the correct form:

Keystroke 1:	ج	→	*Screen 1:*	ج
Keystroke 2:	م	→	*Screen 2:*	جم
Keystroke 3:	ي	→	*Screen 3:*	جمي
Keystroke 4:	ل	→	*Screen 4:*	جميل

When you key a space, the computer detects that this word is finished and the process begins again with the next word.

Anwar's blog مُدَوَّنَة أَنوَر

Anwar and Nur have gone on a Nile cruise for their honeymoon. Anwar is a photographer and has set up a photo blog for the trip. Here is his first entry. *Tip:* **مَركَب** (markab) = boat; **قَمرة** (qamra) = cabin.

Exercise 11

Read Anwar's blog and answer these questions:

1 From which location is Anwar blogging?
2 At what time of day did Anwar take the photo of the River Nile?
3 How does Anwar describe the cabin?
4 How does he describe the bed, the table and the cupboard?
5 Where is the television? How does he describe it?

Exercise 12

Now see if you can find the Arabic words and expressions in the blog that mean the following. Write the Arabic next to the English equivalent.

1 on the boat ______________________

2 in the morning ______________________

3 next to the window ______________________

4 above the cupboard ______________________

5 between Luxor and Aswan ______________________

6 as well ______________________

7 new and unbroken ______________________

8 the River Nile ______________________

You could start your own Arabic blog. Begin by talking about yourself and describing where you are. You can develop the blog as you learn. Invite fellow students or Arab friends to read your blog and add comments.

CD1: 56

Conversation

Dialects

So far you have met some simple Modern Standard Arabic (MSA) phrases for greetings, for introducing yourself and your family, and for asking for things. These phrases will be understood throughout the Arab world. However, spoken dialects vary from one region to another.

MSA is the foundation that underpins all these dialects. Through MSA you will understand the principles that guide the Arabic language. However, there are variations for basic words used in dialects and it is worth recognising the most common. Two of these are the question words 'What?' and 'Where?':

	What's your name?	*Where's the door?*
MSA	ما اسمك؟ (mā ismak)	أين الباب؟ (ayna l-bāb)
Egyptian	اسمك ايه؟ (ismak eh)	فين الباب؟ (fayn il-bāb)
Levant/Gulf	شو اسمك؟ (shū ismak)	وين الباب؟ (wayn il-bāb)

Listen to the dialects and compare them with the standard version.

Structure notes

The genitive case

Nouns that follow positional words, such as في (in) or على (on), are in the *genitive* case. This case is formed in a similar way to the nominative (see Structure notes in Unit 4), but using kasra, not ḍamma:

	Nominative	*Genitive*
Indefinite	بنتٌ (bintun)	بنتٍ (bintin)
Definite	البنتُ (al-bintu)	البنتِ (al-binti)

So the sentence ...

الصورة فوق السرير. (aṣ-ṣūra fawqa s-sarīr) The picture is above the bed.

... would be pronounced as follows, if fully vowelled:

الصُّورَةُ فَوْقَ السَّرِيرِ. (aṣ-ṣūratu fawqa s-sarīri)

The noun الصورة (picture) is nominative whereas the word السرير (bed) is genitive as it follows the positional word فوق (above).

Vocabulary in Unit 6

فِي (fī) in

عَلَى (ɛalā) on

فَوْقَ (fawqa) above

تَحْتَ (taḥta) below

بِجانِب (bijānib) beside

بَيْنَ (bayna) between

هَلْ...؟ (hal) question marker

نَعَم (naɛam) yes

لا (lā) no

أَيْنَ...؟ (ayna) where?

مُدَوَّنَة (mudawanna) blog/journal

صُورَة (ṣūra) picture/photo

مائِدَة (mā'ida) table

كُرْسِيّ (kursī) chair

سَرِير (sarīr) bed

باب (bāb) door

تِلِيفِزْيون (tilīfizyūn) television

شُبّاك (shubbāk) window

خِزانَة (khazāna) cupboard

مَرْكَب (markab) boat

قَمْرَة (qamra) cabin

نَهْر (nahr) river

7 Describing places

Describing your city or town

Look at this picture and read the Arabic labels of the features around town.

Now check your pronunciation of the labels with the audio.

CD1: 57

نهر النيل في وسط القاهرة
nahr an-nīl fī wasaṭ al-qāhira
The River Nile in the centre of Cairo

Exercise 1

Who works where? Match the jobs with the places.

A ممرّضة	1 مَدْرَسَة
B مهندس	2 مُسْتَشفَى
C مدرِّس	3 بَنْك
D محاسب	4 مَصْنَع

Where are they now? Write sentences, as in the example:

1 بدر/محاسب ~~بدر محاسب وهو في البنك.~~

2 زينب/ممرّضة __________

3 زين/مدرّسة __________

4 أحمد/مهندس __________

What's the town like?

Listen to the description of the town on page 83, following the text below.

CD1: 58

هذه صورة مَدينة، وهُناكَ نهر في المدينة،
وبجانب النهر هُناكَ شارِع.
في وَسَط الصورة هُناكَ بنك وبجانب البنك
هُناكَ مدرسة. المدرسة بين البنك والمستشفى.
وعلى يَمين البنك هُناكَ مصنع أسود وقبيح،
وهو مصنع السيّارات، وَلكِن لَيْسَ هُناكَ سيّارات
في الشارع. أمام البنك هُناكَ شجر جميل،
وَلكِن لَيْس هُناكَ شجر أمام المصنع.

web

Practise writing this description with the 'Speed writing' game on the website.

عَلى يَمين ... (ɛalā l-yamīn) on the right of ...

عَلى يَسار ... (ɛalā l-yasār) on the left of ...

أَمام ... (amām) in front of ...

في وَسَط ... (fī wasaṭ) in the centre of ...

هُناك (hunāka) there is/there are

لَيْسَ هُناك (laysa hunāka) there isn't/there aren't

وَلَكِن (wa-lākin) but

هناك شجر أمام البنك.

There are trees in front of the bank.

ليس هناك شجر أمام المصنع.

There aren't any trees in front of the factory.

هناك شجر أمام البنك ولكن
ليس هناك شجر أمام المصنع.

There are trees in front of the bank but
there aren't any trees in front of the factory.

Iḍāfa constructions

Notice these phrases from the description of the town:

صورة مدينة (ṣūrat madīna) picture of a town

مصنع السيّارات (maṣnaɛ as-sayyārāt) car factory ('factory of the cars')

Putting two or more nouns directly together in this way is known as iḍāfa ('addition'). You have also met examples of iḍāfa in Units 3 and 4: بنت أحمد (bint aḥmad), Ahmad's daughter; حقيبة الولد (ḥaqībat al-walad), the boy's bag. Arabic uses iḍāfa to describe a close relationship, where English might use the possessive 's, 'of' ('a bottle of water') or a compound ('the clothes store').

The ta' marbūta is always pronounced on the first noun in an iḍāfa. Only the last noun in an iḍāfa can have al- (the). Whether or not the last noun has al- depends on the meaning. Look at the examples below:

بيت مدرس (bayt mudarris)	a teacher's house
بيت المدرّس (bayt al-mudarris)	the teacher's house
زُجاجة عَصير (zujājat ʿaṣīr)	a bottle of juice
زُجاجة العَصير (zujājat al-ʿaṣīr)	the bottle of juice

An iḍāfa can consist of more than two nouns:

باب بيت المدرّس (bāb bayt al-mudarris)	the door of the teacher's house
اِبن أمير الكُوَيت (ibn amīr al-kuwayt)	the son of the Emir of Kuwait

Exercise 2

Decide whether these sentences about the town on page 83 are true or false.

1 هناك نهر في المدينة. ☐
2 هناك شارع بجانب النهر. ☐
3 ليس هناك بنك في الصورة. ☐
4 هناك مصنع على يمين البنك. ☐
5 هناك مستشفى بين البنك والمصنع. ☐
6 هناك ممرّضة أمام المستشفى. ☐
7 المصنع هو مصنع السيّارات. ☐
8 في وسط الصورة هُناك مستشفى. ☐
9 ليس هناك شجر أمام المستشفى. ☐
10 المصنع أبيض وجميل. ☐

web PPT On the website you can find a PowerPoint presentation to help you remember the key words for places around town.

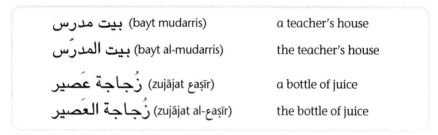

Exercise 3

Make sentences for each picture, as in the example:

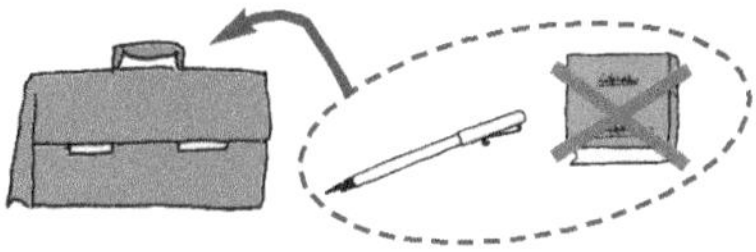

هناك قلم في الحقيبة
ولكن ليس هناك كتاب.

1

2

3

4

CD1: 59

Conversation

Asking for directions

The simplest way to ask for directions is to use the phrase: ... min ayna?, *How do I get to ...?*:

البنك من أين؟ (al-bank min ayna?) How do I get to the bank?

المستشفى من أين؟ (al-mustashfā min ayna?) How do I get to the hospital?

In directions you are given, you might hear these expressions:

على طول (ɛalā ṭūl) Straight on

خذ/خذي ... (khudh/khudhī...) Take ... *(talking to a male/a female)*

أوّل شارع (awwal shāriɛ) the first street

ثاني شارع (thāni shāriɛ) the second street

على اليسار (ɛalā l-yasār) on the left

على اليمين (ɛalā l-yamīn) on the right

قريب[ة] من ... (qarīb[a] min ...) near to ...

Listen to the expressions on the audio, and then try to ask about and understand directions to other places around town. The audio will help you.

بنك المغرب bank al-maghrib *The Bank of Morocco*

More about plurals

You have seen in Unit 4 how many words which refer to people can be made plural by adding certain endings. Remind yourself of the singular and plural for 'teacher':

	Singular	Plural
Masculine	مُدَرِّس (mudarris)	مُدَرِّسون (mudarrisūn)
Feminine	مُدَرِّسة (mudarrisa)	مُدَرِّسات (mudarrisāt)

The sound masculine plural (-ūn) is only used as a plural for words referring to *male people*. The sound feminine plural (-āt) is used as a plural for words referring to female people, but also as the plural of a number of other words which are *not* people (and which may be masculine or feminine in the singular). Here are some words you already know that can be made plural using the sound feminine plural:

	Singular	Plural
car	سيّارة (sayyāra)	سيّارات (sayyārāt)
bicycle	درّاجة (darrāja)	درّاجات (darrājāt)
television	تليفزيون (tilīfizyūn)	تليفزيونات (tilīfizyūnāt)

Notice that you must remove the tā' marbūṭa before adding the plural ending -āt. There are no absolute rules to tell you which words can be made plural using the sound feminine plural. However, a tip is that this plural is often used with longer Arabic words (for example, mudawannāt, blogs) and with words derived from other languages (for example, tilīfizyūnāt, televisions).

More about adjectives

In the description of the town you met this sentence:

على يمين البنك هناك مصنع أسود وقبيح.
On the right of the bank, there's a black and ugly factory.

Notice that the two adjectives come *after* the noun (and not before, as they would in English). The use of و (wa, and) to separate the adjectives is optional. If you are referring to a specific factory, then you must add الـ (al, the) to the adjectives as well as to the noun:

مصنع أسود قبيح	(masnaع aswad qabīḥ)	*a* black ugly factory
المصنع الأسود القبيح	(al-masnaع al-aswad al-qabīḥ)	*the* black ugly factory

You also add الـ to the adjective if the noun has a possessive ending:

حقيبتي الجديدة	(ḥaqībatī al-jadīda)	my new bag
كلبه الأبيض الثقيل	(kalbuhu al-abyaḍ ath-thaqīl)	his white heavy dog

The presence and position of الـ can change the meaning, and you must take care where you place it when describing things:

البنت جميلة.	(al-bint jamīla.)	The girl is beautiful.
البنت الجميلة	(al-bint al-jamīla)	the beautiful girl
بنت جميلة	(bint jamīla)	a beautiful girl

Exercise 4

Put these sentences in the right order. The first is an example.

المصنع	هناك	أمام	سيّارة	جديدة	1

هناك سيّارة جديدة أمام المصنع.

على	قلم	المائدة	هناك	مكسور	2
سيّارتي	أنا	الجديدة	الجميلة	في	3
هناك	المستشفى	بجانب	ليس	شجر	4
مدرّس	المدرسة	هناك	جديد	في	5
محاسب	البنك	بدر	في	الجديد	6

Exercise 5

CD1: 60

Listen to these six new adjectives:

short (qaṣīr) قَصير	big (kabīr) كَبير
weak (ḍaɛīf) ضَعيف	small (ṣaghīr) صَغير
strong (qawīy) قَوِيّ	long/tall (ṭawīl) طَويل

Now say and write a sentence for each picture, as in the example:

1

هذه الدرّاجة كبيرة.

2

3

4

5

6

CD1: 61

Conversation

Describing your town or your room

Alternative phrases for 'hunāka' and 'laysa hunāka' commonly used in spoken Arabic are 'fīh' and 'mā fīh' (also pronounced 'mā fīsh'). Listen to the example sentences on the audio and then try to describe your town or room in a similar way.

فيه مدرسة كبيرة في المدينة. ما فيه مستشفى. (fīh madrasa kabīra fī l-madīna. mā fīh mustashfā.) There's a big school in the town. There isn't a hospital.

فيه صورة جميلة في غُرفتي. ما فيه تليفزيون. (fīh ṣūra jamīla fī ghurfatī. mā fīh tilīfizyūn.) There's a beautiful picture in my room. There isn't a television.

You'll find a full transcript of the descriptions on the website.

Exercise 6

Your friend is looking for somewhere to live and has asked you to translate this advertisement from the local paper. Can you work out what it says?

Tip: شقّة (shaqqa) = apartment; شرفة (shurfa) = balcony;
نخل (nakhl) = palm trees.

شقّة كبيرة وجميلة!

- في مدينة مَرّاكُش
- شارع شَريف
- قريبة من المستشفى
- بين الجامِعة ومدرسة اِبن سينا
- هناك نَخل جميل أمام البيت وشُرفة كبيرة

تليفون: 442 137891

Exercise 7

CD1: 62

Listen to the audio and draw a picture of the description you'll hear. Play the audio through once without stopping, and then play it again, stopping and repeating as many times as you like until you have finished the drawing.

web

Video: *Mahmoud describes his apartment*

Go to the *Mastering Arabic* website to play the video of Mahmoud introducing himself and talking about his apartment in Cairo (al-qāhira). See if you can answer these questions:

1 What feature of Cairo is near to the apartment ?
2 What is the name of the street?
3 What is there at the start of the street?
4 What is there next to Mahmoud's house?
5 Is there a television or internet in the apartment? Why/Why not?

You'll find a transcript, a translation and an extension activity on the website.

Structure notes

Genitive with iḍāfa

The second word in an iḍāfa construction (see pages 85–6) is always in the genitive case:

صورةُ مدينةٍ (ṣūratu madīnatin) a picture of a town

حقيبةُ الولدِ (ḥaqībatu l-waladi) the boy's bag

Vocabulary in Unit 7

مَدينة (madīna) town/city

بَنْك (bank) bank

مَدْرَسة (madrasa) school

شَجَر (shajar) trees

هُناكَ (hunāka) there is/are

لَيْسَ هُناكَ (laysa hunāka) there isn't/aren't

مَصْنَع (maṣnaع) factory

مُسْتَشْفى (mustashfā) hospital

شارِع (shāriع) street

غُرْفة (ghurfa) room

شَقّة (shaqqa) apartment

شُرْفة (shurfa) balcony

نَخْل (nakhl) palm trees

يَمين (yamīn) right

يَسار (yasār) left

وَسَط (wasaṭ) centre

أَمامَ (amāma) in front of

وَلٰكِن (wa-lākin) but

كَبير (kabīr) big

صَغير (saghīr) small

طَويل (ṭawīl) long/tall

قَصير (qaṣīr) short

ضَعيف (ḍaعīf) weak

قَويّ (qawīy) strong

قَريب (مِن) (qarīb) near (to)

عَلَى طول (ﻉalā ṭūl) straight on

خُذ/خُذي ... (khudh/khudhī ...) Take ... *(talking to a male/a female)*

أَوَّل شارِع (awwal shāriع) the first street

ثاني شارِع (thānī shāriع) the second street

On the website you can find links to interactive audio flashcards that will help you review the key vocabulary in *Mastering Arabic* Units 5–7.

8 Review

Exercise 1

Handwrite these combinations of letters.

1 م + ص + ر = ______________________

2 ع + م + ا + ن = ______________________

3 د + م + ش + ق = ______________________

4 م + س + ق + ط = ______________________

5 ل + ب + ن + ا + ن = ______________________

6 ب + ي + ر + و + ت = ______________________

7 ب + غ + د + ا + د = ______________________

Now listen to the audio and add the vowels to the words you have written.

CD1: 63

شارع في دمشق shāriع fī dimashq
A street in Damascus

Exercise 2

Complete this table, as in the examples:

Word with الـ	Meaning	Sun letter?	Initial letter	Word
(al-bayt) اَلْبَيْت	house	✗	ب	بيت
(an-nahr) اَلنَّهْر	river	✔	ن	نهر
				خيمة
				مدينة
				زجاجة
				شقّة
				تين
				كتاب
				سيّارة
				درّاجة
				قميص
				حقيبة
				يَمين
				صورة
				غُرفة
				جَريدة
				طالِب
				وَلَد

When you've completed the table, try covering all the columns except the right-hand 'Word' column. See if you can remember the meaning and then say the word out loud with الـ, checking your answers one by one.

Exercise 3

Put the names in the correct rows, as in the examples:

أحمد	جيهان	نور	مدحت
زينب	زيد	أنور	حسين
بدر	زين	محمّد	دينا

male ______________________ أحمد

female ______________________ زينب

both ______________________ نور

Exercise 4

CD1: 64

Listen to the description of the family on the audio and fill in the names on the family tree.

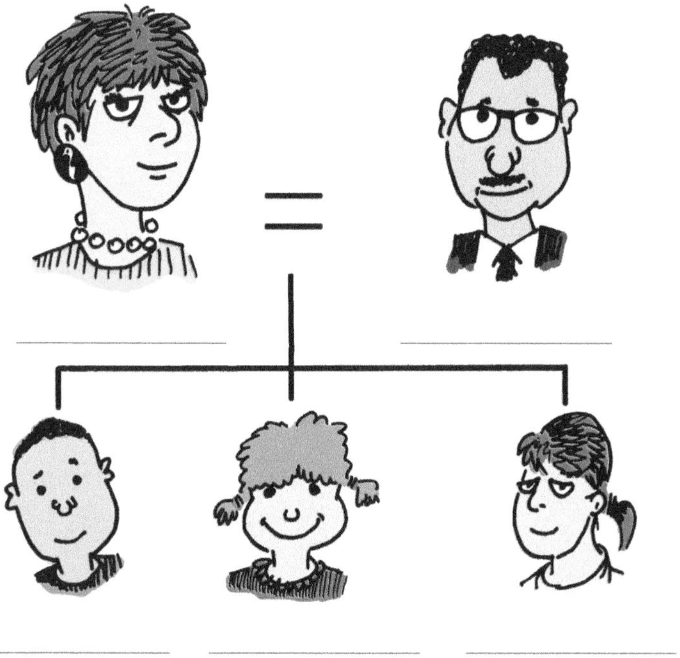

Now draw a family tree for your own family, or the family of a friend, and describe it in a similar way.

Exercise 5

Find the professions in the word square. (The words run either top to bottom or right to left.)

ق	ا	ف	و	ن
م	ث	ظ	م	ي
م	ص	ش	ه	ح
ر	ا	ج	ن	س
ض	ذ	ض	د	ق
ة	م	ت	س	ش
ي	د	خ	ط	ر
و	ر	ب	ه	ن
ب	س	ا	ح	م
ا	ل	ز	ج	و
خ	ط	ت	م	ش

Now write out all the plurals for the words, as in the example:

Feminine pl.	*Feminine sing.*	*Masculine pl.*	*Masculine sing.*
مدرّسات	مدرّسة	مدرّسون	مدرّس

(If you need to remind yourself how to pronounce these professions, look at the vocabulary list on page 50.)

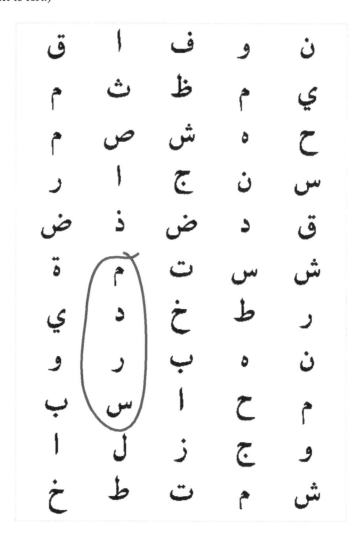

Exercise 6

Find the odd word out in each group of words. The first is an example.

1 حمار كلب جريدة حمامة دجاجة

2 أنا أنتَ هم نحن هل

3 بدر زينب أحمد مدحت أنور

4 هناك في بين فوق بجانب

5 مدرِّس نجّار مصنع خبّاز محاسب

6 بيت شقّة غُرفة أُخت شُرفة

7 كبير صغير ثقيل خفيف كتاب

8 أمّ أب باب أخ بنت

Exercise 7

Write a sentence for each picture, as in the example.

1

هذه سيّارة.

2

3

4

5
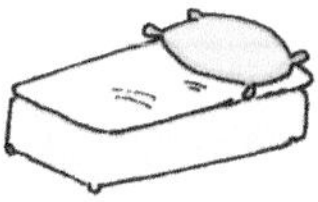

6

7

8

9

10

11

12

CD1: 65

Conversation

Review

Review some of the conversational Arabic you've learned so far by taking part in these two conversations.

Prepare your part first by looking at the guide below. You can look back at the Conversation boxes in Units 1–7 if you want to remind yourself of the conversational phrases.

Conversation 1

– مساء الخير. (masā al-khayr)

Reply.

– ما اسمك؟ (mā ismak)

Say 'I'm ...'.

– ومن هذا؟ (wa man hādhā?)

Introduce a male member of your family.

– تشرفنا (tasharrafna)

Conversation 2

– أهلا! (ahlan)

Say 'Hello to you, Dina.'

– كيف الحال؟ (kayf al-hāl?)

Reply.

– هل هذا قلمك؟ (hal hādhā qalamak?)

Say 'No, that's my sister's pen. My pen is black.'

– أين أختك؟ (ayna uhktak?)

Say 'In the house.'

– تفضل. (tafaḍḍal)

Thank Dina and say goodbye.

Now say your part in the pauses on the audio. You could vary the conversations, changing the person you introduce or the item you are describing. You could also practise with a native speaker, another learner or a teacher if this is possible.

web You'll find a full transcript of the conversations on the website.

Exercise 8

You'll find a large printable version of this activity on the website.

Look at this picture of a bedroom:

Now cut out these pictures and stick them in the bedroom.

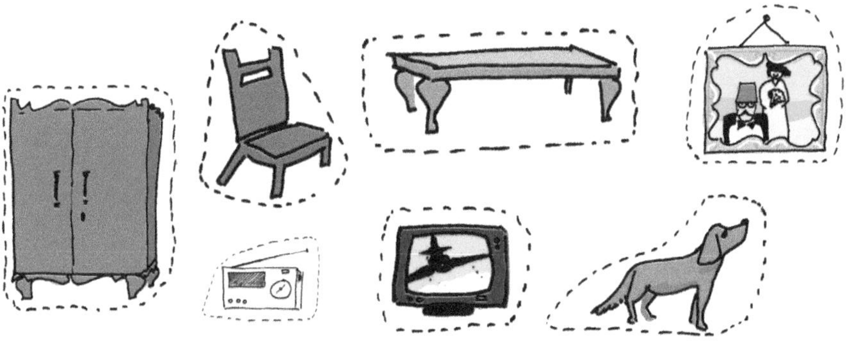

Using some of the words in the box below, make sentences to describe your picture. Start your sentences with هناك.

فوق تحت في على بجانب بين

أمام على يسار... على يمين... في وسط...

Exercise 9

Match the opposite pairs of adjectives, as in the example:

مكسور	طويل	قبيح	قصير	جديد	
قويّ	قديم	ثقيل	كبير	سليم	صغير
أسود	ضعيف	جميل	خفيف	أبيض	

Now choose one of these adjectives to fit into each gap in the description of the picture below. Remember to add tā' marbūṭa and/or al- if necessary. You can use an adjective more than once.

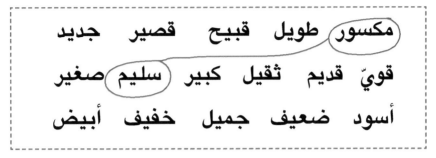

هذه صورة بيت جميل، وعلى يمين البيت هناك

شجرة ______ . لَون (colour) هذا البيت الجميل

______ ، ولكن الباب ______ . أمام البيت هناك

سيّارة ______ ولكن على يسار السيّارة هناك

درّاجة ______ ، والدرّاجة أمام الشجرة ______ .

هناك دجاجة ______ تحت السيّارة. على يمين الصورة

هناك حمار ______ ، وبين الحمار ______ والسيارة

هناك كلب ______ و______.

Exercise 10

Now make questions and answers about the picture in Exercise 9 using the prompts given, as in the example:

1 حمار / قبيح

هل الحمار قبيح؟ لا، هو جميل.

2 سيارة / أمام / بيت

3 كلب / جميل

4 دراجة / سليم

5 دجاجة / على / سيّارة

6 الباب / البيت / الأبيض

7 الشجرة/الصغيرة / على يسار / بيت

8 كلب / بين / حمار / سيّارة

Exercise 11

Look again at these characters you met in Unit 2.

زَيْد

دينا

زَين

نادِر

زَيْنَب

Read the examples describing Zainab's dog and Zaid's bag:

هذا كلب زينب.
هذا كلبُها.

هذه حقيبة زيد.
هذه حقيبتُه.

Now say and write similar sentences for the other characters.

1

2

3

4

9 Countries and people

The Middle East الشّرْق الأوْسَط

Look at this map of ten countries in the Middle East (الشّرْق الأوْسَط, ash-sharq al-awsaṭ) and then listen to the names of the countries. The key to the countries is below the map, together with the relevant national flags.

CD1: 66

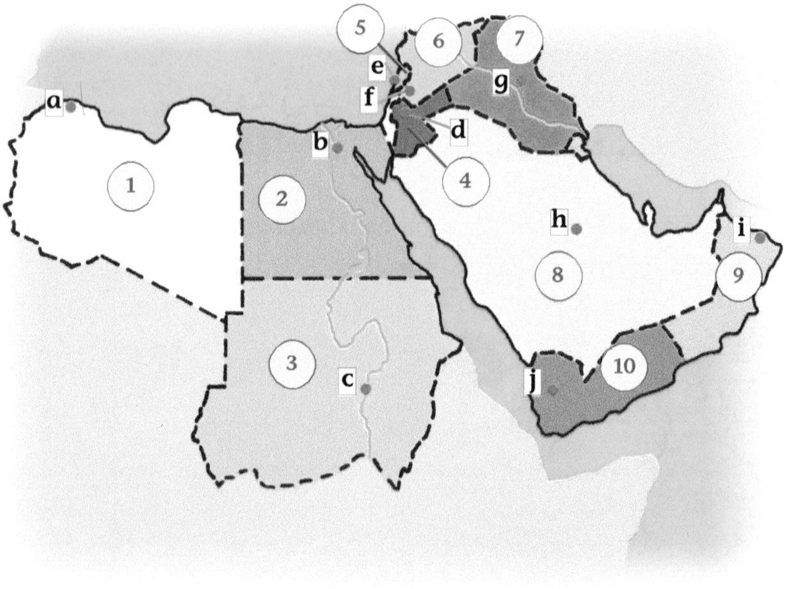

1 ليبيا

2 مِصْر

3 السودان

4 الأردُنّ

5 لُبْنان

6 سوريا

7 العِراق

8 السَّعودِيّة

9 عُمان

10 اليَمَن

web PPT Download a PowerPoint presentation to help you remember the Arab countries.

أنا إماراتيّ من دبي
āna imārātī min dubay
I'm Emirati, from Dubai

Capital city عاصمة

CD1: 67

Now listen to these capital cities, which are also keyed on the map opposite.

a طَرابْلُس
b القَاهِرة
c الخَرْطوم
d عَمَّان
e بَيرُوت
f دِمَشْق
g بَغْداد
h الرِّياض
i مَسْقَط
j صَنْعَاء

Tip: Without the vowels the word عمان could be عُمان (ɛumān), the country of Oman, or عَمَّان (ɛammān), Amman, the capital of Jordan. Watch for the context to tell you which is being referred to.

Exercise 1

Answer these questions referring to the map. The first is an example. Remember that towns and cities are almost always feminine (see Unit 3).

1 هل القَاهِرة في اليمن؟
لا، هي في مصر.
2 هل بَغْداد في لبنان؟
3 هل الرياض في السُعودِيّة؟
4 أين عَمَّان؟
5 هل الأردن بين السُعودِيّة وسوريا؟
6 أين مَسْقَط؟
7 هل ليبيا بجانب اليمن؟
8 هل اليمن بجانب عُمان؟

Exercise 2

Join the flag with the appropriate country and capital city, as in the example.

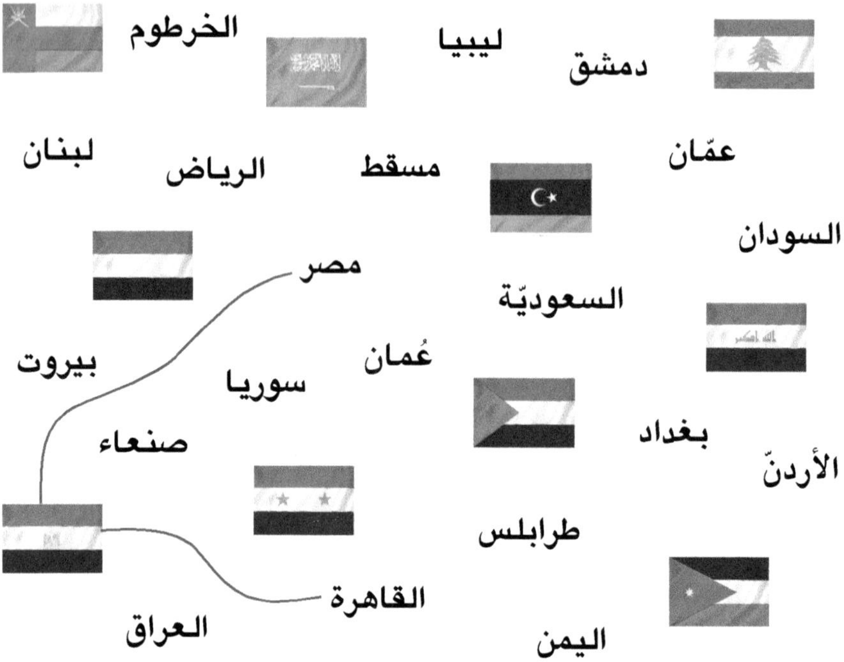

Exercise 3

Now write ten sentences describing the countries and their capitals. The first is an example:

1 القاهرة في مصر وهي عاصِمة مصر.

(al qāhira fī miṣr wa-hiya ɛāṣimat miṣr)

Cairo is in Egypt and it's the capital of Egypt.

Geographical position

Look at the compass with the Arabic for the different directions.

north
شَمال (shamāl)

west
غَرب (gharb)

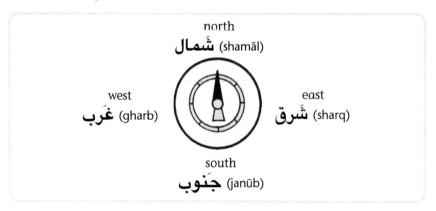

east
شَرق (sharq)

south
جَنوب (janūb)

CD1: 68

Now listen to these descriptions:

مسقط في شمال عُمان.

بيروت في غرب لبنان.

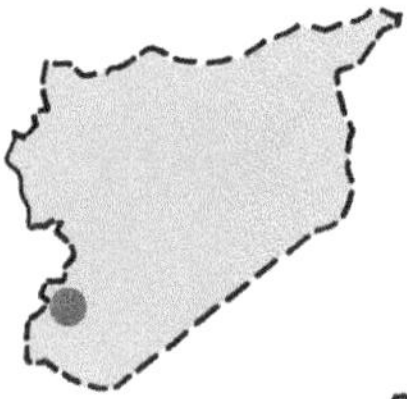

دمشق في جنوب سورية.

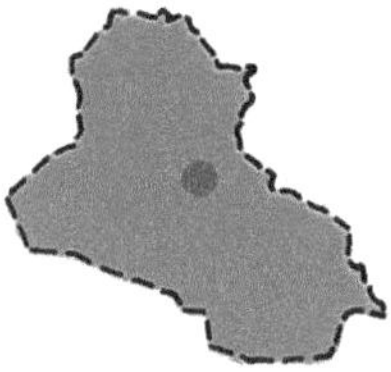

بغداد في شرق العراق.

Notice that in Arabic you use the iḍāfa construction (see page 85) to describe geographical position, putting the position (شمال shamāl, north) directly in front of the place (عمان ɛumān, Oman) with the meaning 'the north *of* Oman': مسقط في شمال عمان (musqaṭ fī shamāl ɛumān, Musqat is in the north of Oman).

Exercise 4

Look at the map of Egypt and read the four towns marked (Alexandria, Port Said, Siwa and Aswan). Then fill the gaps in the descriptions.

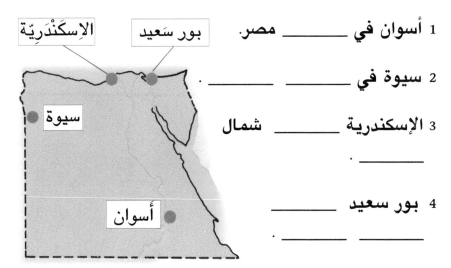

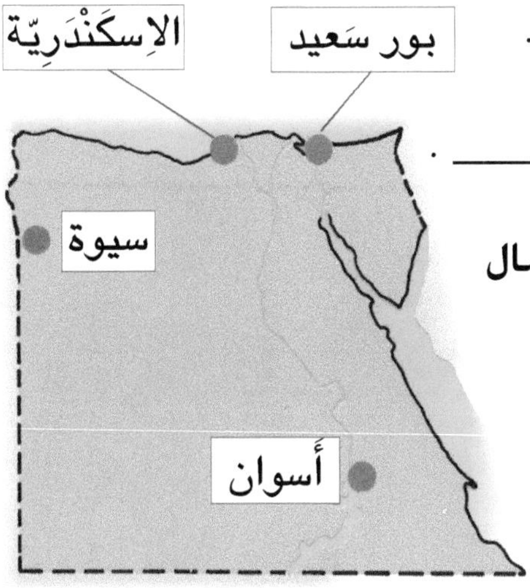

1 أسوان في ______ مصر.

2 سيوة في ______ ______.

3 الإسكندرية ______ شمال ______.

4 بور سعيد ______ ______ ______.

Other countries of the world

Arabic names for foreign countries often end in a long ā sound. As you become more aware of patterns in the Arabic language, you will recognise these foreign names since they stand out as different. There are some variations in how Arabic-speakers say the adopted names for countries, but most pronunciations are more or less similar.

Exercise 5

Try to read the names of the countries in Arabic and then see whether you can match them to their English equivalents, as in the example.

أَمريكا	1 → C	A	China	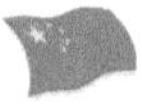
الصِّين	2	B	Spain	
روسْيا	3	C	America	
اليابان	4	D	Italy	
إنجِلتَرا	5	E	Japan	
فَرَنسا	6	F	Russia	
أَلمانيا	7	G	England	
أَسبانيا	8	H	France	
إيطاليا	9	I	Germany	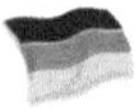

Now check your pronunciation of the Arabic against the audio.

CD1: 69

أنا من برادفورد في إنجلترا
āna min brādfūrd fī injiltarā
I'm from Bradford in England

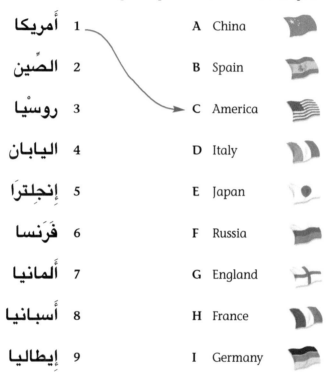

Nationalities

CD1: 70

Listen to the audio, looking at the pictures and following the Arabic.

1 هو مِنْ أين؟

هو من مسقط.

هو عُمانِيّ.

2 هو مِنْ أين؟

هو من الرياض.

هو سعوديّ.

3 هي من أين؟

هي من أسوان.

هي مصرِيّة.

4 هُمْ مِنْ أين؟

هُم من طوكيو.

هم يابانِيّون.

5 هُنَّ مِنْ أين؟

هُنَّ من طَرابلُس. هنّ ليبِيّات.

Nisba adjectives

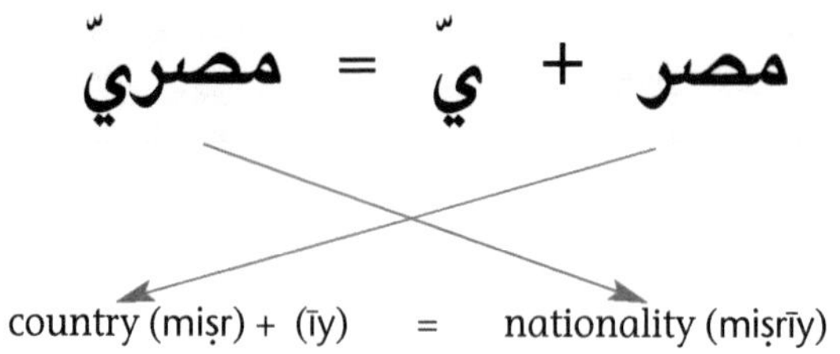

Adjectives describing nationality are made by adding -īy to the noun, in this case the country. This ending has come into English through words adopted from Arabic, such as Kuwaiti, Saudi, Omani and Yemeni.

The -īy adjectival ending is known as نسبة (nisba). Nisba is used to describe nationality, but is also commonly employed to make many other nouns into adjectives, for example turning بيت (bayt), house, into بيتيّ (baytīy), domestic, or شمال (shamāl), north, into شماليّ (shamālīy), northern. Nisba adjectives are a very useful way of expanding your vocabulary quite easily.

There are a few things to remember when adding the nisba ending:

1 If the noun ends in tā' marbūṭa (ة), ā or yā, you need to remove this before adding the nisba ending:

سوريا (sūriyā) Syria	➛	سوريّ (sūrīy) Syrian
أمريكا (amrīkā) America	➛	أمريكيّ (amrīkīy) American
ليبيا (lībyā) Libya	➛	ليبيّ (lībīy) Libyan
مهنة (mihna) profession	➛	مهنيّ (mihnīy) professional
موسيقى (mūsīkā) music	➛	موسيقيّ (mūsīkī) musical

2 If a country starts with al-, remove this before adding the nisba ending:

السودان (as-sūdān) Sudan	➛	سودانيّ (sūdānī) Sudanese
اليابان (al-yābān) Japan	➛	يابانيّ (yābānī) Japanese

3 One nationality is unusual. Take a special note of it:

انجلترا (injiltarā) England	➛	انجليزيّ (injilīzī) English

Exercise 6

Complete the following table, filling in the missing countries and nationalities.

Country الدَّوْلَة		*Nationality* الجِنْسيَّة
الأردنّ		______
______		عِراقيّ
اليابان		______
______		______
أسبانيا		______
______		رُوسيّ
______	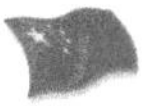	______
______		عُمانيّ
إيطاليا		______
______		سوريّ
______		______
______		مِصْريّ
______		______
فرنسا		______
ألمانيا	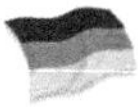	______
______		إنجليزي

Exercise 7

Make sentences about where these people come from, as in the example.

1

هو من الأردن.

هو أردنيّ.

2

3

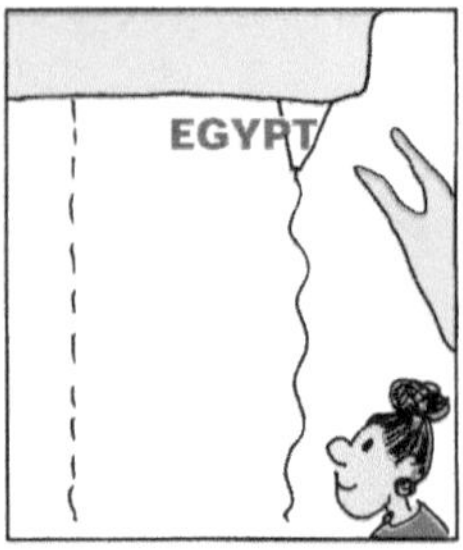

4

5

6

7

8

web

The *Mastering Arabic* website has guidance and links to Arabic dictionaries where you can look up other countries and nationalities. To create a nationality from a country, follow the rules on page 110. You will need to know your nationality in Arabic to take part in the conversation on page 113.

CD1: 71

Conversation

Talking about where you come from

If you want to ask someone where he or she comes from, you can use this question, which literally means 'You from where?':

أنت من أين؟ (anta/anti min ayn?) Where are you from? *(masc./fem.)*

A more formal question would be:

ما جنسيتك؟ (mā jinsīyatak/-ik?) What's your nationality? *(masc./fem.)*

The answer could be either of the following:

أنا من لبنان. (ānā min lubnān) I'm from Lebanon.

أنا لبناني/لبنانيّة. (ānā lubnānīy/lubnānīya) I'm Lebanese. *(masc./fem.)*

You could also be asked:

من أية مدينة؟ (min ayyat madīna?) From which town?

هل هي في الشمال؟ (hal hiya fī sh-shamāl?) Is that in the north?

Now listen to the audio and have a go at answering questions about where *you* come from.

web

You'll find a full transcript of the conversations on the website.

Plural nationalities

As with many of the jobs you met in Unit 4, nationalities and other nisba adjectives can generally be made feminine by adding tā' marbūṭa, and plural by using the sound masculine plural (-ūn) or the sound feminine plural (-āt):

	Masc. sing.	Fem. sing.	Masc. plural	Fem. plural
Egyptian	مصري (miṣrīy)	مصرية (miṣrīya)	مصريون (miṣrīyūn)	مصريات (miṣrīyāt)
French	فرنسي (faransīy)	فرنسية (faransīya)	فرنسيون (faransīyūn)	فرنسيات (faransīyāt)

There are a few exceptions. In these cases the masculine plural is made by *removing* the nisba ending (-īy). The feminine plural is not affected.

	Masc. sing.	Fem. sing.	Masc. plural	Fem. plural
Arab	عربي (ɛarabīy)	عربية (ɛarabīya)	عرب (ɛarab)	عربيات (ɛarabīyāt)
English	انجليزي (injilīzīy)	انجليزية (injilīzīya)	انجليز (injilīz)	انجليزيات (injilīzīyāt)
Russian	روسي (rūsīy)	روسية (rūsīya)	روس (rūs)	روسيات (rūsīyāt)

Exercise 8

CD1: 72

Listen to where these people are from and match the audio to the pictures.

C

description: ____

B

description: 1

A

description: ____

E

description: ____

D

description: ____

Now write about where the people are from. For example:

A هو من نيويورك. هو أمريكيّ.

Tip: The Arabic pronunciation of words of foreign origin can vary, for example amrīkīy or amarikīy for 'American'.

Personal pronouns

Personal pronouns are words such as 'I', 'he' and 'they'. Here is a summary of the important pronouns. You already know most of these, but pay attention to the plural 'you' used when talking to a *group* of people:

	English	Arabic
Singular	I	(āna) أنا
	you *(masc.)*	(anta) أنتَ
	you *(fem.)*	(anti) أنتِ
	he	(huwa) هُوَ
	she	(hiya) هِيَ
Plural	we	(naḥnu) نَحنُ
	you *(plural)*	(antum) أنتُم
	they *(masc.)*	(hum) هُم
	they *(fem.)*	(hunna) هُنَّ

Exercise 9

Create a sentence or question about nationality using the pronoun and flag prompts, as in these examples:

هي  . ← هي لُبنانيّة. (She's Lebanese.)

أنتَ  ؟ ← هل أنتَ صينيّ؟ (Are you Chinese? *masc.*)

1 هو  .

2 أنتِ  ؟

3 هم  .

4 نحن (*masc.*)  .

5 هي  .

6 أنتم  ؟

7 أنتَ  ؟

8 هنّ  .

9 نحن (*masc.*)  .

10 هو  ؟

11 هم  .

12 نحن (*fem.*)  .

13 هي  .

14 هنّ  ؟

15 أنتم  ؟

Exercise 10

CD1: 73

Look at the immigration form and listen to the conversation at the airport. Listen once without writing; then listen again, filling in the missing information on the form. (*Note:* مِهنة mihna = profession.)

الإسم.......أحمد.حسين.....

الجِنسيّة ....

المِهنة ....

اسم الزوجة..............................

جنسية الزوجة............................

مهنة الزوجة.............................

Exercise 11

Read this description of Ahmed and Dina whom you heard at the airport in Exercise 10:

أحمد حسين مُهندس في الرّياض.

أحمد سَعوديّ ولكن زَوجَتُه دينا مِصريّة.

دينا مُدَرّسة في الرّياض.

From the following completed immigration form, write a similar description about Mohammad and Zaynab. *Tip:* طبيب (ṭabīb) = doctor.

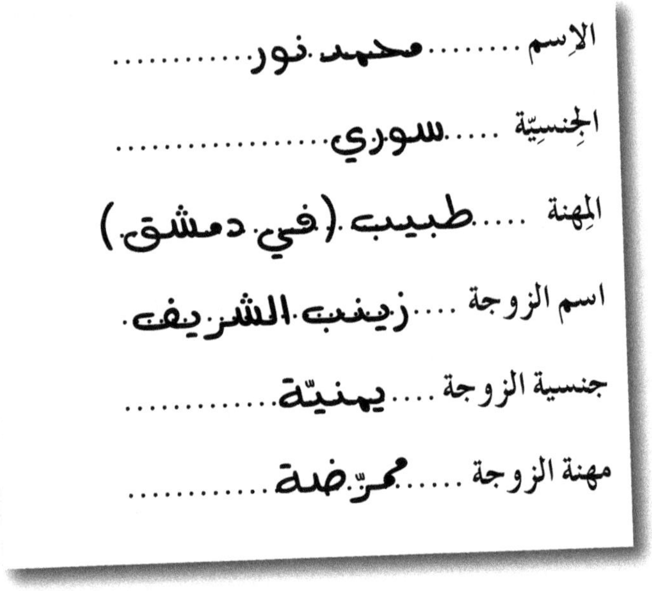

الإسم .... محمد نور ....

الجِنسيّة .... سوري ....

المِهنة .... طبيب (في دمشق)

اسم الزوجة .... زينب الشريف.

جنسية الزوجة .... يمنيّة ....

مهنة الزوجة ..... ممرّضة ....

Video: ***Cyrine talks about herself***

Go to the *Mastering Arabic* website to play the video of Cyrine talking about herself. See if you can answer these questions:

1 What nationality is Cyrine?
2 Which town does she live in?
3 How does she describe her house?
4 What do her parents do?

Don't try to understand everything: just concentrate on the key information. You'll find a transcript, a translation and an extension activity on the website.

Vocabulary in Unit 9

الشَّرْق الأَوْسَط (ash-sharq al-awsaṭ) The Middle East

ليبْيا / ليبيّ (lībyā/lībīy) Libya/Libyan

مِصْر / مِصْريّ (miṣr/miṣrīy) Egypt/Egyptian

السُّودان / سُودَانيّ (as-sūdān/sūdānīy) Sudan/Sudanese

لُبْنان / لُبْنانيّ (lubnān/lubnānīy) Lebanon/Lebanese

سورِيا / سوريّ (sūriya/sūrīy) Syria/Syrian

العِرَاق / عِراقيّ (al-ɛirāq/ɛirāqīy) Iraq/Iraqi

الأُرْدُنّ / أُرْدُنيّ (al-urdunn/urdunnīy) Jordan/Jordanian

السَّعوديّة / سَعوديّ (as saɛūdiyya/saɛūdīy) Saudi (Arabia)/Saudi

عُمان / عُمانيّ (ɛumān/ɛumānīy) Oman/Omani

اليَمَن / يَمَنيّ (al-yaman/yamanīy) Yemen/Yemeni

أمْريكا / أمْريكيّ (amrīkā/amrīkīy) America/American

الصِّين / صينيّ (aṣ-ṣīn/ṣīnīy) China/Chinese

روسْيا / روسيّ (rūsya/rūsīy) Russia/Russian

اليابان / يابانيّ (al-yābān/yābānīy) Japan/Japanese

اِنجلْتَرا* / اِنْجليزيّ (injiltarā/injilīzīy) England/English (*also انكلترا)

فَرَنْسا / فَرَنْسيّ (faransā/faransīy) France/French

أَلْمانيا / أَلْمانيّ (almānyā/almānīy) Germany/German

أَسْبانيا / أَسْبانيّ (asbānyā/asbānīy) Spain/Spanish

إيطالْيا / إيطاليّ (īṭālyā/īṭālīy) Italy/Italian

عاصِمة (ɛāṣima) capital (city)

دَوْلَة (dawla) country, state

جِنْسيّة (jinsiyya) nationality

مِهْنة (mihna) profession

طَبيب (ṭabīb) doctor

أَنْتُمْ (antum) you *(plural)*

شَمال (shamāl) north

جَنوب (janūb) south

غَرْب (gharb) west

شَرْق (sharq) east

مِنْ (min) from

10 Counting things

Arabic numbers 1–10

Europeans adopted Hindu-Arabic numerals in the Middle Ages to replace the clumsy Roman numerals. The set of numerals used most widely in the modern Middle East is the 'Eastern' Arabic set, although the figures more familiar to Europeans are also sometimes used. Compare the Eastern Arabic figures 1 to 10 with their European equivalents.

Eastern Arabic	*European*
١	1
٢	2
٣	3
٤	4
٥	5
٦	6
٧	7
٨	8
٩	9
١٠	10

You can see obvious similarities between the 1 and the 9 in both sets. There is also a theory that the Eastern Arabic ٢ and ٣ were turned on their side to produce the European 2 and 3:

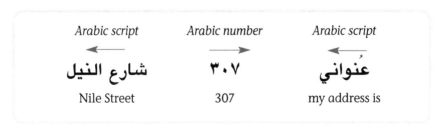

ثلاثة كيلو موز من فضلك
thalātha kīlū mawz, min faḍlak
Three kilos of bananas, please

CD1: 74

Look at the Arabic numbers spelt out below and repeat them after the audio. Each number is given twice:

١	واحِد (wāḥid)	٦	سِتَّة (sitta)
٢	اِثْنان (ithnān)	٧	سَبْعة (sabعa)
٣	ثَلاثَة (thalātha)	٨	ثَمانية (thamānya)
٤	أَرْبَعَة (arbaعa)	٩	تِسْعَة (tisعa)
٥	خَمْسَة (khamsa)	١٠	عَشَرَة (عashara)

Direction of Arabic numbers

One unusual feature of Arabic numbers is that they are written from left to right, in the same direction as English numbers. (Look at the Arabic ١٠ and the English 10.) This is the opposite direction to the rest of the Arabic script. You may see Arabs writing numbers backwards (as if you wrote 12387 starting with the 7 and finishing with the 1). However, writing numbers backwards is a difficult art to master and it is common to leave a space and start the numbers from the left:

Arabic script ←	*Arabic number* →	*Arabic script* ←
شارع النيل	٣٠٧	عُنواني
Nile Street	307	my address is

Exercise 1

Match the figures with the words, as in the example.

1	٦	خمسة
2	٩	ثلاثة
3	٨	سبعة
4	٣	تسعة
5	١٠	واحد
6	٤	ستة
7	١	ثمانية
8	٥	اثنان
9	٢	عشرة
10	٧	أربعة

Now write the vowels on the Arabic spellings of the numbers.

Handwritten numbers

Most Arabic handwritten numbers look similar to the printed ones. The main difference is that the ٢ (2) is usually handwritten as ٢ (see the 'Handwriting practice' panel).

Tip: Watch out for the handwritten ٣ (3). Sometimes the wavy shape at the top becomes smoothed out for the sake of speed, making it look more like a printed ٢. Remember this, especially when reading handwritten prices.

Handwriting practice

Practise writing the numbers, starting at the dot.

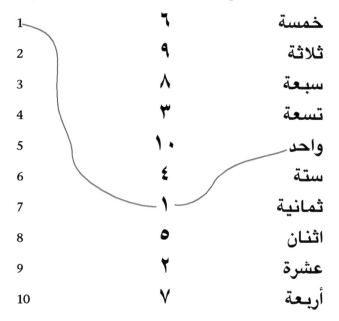

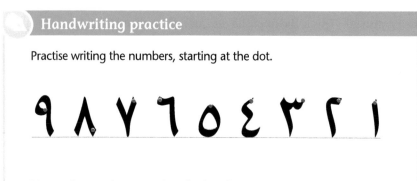

Now write out these numbers by hand: 57, 102, 956, 340, 788.

On the website you can find a worksheet to practise writing the numbers.

CD1: 75

Conversation

Giving your telephone number and address
You can use the numbers to give your telephone number and address. You may also need the Arabic word صفر ṣifr (zero).

رقم تليفوني ٩٧٢٥٠٥ (raqm tilīfunī tisع a, sabع a, ithnān, khamsa, ṣifr, khamsa) My telephone number is 972505.

عُنواني ٧ شارع النيل. (unwānī sabع a shāriع an-nīl)
My address is 7 Nile Street.

If you have a higher number in your address, say the individual digits (e.g. 36 as 'three, six'). You can use the numbers above ten as you learn them.

Listen to the examples on the audio, and then have a go at giving your own address and telephone number.

web You'll find a full transcript of the conversation on the website.

Counting things

Look at the following and listen to the audio:

CD1: 76

مُدَرِّسَة

مُدَرِّس

مُدَرِّسَتان

مُدَرِّسان

ثَلاث مُدَرِّسات

ثَلاثة مُدَرِّسين

The dual

Notice how Arabic uses the plural for 'three teachers', but not for 'two teachers'. This is because there is a special dual ending, ان (-ān), which is added to the *singular*: مدرّسان (mudarrisān), two teachers. There is no need to use the number 2, ithnān, since the dual ending already gives you this information. So 'two dogs' would be كلبان (kalbān), 'two girls' بنتان (bintān), and so on.

An alternative form of the dual ending is -ayn (kalbayn, bintayn). Both forms are possible in Standard Arabic. Dialects usually stick to -ayn.

When the dual ending is added to feminine words ending in ة (tā' marbūṭa), it unties the tā' and so must be pronounced:

Feminine ending with ة	Feminine dual
مدرّسة (mudarrisa) teacher	مدرّستان/تين (mudarrisatān/-tayn)
سيّارة (sayyāra) car	سيّارتان/تين (sayyāratān/-tayn)

Exercise 2

Say and write these words in the dual, as in the example. What do they mean?

١ كتاب كتابان/ين 2 books
٢ مِفتاح ______
٣ مَدرَسة ______
٤ نَهر ______
٥ جَريدة ______
٦ دَولة ______

Plural with numbers

1 The masculine plural مدرّسون (mudarrisūn) becomes مدرّسين (mudarrisīn) when it follows a number. The -īn ending is an alternative sound masculine plural that is sometimes used in Modern Standard Arabic (see 'Structure notes' at the end of this unit for further explanation). Spoken dialects tend to use -īn almost exclusively, so as a beginner you can do the same.
2 You may see the numbers with or without the final tā' marbūṭa, e.g. 'three' as ثلاث (thalāth) or ثلاثة (thalātha). Strictly speaking, a *masculine* noun should be preceded by the number *including* tā' marbūṭa and a *feminine* noun by the number *without* tā' marbūṭa, the opposite to what you might expect:

ثلاثة مدرّسين (thalaathat mudarrisīn) three *(male)* teachers

ثلاث مدرّسات (thalaath mudarrisāt) three *(female)* teachers

This use of tā' marbūṭa with the masculine is an unusual feature that even native speakers can overlook. Spoken dialects tend to simplify the rules, keeping the tā' marbūṭa when the number is pronounced by itself, but dropping it when there is a noun following the number. As a beginner, you can do the same while being aware of the more formal rules.

Exercise 3

Look at the pictures and say how many there are, as in the example.
Tip: balloons = بالونات (bālūnāt)

١

ثلاثة تليفونات

٢

٣

٤

٥

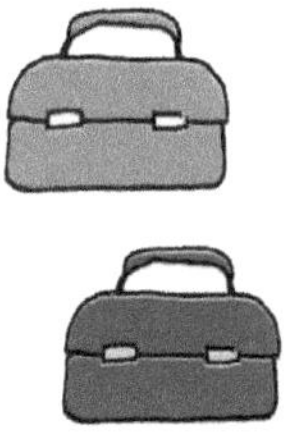

٦

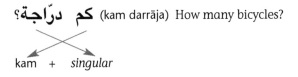

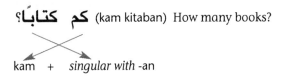

How many? كَم؟

'How many?' is كَم؟ (kam?). In Arabic, this is followed by a *singular* word:

كم درّاجة؟ (kam darrāja) How many bicycles?

kam + *singular*

In addition, if the word following kam does *not* end in tā' marbūṭa (such as almost all masculine nouns), an extra ending is added: اً, pronounced -an.

كم كتاباً؟ (kam kitaban) How many books?

kam + *singular with* -an

Exercise 4

Ask and answer six questions about this picture, as in the example.

هناك كَم سيّارة في الصورة؟ How many cars are there in the picture?

هناك خمس سيّارات. There are five cars.

How much? بِكَم؟

There are many currencies used throughout the Arab world. Here are the most common, together with some of the countries that use them:

CD1: 77

جُنَيْه	(junayh)	Pound (Egypt, Sudan)
رِيال	(riyāl)	Riyal (Saudi, Qatar)
دينار	(dīnār)	Dinar (Kuwait, Bahrain, Iraq, Jordan)
ليرة	(līra)	Lira (Lebanon)
دِرْهَم	(dirham)	Dirham (United Arab Emirates)

Tip: جنيه (junayh, pound) is pronounced with a hard 'g' in Egypt – gunayh. The word is derived from the English word 'guinea'.

Look at the fruit stall and the vocabulary list. Take note of how much each type of fruit costs.

بَطاطِس	(baṭāṭis)	potatoes
بُرتُقال	(burtuqāl)	oranges
مَوز	(mawz)	bananas
طَماطِم	(ṭamāṭim)	tomatoes
تُفَّاح	(tuffāḥ)	apples
مَنجة	(manga)	mangoes

CD1: 78

Now listen to this conversation between the fruit and vegetable trader and his customer. How much are the bananas and how many kilos does she want?

– بِكَم كيلو المَوز من فَضلك؟

– كيلو المَوز بِخَمسة جُنَيهات.

– أريد ثَلاثة كيلو من فَضلك.

– تَفَضَّلي. ثَلاثة كيلو مَوز.

– شُكراً.

بِـ + كَم؟ = بِكَم؟

'with' + 'how many?' = 'how much?'

When you answer the question بِكَم (bikam), 'how much?', you should also put بِـ (bi), 'with', in front of the amount:

بكم كيلو الموز؟ (bikam kīlo l-mawz?)
How much is a kilo of bananas?

كيلو الموز بخمسة جنيهات. (kīlo l-mawz bi-khamsat junayhāt.)
A kilo of bananas is five pounds.

Exercise 5

Look at the question and answer above about the price of a kilo of bananas and make similar exchanges about the other fruit on the stall on page 125.

Exercise 6

Now make up other conversations about the other fruit, based on the conversation above. Vary the fruit, the price and the number of kilos you want.

السوق في المدينة القديمة، القدس
as-sūq fīl-madīna al-qadīma, al-quds
The market in the old city, Jerusalem

In the market في السوق

Here are a few typical souvenirs you might want to buy from the local market. Listen to the words on the audio.

CD1: 79

صَنْدَل	(ṣandal)	sandals
طَبْلَة	(ṭabla)	drum
قِلادة	(qilāda)	necklace
سَلّة	(salla)	basket
تي-شيرت	(tī shīrt)	T-shirt
طَبَق	(ṭabaq)	plate

web PPT Download a presentation to help you remember vocabulary for the market.

Exercise 7

Ask about the price of each of the above items, as in the example.

بكم الصَندَل من فضلك؟

What's it made of?

You can describe what something is made of by putting the material directly after the item:

صَنْدَل جِلد	(ṣandal jild)	leather sandals
قِلادة فِضّة	(qilāda fiḍḍa)	a silver necklace

Exercise 8

Choose a suitable material for each item. (There may be more than one possible material.)

خَشَب (khashab) wood

قُطن (quṭn) cotton

جِلد (jild) leather

زُجاج (zujāj) glass

حَرير (harīr) silk

فضّة (fiḍḍa) silver

ذَهَب (dhahab) gold

نُحاس (nuḥās) copper

Now make requests using أُريد (urīd, I'd like ...). For example:

أريد قلادة ذهب/فضّة من فضلك. (I'd like a gold/silver necklace, please.)

If you are learning in a group, take roles in the market. On the website you can find ideas for role-play.

Describing what you have

Arabic does not generally use a verb to express the meaning of 'have/has'. Instead, a number of prepositions are used: عِند (ɛinda, at), مَع (maɛa, with), and لِ (li, to) are three of the most common prepositions used in this way. The preposition is followed by the possessor, as in the following examples:

عند سارة قلادة ذهب. (ɛinda sāra qilādat dhahab.)
Sarah has a gold necklace. ('at Sarah a gold necklace')

القلم مع أختي. (al-qalam maɛa ukhtī.)
My sister has the pen. ('the pen with my sister')

لمحمد سيّارة جديدة (li-muḥammad sayyāra jadīda.)
Mohammad has a new car. ('to Mohammad a new car')

لِـ (li) is written as part of the word that follows. If it is put before al-, the combination becomes ...للـ (lil-):

للمُحاسِب كمبيوتر قديم. (lil-muḥāsib kompyūtir qadīm.)
The accountant has an old computer.

With attached pronouns

You can use these prepositions with the attached pronouns (see Unit 5), but notice that لِـ (li) then changes to لَ (la) except for لي (lī, I have):

لي أخ في البرازيل. (lī akh fī l-barāzīl.)
I have a brother in Brazil.

لها أخت في قطر. (lahā ukht fī qaṭar.)
She has a sister in Qatar.

عنده كلب صغير. (ع indahu kalb ṣaghīr.)
He has a small dog.

معك كبريت؟ (maعak kibrīt?)
Do you (*masc.*) have matches [with you]?

So far you have met the singular attached pronouns. The most common plural attached pronouns are كم (-kum) your *(plural)*, نا (-nā) our, and هم (-hum) their. These can also be attached to nouns or prepositions in the same way as the singular pronouns.

هل عندكم تين؟ (hal عindakum tīn?)
Do you *(pl.)* have figs?

بيتنا كبير ولكن بيتهم أكبر. (baytunā kabīr walākin baytuhum akbar.)
Our house is large but their house is larger.

عندهم طبق نحاس جميل. (عindahum ṭabaq nuḥās jamīl.)
They have a beautiful copper plate.

Exercise 9

How could you say these in Arabic?

١ Sarah has a large car.
٢ I have a sister in Morocco.
٣ Mohammed has a new bag.
٤ We have a beautiful silver plate.
٥ They have three televisions.
٦ Anwar has a small black dog.
٧ I have two keys [with me].
٨ Do you (*pl.*) have oranges?
٩ Do you (*masc.*) have a pen [with you]?
١٠ Do you (*fem.*) have a car?

سوق الذهب، دبي sūq adh-dhahab, dubay
The gold market, Dubai

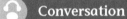

CD1: 80

Conversation

Buying a ring in the market
Put all you've learnt in this unit to good use in the market.

You're going to buy a ring from one of the stalls in the market. You'll need to think about how to say the following in Arabic:

- Good evening.
- I'd like a silver ring, please.
- How much is the ring?
- Here you are. Seven pounds.
- Do you have a bag*?
- Thank you. Goodbye.

Now join in the conversation on the audio, saying your part in the pauses.

* *Tip*: A bag to take away purchases is كيس (kīs) whereas حقيبة (ḥaqība) is a handbag, a suitcase, etc.

web

You'll find a full transcript of the conversation on the website.

Structure notes

Sound masculine plural case endings

The sound masculine plural does not have the same case endings as other nouns. The nominative is mudarris<u>ūn</u>, but the genitive is mudarris<u>īn</u>.

The numbers 3 to 10 are always followed by a plural noun in the *genitive*. This is why the sound masculine plural ending changes from -ūn to -īn.

هناك محاسبون في البنك. (hunāka muḥāsib<u>ūn</u> fī l-bank)
There are accountants in the bank.

هناك ستّة محاسبين في البنك. (hunāka sitta muḥāsib<u>īn</u> fī l-bank)
There are six accountants in the bank.

This change is one of the relatively few instances when a case ending affects the spelling, so it is important to know when it is used.

Vocabulary in Unit 10

صِفْر (ṣifr) zero

واحِد (wāḥid) one

اِثْنان (ithnān) two

ثَلاثَة (thalātha) three

أَرْبَعَة (arbaعa) four

خَمْسَة (khamsa) five

سِتَّة (sitta) six

سَبْعَة (sabعa) seven

ثَمانِيَة (thamānya) eight

تِسْعَة (tisعa) nine

عَشَرَة (عashara) ten

كَمْ؟ (kam) how many?

تِليفون (tilīfūn) telephone

رَقْم تِليفون (raqm tilīfūn) telephone number

عُنْوان (عunwān) address

بِكَمْ؟ (bikam) how much?

جُنَيْه (junayh) Pound

رِيال (riyāl) Riyal

دينار (dīnār) Dinar

ليرة (līra) Lira

دِرْهَم (dirham) Dirham

كيلو (kīlū) kilo

طَماطِم (tamātim) tomatoes

بَطاطِس (baṭāṭis) potatoes

مَنْجَة (manga) mangoes

تُفّاح (tuffāḥ) apples

بُرْتُقال (burtuqāl) oranges

مَوْز (mawz) bananas

سوق (sūq) market

صَنْدَل (ṣandal) sandals

طَبْلة (ṭabla) drum

قِلادة (qilāda) necklace

سَلّة (salla) basket

تي-شيرت (tī shīrt) T-shirt

طَبَق (ṭabaq) plate

ذَهَب (dhahab) gold

فِضّة (fiḍḍa) silver

نُحاس (nuḥās) copper

خَشَب (khashab) wood

قُطْن (quṭn) cotton

جِلْد (jild) leather

زُجاج (zujāj) glass

حَرير (ḥarīr) silk

كُمْبيوتر (kumbyūtir) computer

كِبْريت (kibrīt) matches

بالونات (bālūnāt) balloons

11 Plurals and colours

Word roots جُذور الكَلِمات

Look at the following words with their translations:

كِتاب	a book
مَكْتَب	an office/a desk
كِتابة	writing
كَتَبَ	(he) wrote
كاتِب	writer/clerk
يَكْتُب	(he) writes
مَكْتوب	(something) written down; a letter (correspondence)
كُتَيِّب	a booklet
مَكْتَبة	a library/bookshop

All these words have a connection with writing. Can you find the three Arabic letters that occur in all these words? You should be able to pick out the three common letters:

ك	kāf
ت	tā'
ب	bā'

مكتبة الكتاب maktabat al-kitāb
The 'Al-Kitaab' Bookshop

Notice how the letters always appear in the same order. The bā' does not come before the tā' in any of the words, nor the kāf after the tā', etc. So we can say that if the sequence of letters ك/ت/ب (reading from right to left) appears in a word, the word will have something to do with the meaning of 'writing'. These three letters are the *root* (الجذر, al-jadhr) connected with writing.

The nine words on page 133 each have the string of three root letters ك/ت/ب, with different long and short vowels between them. Sometimes extra letters are added before or after the root letters, or both:

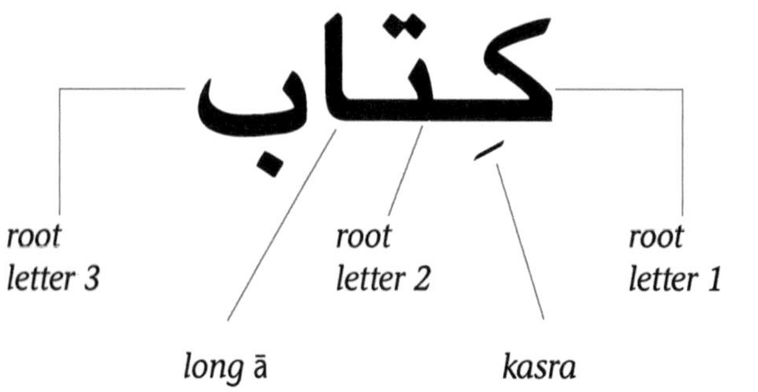

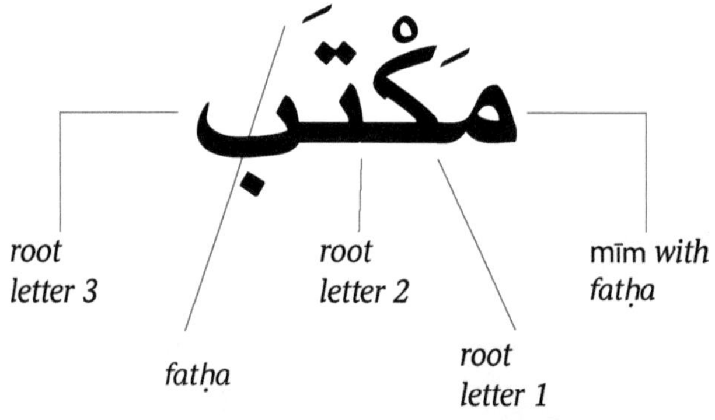

The great majority of Arabic words are formed around a sequence of three root letters, so learning to recognise these will help you enormously with learning the language.

You can often (but not always) find the root of a word by ignoring the vowels (long and short) and removing the extra letters at the beginning and end. As you learn more about the structure of Arabic, you will learn to recognise these extra letters. For the moment, it is enough to know that mīm is a common extra letter at the front of a sequence (*prefix*) and tā' marbūta is a common extra letter at the end (*suffix*).

Exercise 1

Try to write the three root letters for these words which you already know, as in the example. The left-hand column tells you the general meaning of this root.

General meaning	Root	Word
calculating	ح/س/ب	محاسب
bigness	/ /	كبير
carving (wood)	/ /	نجّار
opening	/ /	مفتاح
sealing (a letter)	/ /	خاتم
moving along	/ /	درّاجة
producing	/ /	مصنع
falling sick	/ /	ممرّضة
studying	/ /	مُدرّس + مَدرَسة

web You'll find more details about the Arabic root system, plus a list of common Arabic roots and their general meanings, on the companion website.

External and internal plurals

You already know two ways of making words plural:

1 *Sound masculine plural*. This can be used only with some words that refer to male people:

مدرّس (mudarris) ← مدرّسون/مدرّسين (mudarrisūn/mudarrisīn)

2 *Sound feminine plural*. This can be used with most words that refer to female people, and with some other masculine and feminine words:

ممرّضة (mumarriḍa, nurse) ← ممرّضات (mumarriḍāt)

سيّارة (sayyāra, car) ← سيّارات (sayyārāt)

خطاب (khiṭāb, letter) ← خطابات (khiṭābāt)

These plurals are *external* plurals. However, many Arabic words cannot be made plural with these external endings. They are made plural by following different *internal* patterns which you will learn in the next few chapters.

Internal plurals (also known as 'broken' plurals) are similar to English plurals such as 'mouse'/'mice' or 'goose'/'geese'. However, Arabic has a number of different internal plural patterns and they are much more common than their English equivalents. It's easier to learn these patterns a few at a time so that you get a feel for the way Arabic internal plurals work.

Plural patterns 1 and 2

CD2: 01

Look at the pictures and listen to the audio:

١

قَلَم

أَقْلام

٢

وَلَد

أَوْلاد

٣

فيلم أَفْلام

٤

بَيْت بُيوت

٥

بَنْك

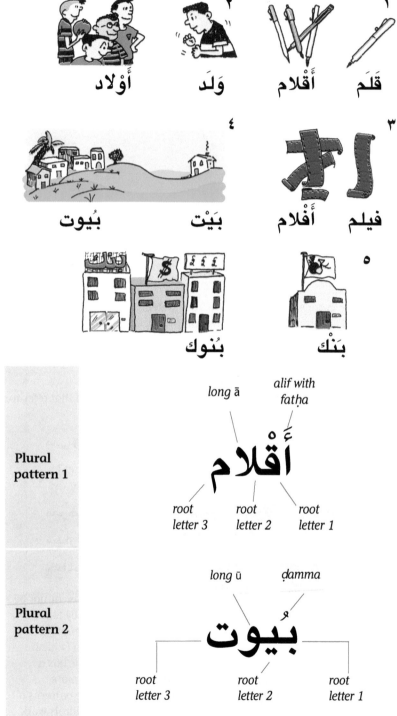

بُنوك

Plural pattern 1

أَقْلام

- *alif with fatḥa*
- *long ā*
- *root letter 1*
- *root letter 2*
- *root letter 3*

Plural pattern 2

بُيوت

- *ḍamma*
- *long ū*
- *root letter 1*
- *root letter 2*
- *root letter 3*

Exercise 2

Match the singular with its plural, plural pattern and meaning, as in the example.

بيت	أقلام	*pattern 1*	films
قلم	أفلام	*pattern 2*	boys
بنك	بيوت	*pattern 1*	pens
فيلم	أولاد	*pattern 1*	banks
ولد	بنوك	*pattern 2*	houses

Now write the vowels on the Arabic singular and plural words.

More about patterns 1 and 2

These two patterns are important internal or 'broken' plurals. The word is 'broken apart' and different long and short vowels are arranged around the root letters, as we have just seen. These two patterns are used to make a number of common short words plural.

Notice that although the vowels on the singular words may vary, they are always the same in the plural pattern. Arabic contains a number of loan words borrowed from other languages, such as 'film' and 'bank': if these have three *consonants* (i.e. letters that are not vowels), they often have broken plural patterns.

There are about a dozen significant different broken plural patterns, seven or eight of these being the most common. You will gradually be introduced to the different patterns.

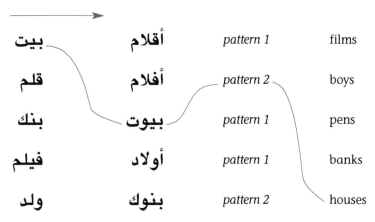

بيوت في قرية تونسية قديمة
buyūt fī qarya tūnisīya qadīma
Houses in an old Tunisian village

Exercise 3

The following words make their plurals according to pattern 1. Write out their plurals, as in the example.

Plural	*Singular*
ألوان	لَوْن (lawn) colour
________	طَبَق (ṭabaq) plate
________	صاحِب (ṣāḥib) owner/friend
________	شَكْل (shakl) shape
________	وَقْت (waqt) time
________	سِعْر (siɛr) price
________	عَلَم (ɛalam) flag
________	كوب (kūb*) glass/tumbler
________	عام (ɛām*) year

* In these cases, و is the 2nd root letter.

These words fit into pattern 2. Write out their plurals.

Plural	*Singular*
سُيوف	سَيْف (sayf) sword
________	قَلْب (qalb) heart
________	مَلِك (malik) king
________	شَمْعة (shamɛa) candle
________	شَيْخ (shaykh) sheikh

Now check your answers with the audio or in the answer section.

CD2: 02

Vocabulary learning

From now on, try to learn each word with its plural. If you are using the card system or an electronic equivalent (see Unit 1), include the plural with the singular.

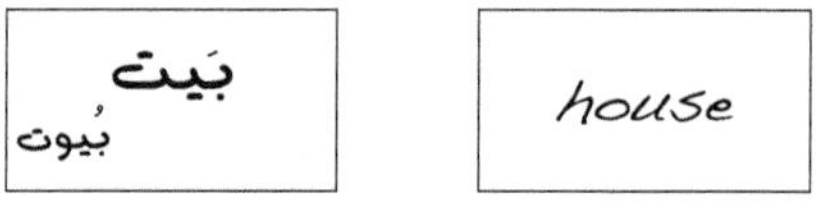

Tip: Just writing or keying the plural will help you to remember it. Make sure that you can remember both the singular and the plural before you pass the vocabulary card to the next stage.

web PPT

Download a PowerPoint presentation from the website to help you remember words that use plural patterns 1 and 2.

What are these?

CD2: 03

Look at the pictures and listen to the audio:

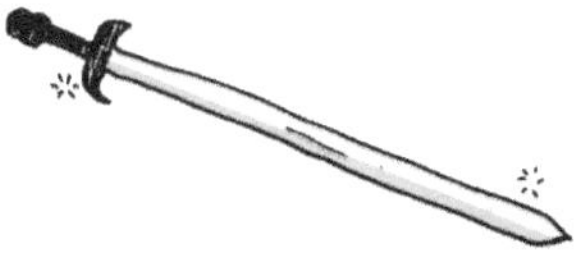

هذا سيف.

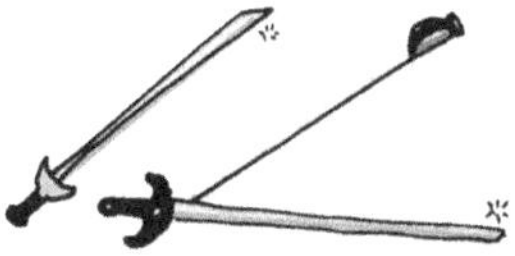

هذه سيوف.

هذا قلم.

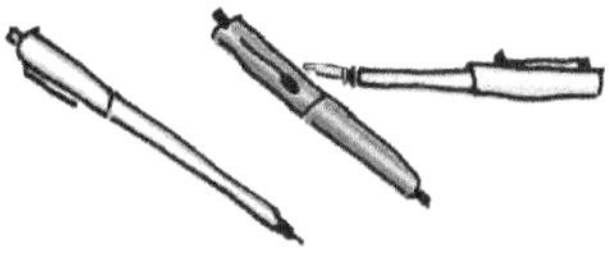

هذه أقلام.

هذا ملك.

هؤُلاءِ ملوك.

هذا سَيف This is a sword.

هذا (hādhā) + *masculine singular*

هذِهِ سُيوف These are swords.

هذه (hādhihi) + *feminine singular* or *non-human plurals*

هؤُلاءِ مُلوك These are kings.

هؤلاء (hā'ulā'i) + *human plurals*

When forming the plural, there are two different ways of saying 'these': هؤلاء (hā'ulā'i) and هذه (hādhihi). Look at these singulars and their plurals:

هذه ممرّضة. هؤلاء ممرّضات.	This is a nurse. These are nurses.
هذه حقيبة. هذه حقائب.	This is a bag. These are bags.
هذا مَلِك. هؤلاء ملوك.	This is a king. These are kings.
هذا قلم. هذه أقلام.	This is a pen. These are pens.

It is important to note that هؤلاء (hā'ulā'i):

1 is only used when referring to *people*; and
2 is the 'people' plural of both هذه (hādhā) and هذه (hādhihi).

In the singular, هذه (hādhā) and هذه (hādhihi) can be used for both humans and non-humans alike, but not in the plural. The reason for this becomes clear when you consider how the Arabic plural system works. Arabic grammar divides plurals into:

1 Humans (the plurals follow gender in a straightforward way).
2 Non-humans (including ideas, animals, objects, etc.), which are all considered and treated as feminine singular. Use feminine singular adjectives, verbs, etc. with non-human plurals. For example, you need to use an adjective with a tā' marbūṭa: البيوت جميلة (The houses are beautiful).

Modern Standard Arabic grammar treats all non-human plurals as feminine singular. There is no exception to this rule.

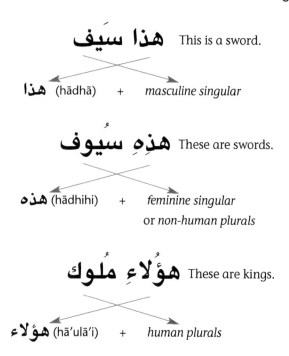

Exercise 4

Write sentences, as in the example.

١

هذه قُلوب.

٢

٣

٤

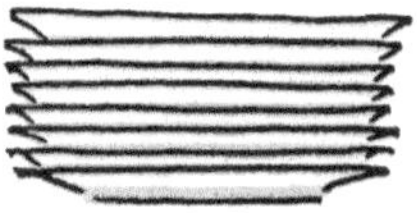

٥

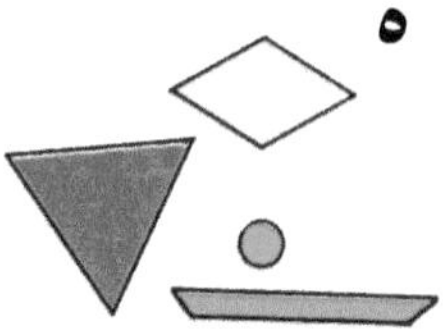

٦

Exercise 5

Make these sentences and questions plural, as in the example:

١ هذا بَيت. هذه بُيوت.

٢ هذا وَلَد.

٣ هل هذا سَيف؟

٤ هذا الكوب مَكسور.

٥ هذه الشَّمعة جَميلة.

٦ أين البَنك؟

٧ الدَرّاجة خفيفة.

٨ هذا العَلَم من أين؟

٩ هَل هذا مُدَرِّس؟

١٠ لا، هو مُحاسِب.

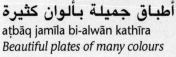

أطباق جميلة بألوان كثيرة
aṭbāq jamīla bi-alwān kathīra
Beautiful plates of many colours

The party الحفَلة

CD2: 04

Salwa is arranging a party for her son's fifth birthday. Listen to the items she needs for the party:

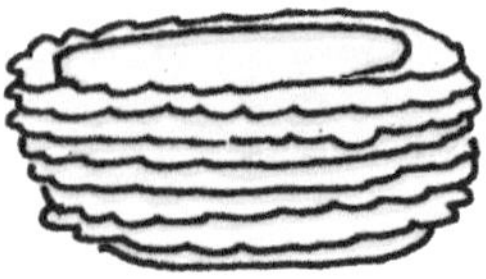

أطباق وَرَق

أكواب بلاستيك

قُبَّعات وَرَق

زجاجات كولا

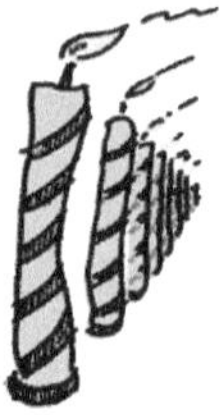

شُموع

أكياس بلاستيك

Exercise 6

Salwa has made a list of how many of each item she needs. Ask the shopkeeper for each item, as in the example.

أطباق ورق ٦
أكواب بلاستيك ١٠
قبعات ٦
زجاجات كولا ٧
شموع ٥
أكياس بلاستيك ٩

أريد ستّة أطباق ورق، من فضلك.

(urīd sittat aṭbāq waraq, min faḍlak)

I'd like six paper plates, please.

Now listen to Salwa buying some of these items in a party shop:

CD2: 05

– صباح الخير. أريد أطباق
وقبّعات ورق وأكواب
بلاستيك من فضلك.

– حاضِر يا مَدام. أيّ لون؟
عِندَنا كُلّ الألوان: أبيَض، أحمَر،
أَخضَر، أزرَق...

– أُفَضِّل القبّعة الزَرقاء والطبَق
الأَحمَر.

– كَم يا مدام؟

– ٦ من فضلك، و١٠ أكواب بيضاء.

– طيِّب... ٦ قُبّعات زَرقاء و٦ أطباق
حَمراء و١٠ أكواب بَيضاء...
خمسة جنيهات من فضلك.

– تَفَضَّل.

– شُكراً. مَعَ السلامة يا مدام.

حاضِر (ḥāḍir) certainly

أيّ ...؟ (ayy ...) which ...?

كُلّ ... (kull ...) all ...

أُفَضِّل (ufaḍḍil) I prefer

CD2: 06

Conversation

Going shopping

Make up a similar conversation but ask for the other three items on the list (plastic bags, cola bottles and candles). Decide which colours you want the items to be. You could start like this:

أريد أكياس بلاستيك وزجاجات كولا وشموع من فضلك.

(urīd akyās bilastīk wa-zujājāt kūlā wa shumūع, min faḍlak)

I'd like some plastic bags, cola bottles and candles, please.

Once you've decided what to say, take the role of the customer.

You'll find a full transcript of the conversation on the website.

Colours الألوان

You can usually make an adjective feminine by adding tā' marbūṭa: for example السرير جديد (as-sarīr jadīd), the bed is new; الحقيبة جديدة (al-ḥaqība jadīda), the bag is new. Six adjectives for basic colours are the main exception to this and have their own feminine forms.

Look at the masculine and feminine adjectives below and the three root letters that occur in both. (Remember to ignore long and short vowels.)

Root letters	Feminine adj.	Masculine adj.	Colour
ب / ي / ض	(bayḍā') بَيضاء	(abyaḍ) أبيَض	white
ح / م / ر	(ḥamrā') حَمراء	(aḥmar) أحمَر	red

We can now see the pattern for the colour adjectives:

Masculine colour adjective

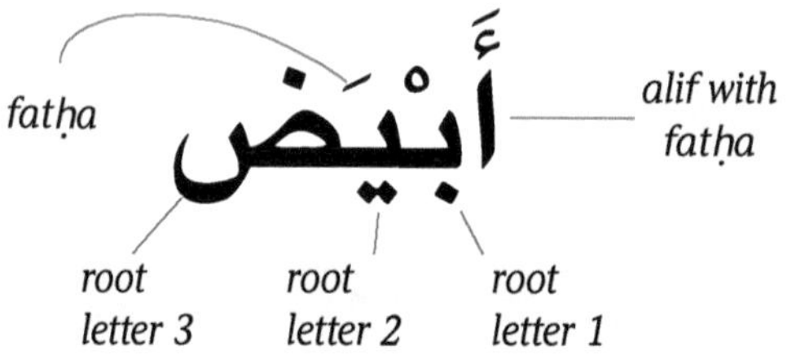

Feminine colour adjective

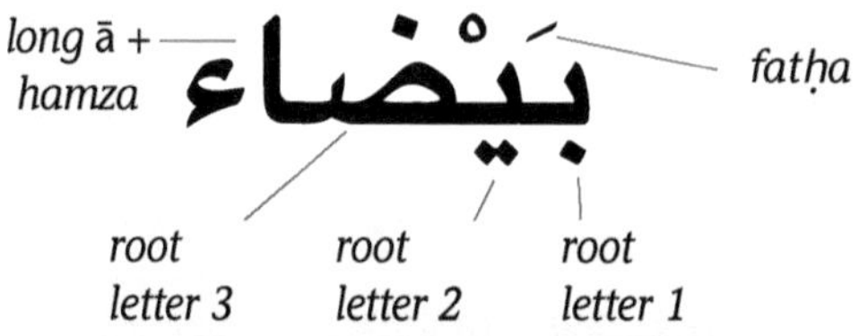

Remember that feminine adjectives are also used with non-human plurals, so it's an important form to learn:

(ṭabaq aḥmar) طبق أحمر	a red plate
(aṭbāq ḥamrā') أطباق حمراء	red plates
(al-qubbaع a aṣ-ṣafrā') القبّعة الصفراء	the yellow hat
(al-qubbaعāt aṣ-ṣafrā') القبّعات الصفراء	the yellow hats

Exercise 7

Here is a table for the four other basic colours, showing the masculine adjectives. Fill in the columns for the feminine adjectives and the root letters:

Root letters	Feminine adj.	Masculine adj.	Colour
		أخضَر	green
		أزرَق	blue
		أسوَد	black
		أصفَر	yellow

Now check your answers with the audio or in the answer section.

CD2: 07

Exercise 8

Say and write these in Arabic, as in the example.

1 a red shirt قَميص أحمر
2 a red car ________________
3 white plates ________________
4 green bottles ________________
5 yellow bags ________________
6 the black dog ________________
7 the blue bicycle ________________
8 the yellow candles ________________

Play the 'Colour' game. You can find instructions on the website.

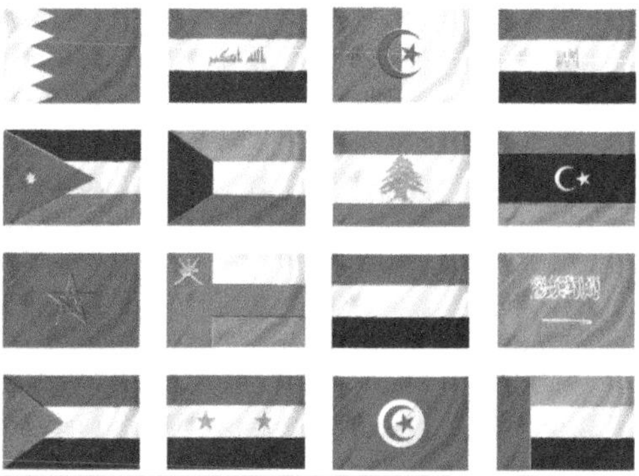

أعلام عربية ألوانها حمراء وسوداء وخضراء.
aع lām عarabīya alwānhā ḥamrā' wa-sawdā' wa-khaḍrā'
The colours of Arab flags are red, black and green.

Back to school

You have spotted this advertisement for back-to-school items ('Fantastic Prices for the New Year').

Exercise 9

Scan the advertisement for the following information:

1 What is the address of the school shop? Where is it next to?
2 What is the question posed on the second line of the advertisement?
3 When does the sale end?
4 Does the company have a website?
5 What is the most expensive item advertised?
6 What is the cheapest item?

Exercise 10

Fill in the items, colours and prices in the following table, as in the example.

Tip: Arabic numbers read left to right and a comma is used as the decimal point.

Item	Price
pens (blue)	4.75

Exercise 11

See if you can find the Arabic words and expressions in the advertisement that mean the following. Write the Arabic next to the English equivalent.

trousers	______________	١
shoes	______________	٢
until	______________	٣
fantastic prices	______________	٤
for sport	______________	٥
for the new year	______________	٦
the best prices in town	______________	٧
our website on the internet	______________	٨

Exercise 12

Pretend you are a trader and make an advertisement yourself using the one on page 146 as a model. You could do this on a computer or by hand. Use household items, toys or clothing in different colours and write the descriptions and prices in Arabic according to what you have chosen.

Structure notes

The accusative case

The third, and final, case in Arabic is the *accusative* (النَّصب, an-naṣb). This is made by adding two fatḥas (ـً) on the end of the word for the *indefinite* (pronounced 'an') and one fatḥa for the *definite* (pronounced 'a').

The table below is a summary of all the case endings:

	Indefinite	*Definite*
Nominative	بنتٌ (bint<u>un</u>)	البنتُ (al-bint<u>u</u>)
Accusative	بنتاً (bint<u>an</u>)	البنتَ (al-bint<u>a</u>)
Genitive	بنتٍ (bint<u>in</u>)	البنتِ (al-bint<u>i</u>)

Note that the accusative indefinite has an extra alif written on the end of the word, called 'alif tanwīn'. The alif tanwīn is not written if the word ends in a tā' marbūṭa:

مدينةً (madīnatan) سيّارةً (sayyāratan)

The alif tanwīn is one of the relatively few instances when a case ending can affect the basic spelling, so it helps if you understand why it is used.

The accusative case is used for the *object of a verb*:

أريد شموعاً. (urīd shumūɛ<u>an</u>) I'd like some candles.

أُفَضِّل القبّعةَ الكبيرة. (ufaḍḍil al-qubbaɛat<u>a</u> l-kabīra) I prefer the big hat.

and for *adverbial phrases* where the meaning is 'with', 'by', 'in the', and so on:

شُكراً	(shukr<u>an</u>)	with thanks (i.e. 'thank you')
صَباحاً	(ṣabāḥ<u>an</u>)	in the morning

The accusative is also used after the *question word* كم؟ (kam, how many?). This explains the extra alif which appears when a noun not ending in tā' marbūṭa follows kam:

كم ولداً؟	(kam walad<u>an</u>)	how many boys?
كم مدينةً؟	(kam madīnat<u>an</u>)	how many towns?

Almost all nouns and adjectives, whether they are singular, dual, plural, masculine or feminine, have case endings in formal Arabic. The main exception to this is words of foreign origin (e.g.: راديو rādyū) when, although theoretically possible, case endings would be very clumsy.

Vocabulary in Unit 11

صَاحِب (أصْحَاب) (ṣāḥib, aṣḥāb) friend/owner

سوق (أسْواق) (sūq, awsāq) market

سِعْر (أسْعار) (siعr, asعār) price

فيلم (أَفْلام) (fīlm, aflām) film

وَقْت (أَوْقات) (waqt, awqāt) time

عام (أَعْوام) (عām, aعwām) year

عَلَم (أَعْلام) (عalam, aعlām) flag

شَكل (أَشْكال) (shakl, ashkāl) shape, likeness

سَيْف (سُيوف) (sayf, suyūf) sword

قَلْب (قُلوب) (qalb, qulūb) heart

مَلِك (مُلوك) (malik, mulūk) king

شَيْخ (شُيوخ) (shaykh, shuyūkh) sheikh

شَمعة (شُموع) (shamعa, shumūع) candle

حَفْلة (حَفْلات) (ḥafla, ḥaflāt) party

كوب (أَكْواب) (kūb, akwāb) glass, tumbler

طَبَق (أَطْباق) (ṭabaq, aṭbāq) plate

كيس (أَكْياس) (kīs, akyās) bag (plastic, etc.), sack

قُبَّعَة (قُبَّعَات) (qubbaعa, qubbaعāt) hat

سِرْوال (سَراويل) (sirwāl, sarāwīl) trousers

حِذاء (أَحْذِية) (ḥidhā', aḥdhiya) shoe

كولا (kūlā) cola

بَلاَسْتيك (bilāstīk) plastic

وَرَق (waraq) paper

مَوْقِع (mawqiع) [web]site

رائِع (rā'iع) great

أَفْضَل (afḍal) best

أيّ (ayy) which?/any

كُلّ (kull) all/every

حَتَّى (ḥatta) until

هؤلاءِ (hā'ulā'i) these (for people only)

حاضِر (ḥāḍir) certainly

أُفَضِّل (ufaḍḍil) I prefer

لَوْن (أَلْوان) (lawn, alwān) colour

أَبْيَض (بَيْضاء) (abyaḍ) white (*fem.* bayḍā')

أَسْوَد (سَوْداء) (aswad) black (*fem.* sawdā')

أَخْضَر (خَضْراء) (akhḍar) green (*fem.* khaḍrā')

أَحْمَر (حَمْراء) (aḥmar) red (*fem.* ḥamrā')

أَزْرَق (زَرْقاء) (azraq) blue (*fem.* zarqā')

أَصْفَر (صَفْراء) (aṣfar) yellow (*fem.* ṣafrā')

web On the website you can find links to interactive audio flashcards to help you review the key vocabulary in *Mastering Arabic 1,* Units 9–11.

12 Eating and drinking

At the grocer's عِنْدَ البَقّال

Look at the pictures and listen to the audio:

CD2: 08

١

جُبْنَة

٢

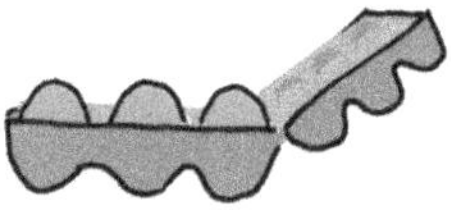

بَيْض

٣

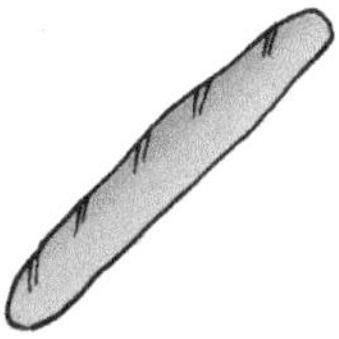

خُبْز

٤

مَعْجون الأَسْنان

٥

حَليب

٦

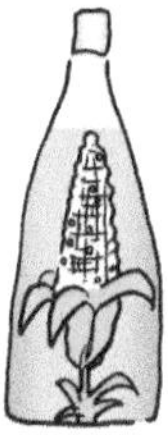

زَيْت

٧

عَصير بُرْتُقال

٨

مَسْحوق الغَسيل

٩

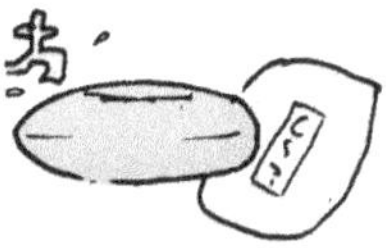

صابون

Download a PowerPoint presentation to help you remember these useful words.

Exercise 1

Here are some more things you might buy in a grocer's shop. The Arabic is very similar to the English. Can you match them, as in the example?

biscuits	أَرُزّ
shampoo	سُكَّر
rice	مَكَرُونَة
cake	شَامْبُو
sugar	بَسْكَوِيت
macaroni	كَعْك

Describing packaging

Here are some useful words to describe food and grocery packaging.

زُجاجة	(zujāja)	bottle
أنبوبة	(unbūba)	tube
عُلبة	(ɛulba)	box/packet/tin/carton
كيس	(kīs)	bag/sack
قِطعة	(qiṭɛa)	piece

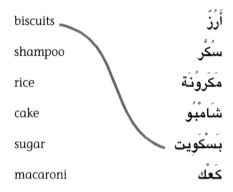

طعام أساسيّ ṭaɛām asāsīy
Basic food

CD2: 09

Now listen to these examples:

زُجاجة زَيت

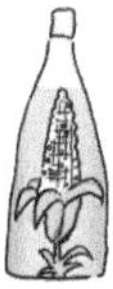

عُلبة بَسكَويت

أنبوبة مَعجون الأسنان

كيس سُكّر

قِطعة جُبنة

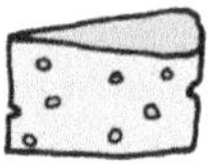

These are iḍāfa phrases, so tā' marbūṭa is pronounced -at if the first word is feminine: zujāj<u>at</u> zayt (a bottle of oil); ع ulb<u>at</u> baskawīt (a packet of biscuits), etc.

Exercise 2

Copy the table below and write the words in the box in an appropriate column, as in the example. The purpose of the exercise is to create reasonable combinations. There is no single correct answer and the items could appear in more than one column.

عصير برتقال	كولا	جبنة	~~حليب~~
مسحوق الغسيل	تين	سكّر	شامبو
معجون الطماطم	كعك	بُنّ	طماطم
مكرونة	بيض	تفّاح	أرزّ

أنبوبة	قطعة	كيس	علبة	زجاجة
			حليب	

CD2: 10

Listen to a customer buying some provisions at the grocer's.

– صَباح الخَير.

– صباح النور يا مَدام.

– أَعْطِني من فضلك علبة طماطم...

– تَحْتَ أَمرِك.

– وكيس سكّر.

– تَفَضَّلي.

– وقطعة جبنة بَيضاء من فضلك. نصف كيلو. كَم الحِساب؟

– أَربعة جنيهات ونصف من فضلك.

– تفضّل.

– شكراً... مَعَ السَّلامة.

– اللّه يُسَلِّمك.

أعطِني	(aɛṭinī)	give me
تَحت أَمرك	(taḥt amrak/-ik)	at your service *(to a male/female)*
الحساب	(al-ḥisāb)	the bill ('the calculation')
مَعَ السلامة	(maɛa s-salāma)	goodbye
الله يُسَلِّمك	(allāh yusallimak/-ik)	goodbye *(reply to man/woman)*

Tip: For the moment, learn phrases you will meet in this unit such "give me", "I (don't) like", "I'll have" and "I'll try" as useful individual expressions. You will learn more about how verbs work as you progress through this course.

Exercise 3

Test your understanding of the conversation above. Answer these questions.

1 What time of day does the conversation take place?
2 The customer wants a tin of something. What is it?
3 She also wants a bag of something. What is this?
4 What type of cheese does she want, and what quantity?
5 How much is the bill?

Exercise 4

Read the speech bubbles and think about which order they should be in:

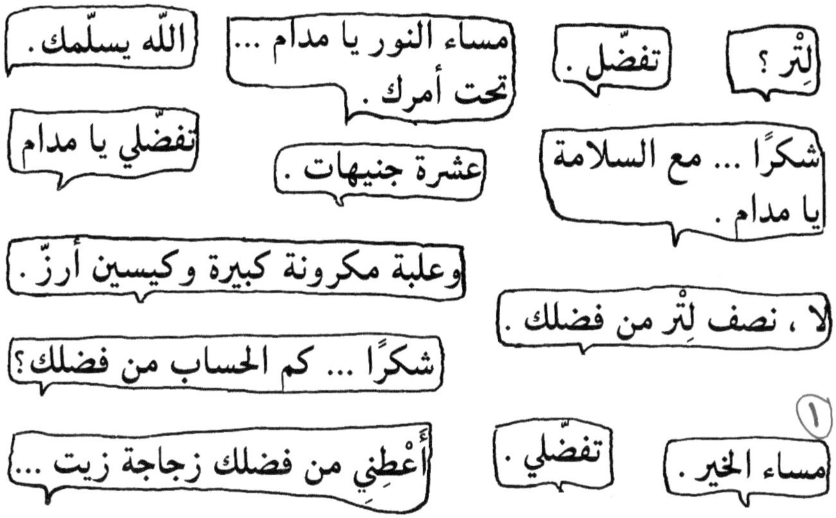

Now listen to the dialogue on the audio, and write numbers next to the bubbles in the correct order. The first is done for you.

CD2: 11

My favourite dish طَبَقي المُفَضَّل

Listen to these useful words and expressions for talking about what you like to eat and drink:

CD2: 12

دَجاج مَشويّ	(dajāj mashwī)	grilled chicken
سَمَك مَقليّ	(samak maqlī)	fried fish
لَحم في الفُرن	(laḥm fil-furn)	[roast] meat in the oven
بطاطس مُحمَّرة	(baṭāṭis muḥamarra)	chips/fries
خَضروَات	(khaḍrawāt)	vegetables
فَواكه	(fawākih)	fruit
قَهوة	(qahwa)	coffee
شاي	(shāy)	tea
أنا أُحبّ ...	(anā uḥibb …)	I like …
أنا لا أُحبّ ...	(anā lā uḥibb …)	I don't like …
طَبَقي المُفَضَّل هو ...	(ṭabaqī al-mufaḍḍal huwa …)	My favourite dish is …

Exercise 5

Read about three people and their favourite foods. Fill in the chart in English according to what they say.

أنا اسمي جَمال وأنا أُحِبّ الدجاج واللحم في الفُرن.
أحبّ الأرزّ والبطاطس كَذلِك ولكن لا أحبّ الجُبنة أو
الحليب. طَبَقي المُفَضَّل هو الدجاج المَشوي مَعَ الأرز.

اسمي كَريمة وأنا لا أحبّ اللحم أو الدجاج،
أُفَضِّل السَمَك والخَضرَوات. طَبَقي المُفَضَّل
هو السَمَك المَقلي في الزَيت مع سَلَطَة الطماطم.

أنا ميدو وطَبَقي المُفَضَّل هو البيتزا! أُحبّ أيضاً
الدجاج المَقلي والبطاطس المُحَمَّرة والكولا
ولكن لا أحبّ الخَضرَوات أو الفَواكِه.

Name	Likes	Dislikes	Favourite dish
Jamal			

Now make notes about *your* likes and dislikes and favourite dish. If you haven't yet met the vocabulary, try to find out what the foods and dishes are called in Arabic. Talk out loud using your notes and then try to write a similar paragraph about yourself.

Group words

Group words (*collective nouns*) are singular but have a plural or general meaning. Most group words refer to things that are naturally found together in groups, for example plants or animals. If a tā' marbūṭa is added to the word, then the group word refers to only one of the group.

a chicken (dajāja) دجاجة ← chickens/chicken (food) (dajāj) دجاج

a fish (samaka) سمكة ← fish (shoal or food) (samak) سمك

a banana (mawza) موزة ← bananas (mawz) موز

an onion (baṣala) بصلة ← onions (baṣal) بصل

Exercise 6

Here are some more group words, some of which are familiar. Read the words and then make them refer to just one of the group, as in the example.

١ figs (tīn) تين ← a fig (tīna) تينة

٢ roses (ward) وَرد

٣ pigeons/pigeon meat (ḥamām) حَمام

٤ trees (shajar) شَجَر

٥ almonds (lawz) لَوْز

٦ apples (tuffāḥ) تفّاح

Exercise 7

Here are three dishes from the Arab world:

كَباب kebab

مَهَلَبيّة mohalabeyya

كُشَريّ koshari

Mark the ingredients you think the dishes contain, as in the example.
Tip: The middle dish is a dessert.

كَباب	مَهَلَبيّة	كُشَريّ	
			دجاج / لحم
		✔	مكرونة / أرزّ
			حليب
			بَصَل
			بطاطس
			سكّر

Which of the dishes do you think the people on page 156 would like? What about *you*? Which do you think you would prefer?

Waiter! يا جرسون!

Listen to the dialogue between a customer (أ) and a waiter (ب). The customer orders three courses and a drink.

CD2: 13 Listen once without looking at the text. Can you make out some of the dishes the customer wants? Then listen again, following the Arabic.

أ – يا جرسون! من فضلك!

ب – نعم!

أ – واحد سلطة طماطم بالبيض...

وبعد ذلك سمك بالأرز.

ب – تحت أمرك يا سيّدي. والمشروب؟

أ – آخذ عصير تفاح بارد من فضلك.

ب – تحت أمرك. هل تجرّب حلوياتنا الشهية بعد ذلك؟

أ – نعم. آخذ بعد ذلك آيس كريم بطعم الفانيليا.

ب – تحت أمرك.

يا جرسون!	(yā gārsūn)	waiter!
آخُذ ...	(ākhudh)	I'll have/I'll take ...
بارد	(bārid)	cold
هل تُجَرِّب ...؟	(hal tujarrib)	will you try ...?
حلَوياتنا الشهيّة	(ḥalawīyātnā ash-shahīyya)	our delicious desserts

Exercise 8

Put a tick on the menu next to what the customer orders, as in the example.

الطبق الأوّل

✔ سلطة طماطم بالبيض .... ٣٠ ريالاً

سلطة دجاج بالمايونيز .... ٥٠ ريالاً

الطبق الرئيسي

لحم بالبطاطس .... ٦٠ ريالاً

سمك بالأرز .... ٧٠ ريالاً

مكرونة بالطماطم والجبنة .... ٤٥ ريالاً

الحلويات

آيس كريم .... ٢٥ ريالاً

كعك باللوز .... ٢٨ ريالاً

المشروبات

قهوة ١٣ ريالاً — شاي بالحليب ١٧ ريالاً

شاي ١٥ ريالاً — عصير برتقال ١٨ ريالاً

كولا ١٤ ريالاً — عصير تفاح ٢٠ ريالاً

Exercise 9

Here is the customer's bill. Look at the menu and fill in the prices.

____	سلطة طماطم
____	سمك بالأرز
____	آيس كريم
____	عصير تفاح
____	المجموع
____	+ خدمة ١٠٪
____	المجموع بالخدمة

Tip: مجموع (majmūع) = total
خدمة (khidma) = service

Tip: Don't worry about saying the numbers out loud for the moment. Just concentrate on writing the figures. You will learn more about higher numbers in Unit 14.

Exercise 10

Now imagine this is your bill, with some of the prices and dishes missing. Referring to the menu again, complete your bill:

٥٠	____
____	لحم بالبطاطس
٢٨	____
____	شاي بالحليب
____	المجموع
____	+ خدمة ١٠٪
____	المجموع بالخدمة

web: You'll find a large printable version of these activities on the website.

CD2: 14

Conversation

At the restaurant

Use your completed bill from Exercise 10 and imagine that you are ordering this meal from the waiter. Using the dialogue on page 158 as a model, prepare what you're going to say and then play the part of the customer on the audio.

web: You'll find a full transcript of the conversation on the website.

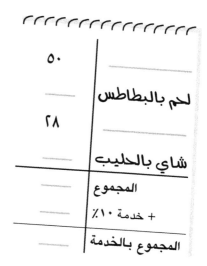

Using a dictionary

You have now reached the point at which you should buy one or more dictionaries to help you expand your vocabulary by yourself and to look up words that you come across in magazines, newspapers, etc.

It is possible to put Arabic in alphabetical order in two ways:

1 According to the order of the letters in a word, as we do in English.
2 According to the order of the *root letters* in a word (see pages 133–4).

For example, imagine you want to look up the word مكتب (maktab, office).

- with method 1 you would look under م/ك/ت/ب (reading right to left).
- with method 2 you would look under ك/ت/ب, the root letters (also reading right to left).

Although the first method is becoming more common, especially as it means that alphabetisation can be carried out by a computer, the second method is still the standard for many comprehansive reference works. The table on pages 282–3 lists the Arabic letters in alphabetical order and will be a useful reference when you are using a dictionary.

So far, we have written the root letters separately: ك/ت/ب. For the sake of convenience, most linguists and dictionaries write the root letters joined up together.

So we can say that كتب is the root of كتاب (kitāb, book) and مكتب (maktab, office); or that درس is the root of مدرسة (madrasa, school) and درس (dars, lesson).

There are a number of Arabic–English dictionaries on the market. Some are designed mainly for native speakers and do not always show the Arabic vowels or plurals (Arabic-speakers are expected to know them). Other dictionaries also have learners of Arabic in mind and these are the most suitable for your purposes.

The two most comprehensive dictionaries designed with learners in mind are the more recent bilingual *Oxford Arabic Dictionary* (OUP, 2014) and the established but older *A Dictionary of Modern Arabic* by Hans Wehr (Otto Harrassowitz, 1993). The *Oxford Arabic Dictionary* includes both Arabic–English and English–Arabic sections. Wehr's *A Dictionary of Modern Arabic* only includes Arabic–English. These two dictionaries differ somewhat in how they present the information and lay out the entries. However, what both dictionaries share is that they organise Arabic words according to the *root letters*, so you will need to identify the root of an Arabic word in order to look it up. The page opposite shows sample entries from both dictionaries under the root درس.

The *Oxford Arabic Dictionary* also has an online version which identifies possible alternative meanings and roots for words you input (including broken plurals and verbs with different prefixes and endings).

web

On the website you'll find more guidance on using Arabic dictionaries, links to the online sites and additional activities to help you look up words.

Oxford Arabic Dictionary (Oxford University Press, 2014)

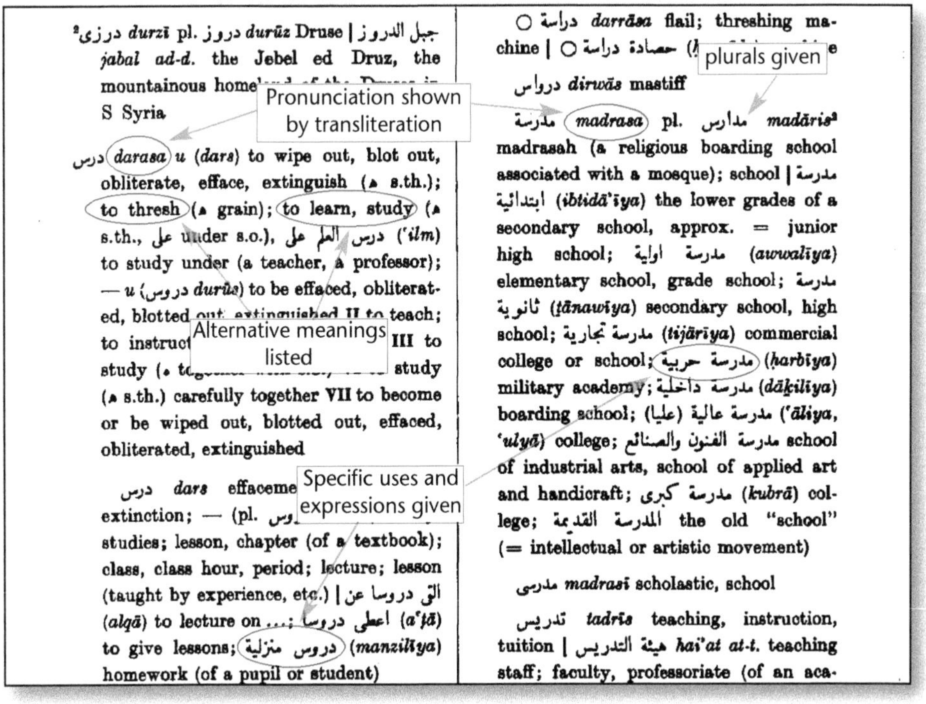

A Dictionary of Modern Arabic (Hans Wehr, Otto Harrassowitz, 1993)

Words for places

Many Arabic words for places begin with ma- (مَـ), for example مَطعم (maṭɛam, restaurant). These words are called *nouns of place* and indicate the place where an activity happens. The root letters طعم (ṭ-ع-m) are connected with feeding, and so the noun of place, مطعم (maṭɛam, 'place of feeding'), has come to mean 'restaurant'.

The pattern starts with ma- (مَـ), followed by the three root letters and a fatḥa, or sometimes a kasra, over the second root letter. A tā' marbūṭa may be added to the end of a noun of place. Here are some more examples:

مَدْرَسَة	'place of study', i.e. school, from root درس
مَكْتَب	'place of writing', i.e. office or desk, from root كتب
مَصْنَع	'place of manufacture', i.e. factory, from root صنع
مَتْحَف	'place for works of art', i.e. museum, from root تحف
مَجْلِس	'place of sitting', i.e. sitting area or council, from root جلس

CD2: 15

The plurals of nouns of place are predictable. Listen to these plurals and repeat the pattern.

مَدْرَسَة	←	مَدَارِس
مَكْتَب	←	مَكاتِب
مَصْنَع	←	مَصانِع
مَتْحَف	←	مَتاحِف
مَجْلِس	←	مَجالِس

متحف الفنّ الإسلاميّ في الدوحة، قطر
matḥaf al-fann al-islāmīy fīd-dūḥa, qaṭar
The Museum of Islamic Art in Doha, Qatar

Exercise 11 Dictionary work

Using your existing knowledge and your dictionary, complete this table.

Plural	Noun of place meaning	Root meaning
مَلاعِب	مَلعَب playground/court	لعب playing
______	______ ______	عرض showing
______	مَدخَل ______	______ coming in
______	______ ______	خرج going out
______	مَخبَز ______	______ ______
______	______ ______	طبخ ______
______	______ ______	غسل ______
______	مَسجِد ______	______ kneeling in prayer

Practise nouns of place with the 'Places' game on the website.

Video: *Mahmoud talks about his favourite food*

Go to the *Mastering Arabic* website to play the video of Mahmoud talking about his favourite food and dishes.
See if you can answer these questions:

1. What does Mahmoud like to eat?
2. What does he not really like?
3. What is his favourite dish called?
4. Can you name some of the ingredients?

Try to pick out the key information.
You'll find a transcript, a translation and an extension activity on the website.

Vocabulary in Unit 12

بَقَّال (baqqāl) grocer

طَعام (ṭaɛām) food

جُبْنَة (jubna) cheese

حَليب (ḥalīb) milk

بَيْض (bayḍ) eggs

زَيْت (zayt) oil

خُبْز (khubz) bread

عَصير (ɛaṣīr) juice

أَرُزّ (aruzz) rice

سُكَّر (sukkar) sugar

مَكَرونَة (makarūna) macaroni

بَسْكَويت (baskawīt) biscuits

كَعْك (kaɛk) cake

مَسْحوق الغَسيل (masḥūq al-ghasīl) washing powder

مَعْجون الأَسْنان (maɛjūn al-asnān) toothpaste

صابون (ṣābūn) soap

شامْبو (shāmbū) shampoo

أُنْبُوبَة (unbūba) tube

قِطْعَة (qiṭɛa) piece

لَحْم (laḥm) meat

دَجاج (dajāj) chicken

سَمَك (samak) fish

حَمام (ḥamām) pigeons/pigeon meat

بَصَل (baṣal) onions

خَضرَوات (khaḍrawāt) vegetables

فَواكِه (fawākih) fruit

بَطاطِس مُحَمَّرَة (baṭāṭis muḥamarra) chips/fries

كَباب (kabāb) kebab

سَلَطَة (سَلَطَات) (salaṭa, salaṭāt) salad

حَلَوِيّات (ḥalawīyāt) desserts

آيس كِريم (āyis krīm) ice-cream

شاي (shāy) tea

قَهْوَة (qahwa) coffee

لَوْز (lawz) almonds

وَرْد (ward) roses

بارِد (bārid) cold

شَهيّ (shahī) delicious

مَقْليّ (maqlī) fried

مَشْويّ (mashwī) grilled

في الفُرْن (fīl-furn) in the oven/roasted

أنا [لا] أُحِبّ (anā [lā] uḥibb) I [don't] like

مُفَضَّل (mufaḍḍal) favourite

جَرسون (garsūn) waiter

تَحت أمْرَك / أمْرِك (taḥt amrak/-ik) at your service *(to a man/woman)*

يا مَدام (yā madām) Madam

يا سَيِّدي (yā sayyidī) Sir

أَعْطِني (aعṭinī) give me

آخُذ (ākhudh) I'll have/I'll take

هَلْ تُجَرِّب؟ (hal tujarrib) will you try?

اللّه يسَلِّمك (allāh yusallimak/ik) 'May God keep you safe' *reply to goodbye (to a man/woman)*

حِساب (حِسابات) (ḥisāb, ḥisābāt) bill/account

خِدْمَة (خِدْمات) (khidma, khidmāt) service

مَجْموع (مَجموعات) (majmūع) total

مَطْعَم (مَطاعِم) (maṭعam, maṭāعim) restaurant

مَكْتَب (مَكاتِب) (maktab, makātib) office/desk

مَتْحَف (مَتاحِف) (matḥaf, matāḥif) museum

مَجْلِس (مَجالِس) (majlis, majālis) sitting area/council

ملْعَب (مَلاعِب) (malعab, malāعib) playground/court/stadium

مَعْرَض (مَعارِض) (maعraḍ, maعāriḍ) exhibition

مَخْبَز (مَخابِز) (makhbaz, makhābiz) bakery

مَطْبَخ (مَطابِخ) (maṭbakh, maṭābikh) kitchen

مَدْخَل (مَداخِل) (madkhal, madhākhil) entrance

مَخْرَج (مَخارِج) (makhraj, makhārij) exit

مَسْجِد (مَساجِد) (masjid, masājid) mosque

مَغْسَلَة (مَغاسِل) (maghsala, maghāsil) laundry

13 What happened yesterday?

What happened yesterday? ماذا حَدَثَ أَمْسِ؟

Look at the today's front page and headline:

سرقة مليون دولار من البنك الكويتي في عمّان أمس!

التحقيق مع لصَّين

زينب شوقي   أحمد حمدي

Exercise 1

See whether you can match these Arabic words from the headline to the English, as in the example:

thief/robber	دولار
dollar	كُوَيتيّ
yesterday	مَعَ
theft/robbery	تَحْقيق
with	لِصّ
investigation	سَرِقة
Kuwaiti	أَمْس

Now answer these questions in English:

1 Where is the bank?
2 How much money was stolen?
3 When did the robbery take place?
4 What is the name of the bank?
5 How many thieves are under investigation?

CD2: 16

The two suspects both deny carrying out the robbery. Listen to Ahmed Hamdi's alibi. (Follow the story from top right, starting on page 169 and using the numbers on the frames.)

ذَهَبْتُ إلى مَطْعَم عربيّ...

وأَكَلْتُ سَمَكاً.

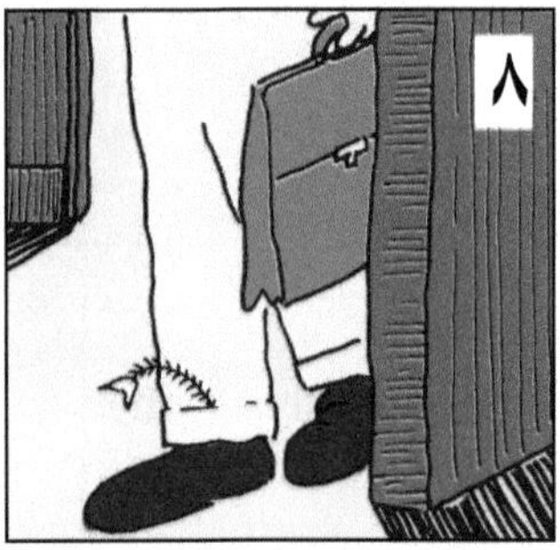

رَجَعْتُ من المكتب
إلى بيتي مَساءً...

وسَمِعْتُ عَن السرقة في التليفزيون.

Download a PowerPoint presentation of Ahmed's alibi to help you follow the frames.

Start here

أنا أحمد حمدي وبيتي في جنوب مدينة عمّان.

أمس خَرَجْتُ من بيتي صَباحاً...

...وذَهَبْتُ إلى مَكْتَبي في وَسَط المدينة.

كَتَبْتُ خِطابات...

وشَرِبْتُ فِنْجان قَهوة.

Look at these sentence tables. See how many different sentences you can make by choosing one word from each column, reading *from right to left*.

صباحًا. (ṣabāḥan) in the morning	البيت (al-bayt) the house	إلى (ilā) to	البيت (al-bayt) the house	من (min) from	ذهبتُ (dhahabtu) I went
مساءً. (masā'an) in the evening	المكتب (al-maktab) the office	من (min) from	المكتب (al-maktab) the office	إلى (ilā) to	رجعتُ (rajaعtu) I returned
	البنك (al-bank) the bank		البنك (al-bank) the bank		

بيتي. (baytī) my house	في (fī) in	شاي (shāy) tea	فنجان (finjān) a cup of	شربتُ (sharibtu) I drank
مكتبي. (maktabī) my office		قهوة (qahwa) coffee	زجاجة (zujājat) a bottle of	
		كولا (kolā) cola	كوب (kūb) a glass of	
		ماء (mā') water		

Now look back at pages 168–9 and listen again to the story, following the words carefully.

CD2: 16
(replay)

شربتُ كوب شاي صباحاً.
sharibtu kūb shāy ṣabāḥan
I drank a glass of tea in the morning.

Asking questions about the past

CD2: 17

A policeman is checking Ahmed's alibi at the police station:

Exercise 2

Make more questions and answers about Ahmed's alibi, as in the example:

١ كتبت خِطابات / مكتب

هل كَتبتَ خِطابات في مكتبك؟

نعم، كَتبتُ خِطابات في مكتبي.

٢ ذهبت / مطعم أمريكيّ؟

٣ أكلت سمكاً / مطعم؟

٤ رجعت / بيت مساءً؟

٥ سمعت /سرقة /راديو؟

Exercise 3

The female suspect, Zaynab Shawqi, is a clerk in the Kuwaiti bank. Read her alibi once *without* writing. Then read it again, filling in the missing words. (Start at picture 1, top right on page 173.)

______ إلى مَطْعَم ______ ...

وفي المطعم سَمِعْتُ ______
السرقة في ______.

رَجَعْتُ ______ المطعم
______ البنك...

ووَجَدْتُ ______.المكسور!

Start here

أنا زينب شَوقيّ و_____ أمس ذَهَبْتُ إلى _____ صَباحاً،
في جنوب مدينة عمّان.

و_____ فِنجان شاي. فَتَحْتُ الخَزانة...

وجَلَسْتُ على مَكتَبي. (على مكتبي = *at* my desk)

The policeman is now checking Zaynab's story:

CD2: 18

اسمي زينب شوقيّ. / ما اسمكِ؟

ذهبتُ صباحاً. / مَتَى ذَهَبْتِ إلى البنك؟

فتحتُ الخزانة وجلستُ على مكتبي. / ماذا فَعَلْتِ في البنك؟

لا، ذهبتُ إلى مطعم صينيّ. / هل ذهبتِ إلى مطعم عربيّ؟

سمعتُ في المطعم. / أين سمعتِ عن السرقة؟

نعم، رجعتُ. / ورجعتِ إلى البنك؟

وجدتُ الشبّاك المكسور. / وماذا وجدتِ؟

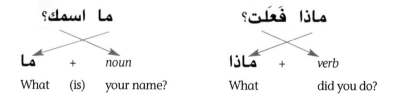

Questions with 'What?'

Arabic has two question words meaning 'what': ما (mā) is used in front of a *noun* and ماذا (mādhā) in front of a *verb*.

ما اسمكَ؟

ما + noun

What (is) your name?

ماذا فَعَلْتَ؟

ماذا + verb

What did you do?

Tip: Arabic verbs are the same whether they are in questions or in sentences. There is no question form *('Did you'/'Did he?', etc.)* in Arabic.

You may have noticed that the past verb endings in the questions vary slightly depending on whether the questions are addressed to a male or a female (compare pages 171 and 174). It's easy to remember:

فعلتَ (faɛal<u>ta</u>) is used for a male أنتَ (an<u>ta</u>)

فعلتِ (faɛal<u>ti</u>) is used for a female أنتِ (an<u>ti</u>)

Exercise 4

Choose a question word from the box to complete each of the questions and answers below. The first one is an example:

أين	متى	ما	ماذا	هل

١ ماذا شَرِبْتَ؟
شربتُ فنجان قهوة.

٢ ______ شَرِبْتَ القهوة؟
شربتُ القهوة في مكتبي.

٣ ______ ذهبتَ إلى مطعم عربي؟
نعم، ذهبتُ إلى مطعم عربي.

٤ ______ أكلتَ في المطعم؟
أكلتُ سمكًا.

٥ ______ فعَلتَ في مكتبك؟
كَتَبتُ خِطابات.

٦ ______ اسمَك؟
اسمي أحمد حمدي.

٧ ______ سَمَعتَ عن السرقة؟
سَمِعْتُ عن السرقة مساءً.

All of the questions above are directed at a male. Say the questions out loud, and then say them again as if you were asking a female rather than a male.

Past Verbs

The verbs you have met in this unit describe things which have happened in the past. They are in the past tense (الماضي al-māḍī). You will have noticed that the end of the verb changes slightly, depending on who carried out the action (that is, depending on the *subject* of the verb).

Look at how this verb changes depending on the subject:

وَجَدْتُ (wajadtu)	I found
وَجَدْتَ (wajadta)	you *(masc.)* found
وَجَدْتِ (wajadti)	you *(fem.)* found
وَجَدَ (wajada)	he found
وَجَدَتْ (wajadat)	she found

Notice that Arabic does not normally use the personal pronouns (هو/أنت/أنا, etc.) with the verb as the *ending* tells you whether the verb relates to 'I', 'you', 'he', etc.

Look again at the list above. You can see that the verb always begins with وَجَد (wajad). This is the *past stem* of the verb and contains the three root letters. (The root letters و/ج/د are connected with the meaning of 'finding'.) The endings added to the stem tell you the subject of the verb:

Ending		Past stem	Subject	Meaning
(-tu) تُ	+	(wajad) وَجَد	أنا	found
(-ta) تَ	+	(dhahab) ذَهَب	أنتَ	went
(-ti) تِ	+	(kharaj) خَرَج	أنتِ	went out
(-a) ـَ	+	(katab) كَتَب	هو	wrote
(-at) ـَتْ	+	(akal) أَكَل	هي	ate
		(rajaع) رَجَع		returned
		(fataḥ) فَتَح		opened
		(jalas) جَلَس		sat
		(faعal) فَعَل		did/made
		(samiع) سَمِع		heard
		(sharib) شَرِب		drank

Tip: In spoken dialects the final vowel of the past tense is often dropped for anā, anta and huwa. So *I found* and *you (masc.) found* both become wajadt, and *he found* becomes wajad.

You may have noticed that without the vowels the word:

وجدت

could have at least four different meanings:

وَجَدْتُ I found	وَجَدْتَ you *(masc.)* found
وَجَدْتِ you *(fem.)* found	وَجَدَتْ she found

There is no automatic way of telling which meaning is intended. However, the context will usually give you a good indication.

Exercise 5

Write the correct form of the verb in the gap. The first is an example:

١ أمس، خَرَجتُ (خرج) من البيت صباحًا. (أنا)

٢ ______ (ذهب) إلى البنك. (هي)

٣ هل ______ (أكل) التُفَّاحة؟ (أنتَ)

٤ أوّلاً، ______ (كتب) خطابات. (هو)

٥ أين ______ (سمع) عن السرقة؟ (أنتِ)

٦ ______ (ذهب) إلى البيت و ______ (جلس) على كرسيّ. (أنا)

٧ ______ (شرب) فنجان قهوة مع أُختها. (هي)

٨ ماذا ______ (فعل) أمس؟ (أنتَ)

Tip: The past stems of the verbs are vowelled mainly with two fatḥas (wajad). Sometimes, however, the second vowel can be a kasra (see the last two verbs in the table). Don't worry too much about this variation. The most important factor is the root letters.

أمس أكلتُ في مطعم سمكٍ.
ams akaltu fī maṭɛam samak
Yesterday I ate in a fish restaurant.

Joining sentences together

CD2: 19

Listen to these words and expressions you can use to link sentences together:

أَوَّلاً (awwalan)	firstly
أَخيراً (akhīran)	finally
بَعْدَ ذلِكَ (baɛda thālika)	after that
قَبْلَ ذلِكَ (qabla thālika)	before that
ثُمَّ (thumma)	then
فـ... (fa)	and/and so

The policeman has written Ahmed's alibi in his notebook. Read what he has written, paying special attention to the linking words and expressions.

التحقيق في سرقة البنك الكويتي

اسمه أحمد حمدي وبيته في جنوب مدينة عمّان. خرج أمس من بيته صباحًا وذهب إلى مكتبه في وسط المدينة. أوّلاً كتب خطابات وبعد ذلك شرب فنجان قهوة. ثمّ ذهب إلى مطعم عربي فأكل سمكًا. رجع إلى بيته مساءً وأخيراً سمع عن السرقة في التليفزيون.

Exercise 6

Unfortunately, the policeman's notes about Zaynab were shredded by mistake. Can you write them out again in the right order?

فرجعَت إلى البنك.

وفتحت الخزانة.

أوّلاً شربَت فنجان شاي...

وبعد ذلك ذهبَت إلى المطعم...

وبيتها في وسط مدينة عمّان.

اسمها زينب شوقي

ثمّ جلسَت على مكتبها.

أخيراً وجدَت الشبّاك المكسور.

أمس ذهبَت إلى البنك الكويتي صباحاً.

وسمعَت عن السرقة في الراديو.

web You'll find a large printable version of this activity on the website.

Exercise 7

Join the two halves to create a meaningful sentence, as in the example.

أكلتُ	ولداً صغيراً بجانب باب المدرسة.
شَرِبَت دينا	إلى بيتي مساءً.
وَجَدْتُ	على كرسيّ خشبيّ.
أولاً، فتحَت زينب	سمكاً في المطعم أمس.
جلَسَت	خزانة البنك الكويتي صباحاً.
أخيراً، رَجَعتُ	زجاجة كولا.

Exercise 8 ماذا فعل الملك أَمْس؟

Below you will find seven things that the king did yesterday.

First, read the sentences and think about the order in which he might have done these things. (Note: قصر (qaṣr) = palace.)

- ☐ ذهب إلى مصنع السيّارات في جنوب المدينة.
- ☐ ذهب إلى مدرسة كبيرة في وسط المدينة.
- ☐ شرب فنجان قهوة مع المهندسين في المصنع.
- ☐ ١ خرج من القصر الملكي.
- ☐ رجع إلى القصر الملكي.
- ☐ جلس مع الأولاد والبنات والمدرّسين.
- ☐ سمِعَ من المهندسين عن السيّارة الجديدة.

CD2: 20

Now listen to the news broadcast and see if you can make out the actual order he did the activities. Write the numbers in the boxes, as in the example.

Using as many of the linking phrases on page 178 as possible, write a newspaper article about what the king did yesterday. Start like this:

أوّلاً خرج الملك من القصر صباحاً و . . .

web

Talk about what *you* did yesterday using the questionnaire on the website.

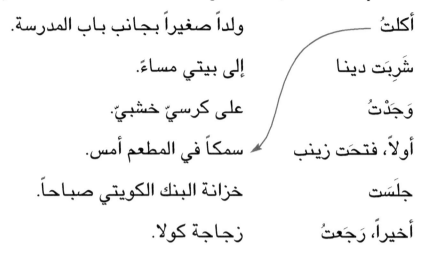

القصر الـملكي في فاس، الـمغرب
al-qaṣr al-malakī fī fās, al-maghrib
The royal palace in Fez, Morroco

Structure notes

Plural and dual case endings

The *sound masculine plural* (SMP) and *dual* case endings vary from the regular case endings. They affect the basic script and the pronounced part of the word. The SMP and dual endings are the same for both the definite and indefinite, so there are only two possible variations for each:

	SMP	*Dual*
Nominative	نجّارون (najjār<u>un</u>)	نجّاران (najjār<u>ān</u>)
Accusative + genitive	نجّارين (najjār<u>īn</u>)	نجّارين (najjār<u>ayn</u>)

The article on page 167 has the title التحقيق مع لصّين (at-taḥqīq maɛa liṣṣayn, The investigation is with two thieves). The dual ending is genitive as لصّين (liṣṣayn) follows the preposition مع (maɛa).

The *sound feminine plural* (SFP) has regular case endings, except for the accusative, which is identical to the genitive:

	Indefinite	*Definite*
Nominative	خطاباتٌ (khiṭābāt<u>un</u>)	الخطاباتُ (al-khiṭābāt<u>u</u>)
Accusative	خطاباتٍ (khiṭābāt<u>in</u>)	الخطاباتِ (al-khiṭābāt<u>i</u>)
Genitive	خطاباتٍ (khiṭābāt<u>in</u>)	الخطاباتِ (al-khiṭābāt<u>i</u>)

Notice that the SFP accusative indefinite, like tā' marbūṭa, does *not* have the extra alif tanwīn:

كتبتُ خطاباً (katabtu khiṭāban)	I wrote a letter.
كتبتُ خطاباتٍ. (katabtu khiṭābātin)	I wrote letters.

Vocabulary in Unit 13

لِصّ (لُصوص)	(liṣṣ, luṣūṣ) thief/robber
سَرِقَة (سَرِقات)	(sariqa, sariqāt) theft/robbery
تَحْقيق (تَحْقيقات)	(taḥqīq, taḥqīqāt) investigation
خِطاب (خِطابات)	(khiṭāb, khiṭābāt) letter
قَصْر (قُصور)	(qaṣr, quṣūr) palace
فِنْجان (فَناجين)	(finjān, fanājīn) cup
كُولا	(kūlā) cola
مَاء	(mā') water
عَنْ	(ʿan) about/concerning
مَعَ	(maʿa) with
إلى	(ilā) to/towards
مَلَكِيّ	(malakī) royal
أَمْس	(ams) yesterday
صَبَاح	(ṣabāḥ) morning
مَسَاء	(masā') afternoon/evening
مَتى؟	(mattā) when?
مَاذا؟	(mādhā) what? (+ *verb*)
خَرَج	(kharaj) went out/exited
ذَهَب	(dhahab) went
كَتَب	(katab) wrote
شَرِب	(sharib) drank
أَكَل	(akal) ate
رَجَع	(rajaʿ) returned/went back
فَتَح	(fataḥ) opened
جَلَس	(jalas) sat down
سَمِع	(samiʿ) heard

فَعَل	(faعal) did/made
وَجَد	(wajad) found
أَوّلاً	(awwalan) firstly
أَخيراً	(akhīran) finally
بَعْدَ ذلِكَ	(baعda dhālika) after that
قَبْلَ ذلِكَ	(qabla dhālika) before that
ثُمَّ	(thumma) then
فَـ...	(fa) and/and so

14 Wish you were here

Plural patterns 3 and 4

Look at the pictures and listen to the audio:

CD2: 21

كَلب كِلاب

رَجُل رِجال

صورة صُوَر

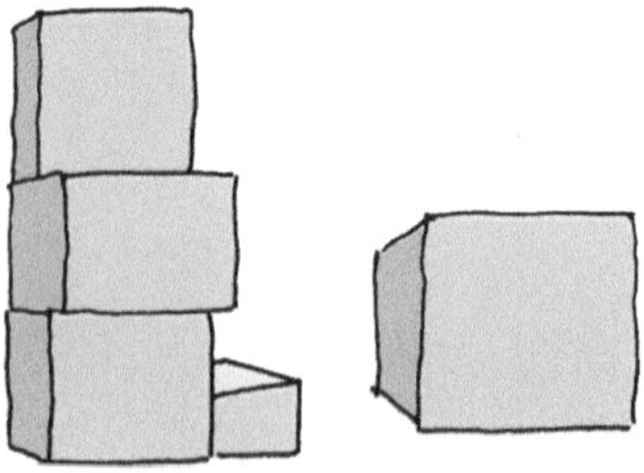

عُلبة عُلَب

To express plural and other patterns in Arabic, the three root letters ف/ع/ل are used as a standard template (فعل = 'to do/to make'). So we can say that plural pattern 3 is the فِعال (fiعāl) pattern, and pattern 4 is the فُعَل (fuعal) pattern.

عُلَب خشب في السوق (القاهرة)
ʕulab khashab fīs-sūq (al-qāhira)
Wooden boxes in the market (Cairo)

Pattern 3: فِعال (fiʕāl)

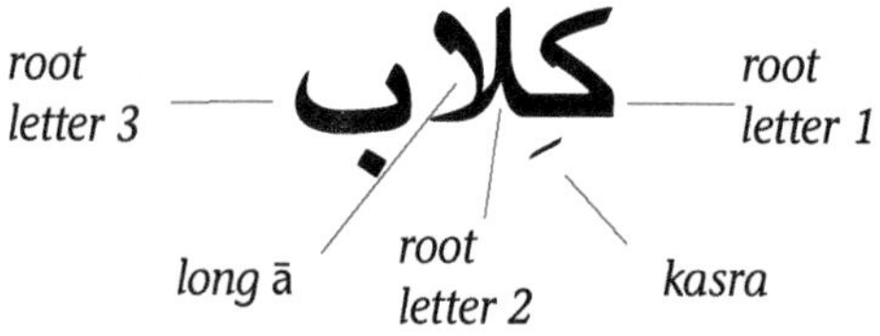

Pattern 4: فُعَل (fuʕal)

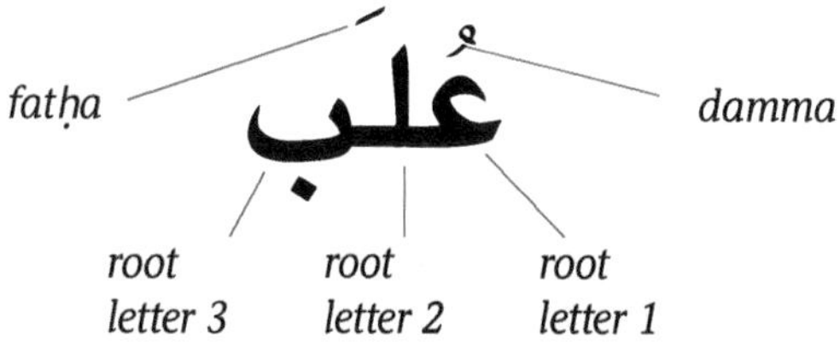

Here are the four broken plural patterns you have met so far:

Pattern			Example		
pattern 1	**أَفْعَال**	(afʕāl)	**قَلَم**	pen	**أَقْلام**
pattern 2	**فُعُول**	(fuʕūl)	**بَيت**	house	**بُيُوت**
pattern 3	**فِعال**	(fiʕāl)	**كَلب**	dog	**كِلاب**
pattern 4	**فُعَل**	(fuʕal)	**عُلبة**	box	**عُلَب**

Exercise 1

Here are some more words that fit into the فِعال (fiعāl) and فُعَل (fuعal) plural patterns. Write the plurals, as in the example.

Plural	Pattern	Singular	
جِبال	فِعال	جَبَل	mountain
	فِعال	جَمَل	camel
	فُعَل	لُعْبَة	toy/game
	فِعال	بَحْر	sea
	فُعَل	تُحْفَة	masterpiece/artefact
	فُعَل	دَوْلَة	nation/state
	فِعال	ريح	wind

CD2: 22

Now check your answers with the audio and repeat the patterns. Do this several times so that you begin to hear the rhythm of patterns 3 and 4.

الجمال في البحر بجانب جبال عُمان
al-jimāl fīl-baḥr bi-jānib jibāl عumān
Camels in the sea beside the mountains of Oman

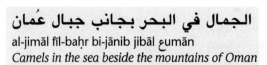

Exercise 2

Make questions and answers, as in the example. Remind yourself of the rules for كم kam ('how many') and for spelling the numbers 3–10 (see pages 122–3).

١

كم كلباً في الصورة؟

هناك أربعة كلاب.

٢

٣

٤

٥

٦

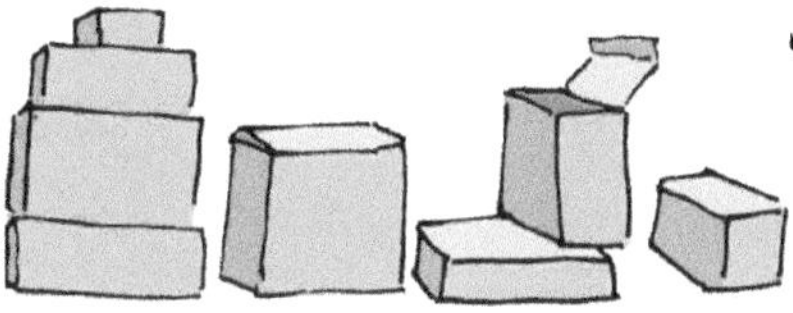

web PPT Download a PowerPoint presentation from the companion website to help you remember words that use plural patterns 3 and 4.

Numbers 11–100

Numbers 11–19

Listen to the audio and repeat the numbers 11–19.

CD2: 23

١١	أَحَد عَشَر	١٦	سِتَّة عَشَر
١٢	اِثْنا عَشَر	١٧	سَبعة عَشَر
١٣	ثَلاثَة عَشَر	١٨	ثَمانية عَشَر
١٤	أَربعة عَشَر	١٩	تِسعَة عَشَر
١٥	خَمسة عَشَر		

The pronunciation of Arabic numbers can vary depending on the accent of the speaker and the formality of the language. In this course you will learn an informal pronunciation that will be understood universally.

Exercise 3

Match the figures and the words, as in the example.

١٤	ستّة عشر	11
١٧	ثلاثة عشر	14
١١	خمسة عشر	16
١٦	أربعة عشر	19
١٩	ثمانية عشر	15
١٢	تسعة عشر	18
١٨	اثنا عشر	17
١٣	سبعة عشر	12
١٥	أحد عشر	13

Exercise 4

Say and write these numbers:

١٥	١٤	٩	٤
٥	١٢	١٦	١٨

Numbers 20–100

CD2: 24

Now listen to the numbers 20 upwards:

٢٠	عِشْرين	٢١	واحد وعِشْرين
٣٠	ثَلاثين	٢٢	اِثنان وعِشْرين
٤٠	أَرْبَعين	٢٣	ثَلاثة وعِشْرين
٥٠	خَمْسين	٥٦	سِتّة وخَمْسين
٦٠	ستِّين	٨٨	ثَمانية وثَمانين
٧٠	سَبْعين	٩٥	خَمْسة وتِسعين
٨٠	ثَمانين		
٩٠	تِسعين		
١٠٠	مِئة		

'Twenty-one', 'fifty-six', etc. in Arabic, are wāḥid <u>wa</u>-ɛishrīn ('one <u>and</u> twenty'), sitta <u>wa</u>-khamsīn ('six <u>and</u> fifty'), etc. The units come *before* the tens.

Tip: The tens from 20 to 90 have an alternative ending, ون (-ūn): ɛishrūn, thalāthūn, etc. However, informally most native speakers use the ين (-īn) ending consistently and so this is the more useful pronunciation to learn initially. See the 'Structure notes' at the end of the unit for more details.

Exercise 5

Write these numbers in figures, as in the example. (Remember: figures go *from left to right*, as they do in English.)

١ ستة وأربعين ← ٤٦

٢ واحد وثمانين

٣ خمسة وثلاثين

٤ مئة وأربعة وعشرين

٥ ثلاثة وتسعين

٦ اثنان وسبعين

٧ مئة وخمسة وثمانين

٨ مئة وسبعة وخمسين

Numbers 11 upwards with a singular noun

The numbers 11 upwards are followed by a *singular* noun. It is as if in English we said 'three cars' but 'thirty car'. This may seem surprising to a learner, but it is important to remember as it is true even of spoken dialects.

٣ سيارات	(thalāth sayyārāt)	three cars
٣٠ سيّارة	(thalāthīn sayyāra)	thirty cars

In addition, the singular noun following a number above 11 will have the extra alif tanwīn (-an ending) if the noun *does not* end in tā' marbūṭa. This is similar to what happens after kam? (how many?).

٤ جبال	(arbaعat jibāl)	four mountains
١٢ جبلاً	(ithnāعasharat jabalan)	twelve mountains

However, it is not necessary to pronounce this -an ending when speaking informally. The singular/plural rule is much more important. High-level Modern Standard Arabic has additional rules about how to spell numbers. As a beginner you can stick to the forms given here. Be prepared, however, to hear or see some variations.

web

You'll find more details about Arabic numbers on the website and further practice activities in the *Mastering Arabic 1 Activity Book*.

Exercise 6

How many are there? Write the answer and then and say it using the informal pronunciation, as shown in the example.

16 x 

58 x 

61 x 

٦١ رجلاً

(wāḥid wa-sittīn rajul)

18 x 

49 x 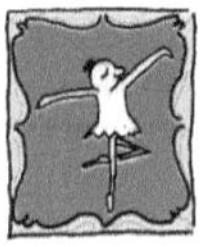

23 x 

93 x 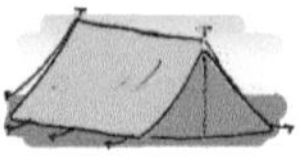

28 x 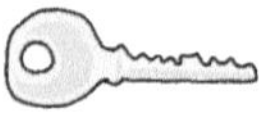

72 x 

What's the weather like? كَيف حـال الطَّقس؟

Temperature دَرَجة الحرارة

Look at the thermometer and the descriptions of the temperatures.

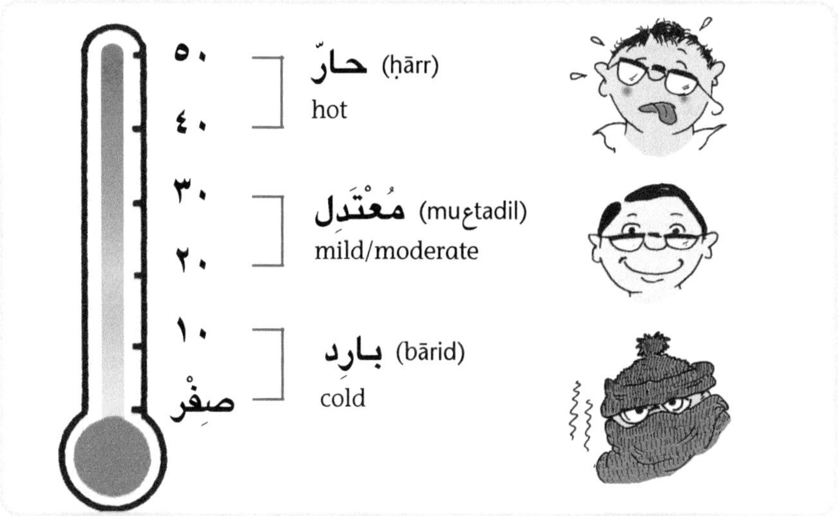

Now listen to the audio and look at the following descriptions:

CD2: 25

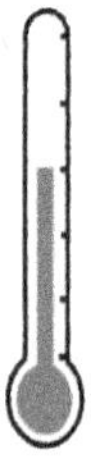

ما هي دَرَجَة الحَرارة؟

دَرَجَة الحرارة ٣٠

الطَّقس مُعْتَدِل.

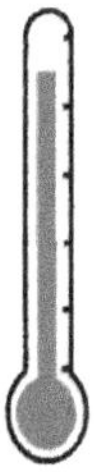

ما هي دَرَجَة الحرارة؟

دَرَجَة الحرارة ٤٥.

الطَّقس حـارّ.

ما هي دَرَجَة الحرارة؟

دَرَجَة الحرارة صِفْر.

الطَّقس بـارِد جِدّاً.

Exercise 7

Following the examples above, make questions and answers for the temperatures shown by these thermometers.

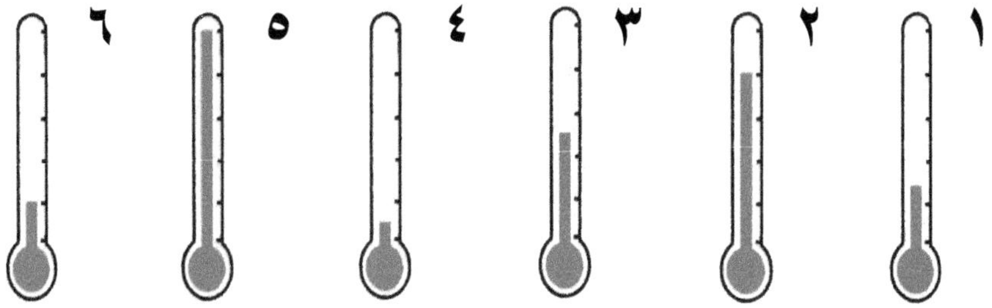

Describing the weather

CD2: 26

Listen to these key words and expressions for talking about the weather:

شَمْس	(shams)	sun
مُشْمِس	(mushmis)	sunny
غَيْم/غُيوم	(ghaym/ghuyūm)	cloud/clouds
غائِم	(ghā'im)	cloudy
مَطَر/أَمْطار	(maṭar/amṭār)	rain/rains
مُمْطِر	(mumṭir)	rainy
شَديد	(shadīd)	strong/heavy (e.g. rain)
فَتْرة/فَتَرات	(fatra/fatarāt)	period/periods
سَماء صافِية	(samā' ṣāfiya)	clear sky

Exercise 8

CD2: 27

Listen to the four weather reports and tick the features that are mentioned.

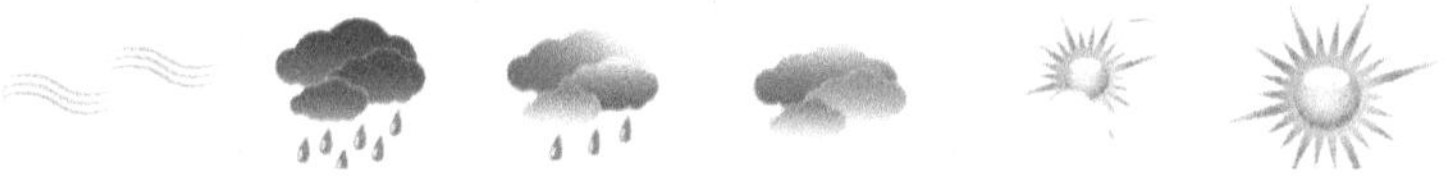

						١
						٢
						٣
						٤

الطقس غائم اليوم.
aṭ-ṭaqs ghā'im al-yawm
The weather is cloudy today.

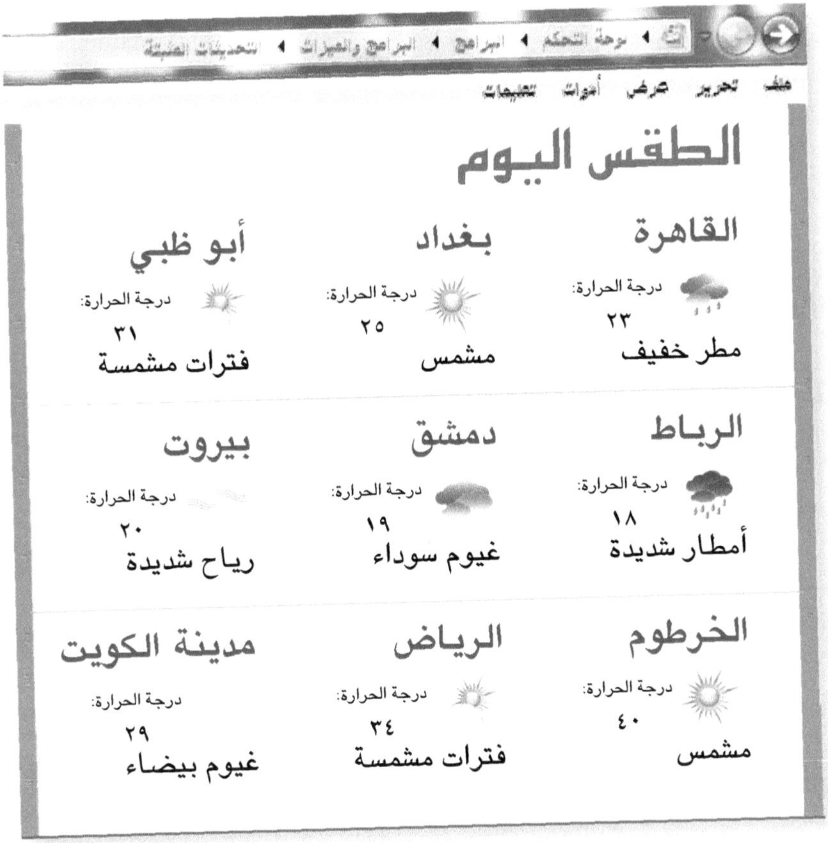

Exercise 9

Above is an Arabic webpage showing the weather today in nine different Arab capitals. Fill in the table below with the details, as in the example. Add your own town or city in the final row.

City	Temperature	Weather
Cairo	23°	light rain
your town		

Exercise 10

Read the description of the weather in Cairo, based on the information on page 193.

الطقس في مدينة القاهرة مُعتَدِل.
درجة الحرارة ٢٣ وهناك مَطَر خفيف.

Write a similar description for Kuwait City and Khartoum. Then try and write a description of the weather for your town or city.

It was an enjoyable trip كانَت رِحلة مُمتِعة

CD2: 28 Tom, a student of Arabic, is in Egypt for a combined study and leisure holiday. Listen to him talking about the weather and what he has been doing recently, following the transcript. There is some additional vocabulary to help you.

أنا في مصر مع صَديقي داني. الشمس شديدة والطقس حارّ جدّاً هنا في القاهرة. درجة الحرارة ٤٥ وليس هناك ريح!

الأُسبوع الماضي ذهبتُ إلى البحر الأحمر بالطائرة. نزلتُ في فُندُق ودرستُ العَرَبيّة لِثلاثة أيّام في مدرسة هناك بجانب الفندق. بعد ذلك ذهبتُ إلى دَيْر سانت كاثرين والجبال هناك وشاهدتُ شُروق الشمس من فوق جبل موسَى.

في آخِر يوم جلستُ بجانب المَسبَح. كانَت رِحلة مُمتِعة لأَنّي أكلتُ سمكاً مشويّاً وأطباق مصريّة لَذيذة في المطاعم. وأخيراً رجعتُ إلى القاهرة أمس!

(ṣadīqī)	صَديقي	my friend	(yawm/ayyām)	يَوم/أيّام	day/days
(al-usbūع al-māḍī)	الأُسبوع الماضي	last week	(dayr)	دَير	monastery
			(shāhadtu)	شاهَدتُ	I watched
(nazaltu fī funduq)	نَزَلتُ في فُندُق	I stayed in a hotel	(masbaḥ)	مَسبَح	swimming pool
(darastu)	دَرَستُ	I studied	(ladhīdh)	لَذيذ	delicious

Exercise 11

Decide whether these sentences about Tom's trip are true or false.

١ توم في مدينة القاهرة مع داني. ☐

٢ الطقس في القاهرة معتدل. ☐

٣ الأُسبوع الماضي ذَهَبَ توم إلى أسوان. ☐

٤ نَزَلَ في فُندُق ودَرَسَ العَرَبيّة في مدرسة. ☐

٥ ذَهَبَ توم إلى دَير سانت كاثرين. ☐

٦ شاهَدَ الغُيوم فوق الجبل. ☐

٧ أَكَلَ دجاجاً مشويّاً وأطباق مصريّة. ☐

٨ رَجَعَ توم إلى القاهرة أمس. ☐

Exercise 12

Look again at the transcript on page 194. Using the context and your existing knowledge, see whether you can find these expressions.

1 on the last day ______ في آخر يوم

2 sunrise ('rising of the sun') ______ شروق الشمس

3 delicious Egyptian dishes ______ أطباق مصرية

4 for three days ______ لثلاثة أيام

5 Mount Moses ______ جبل موسى

6 an enjoyable trip ______ رحلة ممتعة

دير سانت كاثرين، سيناء
dayr sānt kātharīn, sīnā'
St Catherine's Monastery, Sinai

Writing emails and postcards

Look at these useful words and phrases for writing emails or postcards in Arabic.

عَزيزي (azīzī)	Dear ... *(to a male)*
عَزيزتي (azīzatī)	Dear ... *(to a female)*
كَيفَ حالكَ؟ (kayf ḥālak)	How are you? *(to a male)*
كَيفَ حالكِ؟ (kayf ḥālik)	How are you? *(to a female)*
أنا/نَحنُ بِخَير. (anā/naḥnu bi-khayr)	I'm/we're fine.
مَعَ تَحِيّاتي (maɛa taḥiyyātī)	Best wishes ('with my greetings')

Zaynab is on holiday with her family and has written a postcard to her brother.

عزيزي أحمد

كيف حالك؟ أنا بخير. أنا في لندن مع نادر والأولاد. الطقس بارد وغائم. ذَهَبنا أمس صباحاً إلى وسط المدينة وأَكَلنا في مطعم ياباني. بعد ذلك ذهبتُ إلى متحف ولكن نادر والأولاد رَجَعوا إلى الفندق. وأنتُم؟ ماذا فَعَلتُم؟ هل كَتَبتُم لي خطاباً؟

مع تحياتي

زينب

السيد أحمد علي حسين
٤٥ شارع مصنع الثلج
الاسماعيلية
جمهورية مصر العربية

Exercise 13

Answer the questions below about Zaynab's holiday. Don't worry about every word; just try to get the gist.

1 What is Zaynab's brother called?
2 Where is Zaynab on holiday?
3 What's the weather like?
4 Where did Zaynab go yesterday morning?
5 What kind of food did they eat?
6 Where did Zaynab go after eating?
7 What did Nadir and the boys do?
8 What is Zaynab's final question in the postcard?

Past verbs in the plural

The postcard on page 196 contains several examples of verbs in the plural:

ذهبنا إلى وسط المدينة. (dhahabnā ilā wasaṭ il-madīna)	We went to the centre of town.
أكلنا في مطعم ياباني. (akalnā fī maṭɛam yabānī)	We ate in a Japanese restaurant.
رجعوا إلى الفندق. (rajaɛū ilā l-funduq)	They returned to the hotel.
هل كتبتم لي خطاباً؟ (hal katabtum lī khiṭāban?)	Did you *(pl.)* write me a letter?

Example	Ending	Subject
I studied دَرَسْتُ	(-tu) تُ	أنا I
you *(m.)* wrote كَتَبْتَ	(-ta) تَ	you *(m.)* أنتَ
you *(f.)* went ذَهَبْتِ	(-ti) تِ	you *(f.)* أنتِ
he returned رَجَعَ	(-a) ـَ	he هُوَ
she ate أَكَلَتْ	(-at) ـَتْ	she هِيَ
we opened فَتَحْنا	(-nā) نا	we نَحنُ
you *(pl.)* did فَعَلْتُمْ	(-tum) تُمْ	you *(pl.)* أنتُم
they went out خَرَجوا*	(-ū) وا*	they هُم

* *The alif is a spelling convention and is not pronounced.*

Exercise 14

Zaynab has now moved on to Paris and has sent this postcard to her friend, Sara. Fill in the gaps in her message.

______ سارة

كيف ______؟ نحن ______ باريس

والطقس حارّ و______. ______ أمس

صباحاً إلى متحف كبير. ثمّ ______

في مطعم فرنسي في وسط ______.

بعد ______ أنا ______ الى البنك

ولكن نادر والأولاد ______ الى المتحف.

وأنتِ؟ هل كتبتِ لي ______؟

مع ______

زينب

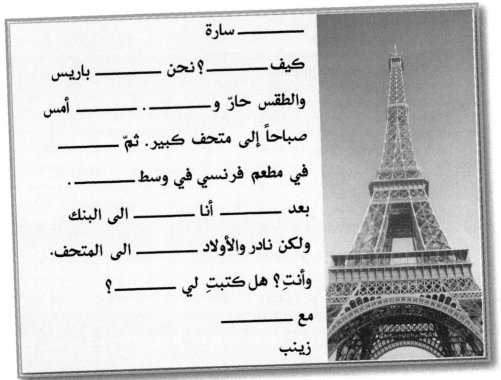

CD2: 29

Conversation

Talking about a vacation

Imagine you are Zaynab and have just come back from your vacation in London and Paris. A friend has rung to ask you about your trip.

Review the information in the postcards from London and Paris, and then play the role of Zaynab in the telephone conversation on the audio.

web

You'll find a full transcript of the conversation on the website.

Why don't you have a go at writing a reply to Zaynab? Tell her about where you are, what the weather is like, and what you did recently with your family or friends.

web

Practise talking about the past with the 'One-word story' game. You can find instructions on the website.

Video: *Amani talks about her trip*
Go to the *Mastering Arabic* website to play the video of Amani talking about a trip. See if you can answer these questions:

1 Where did Amani go last summer?
2 With whom did she go?
3 What did she study? Where was the school?
4 Where did she stay?
5 Where did she visit by train and what did she see there?

You'll find a transcript, a translation and an extension activity on the website.

Vocabulary in Unit 14

عُلبَة (عُلَب)	(ɛulba, ɛulab) box/tin/packet
لُعبَة (لُعَب)	(luɛba, luɛab) toy/game
تُحْفَة (تُحَف)	(tuḥfa, tuḥaf) masterpiece/artefact
دَوْلَة (دُوَل)	(dawla, duwal) nation/state
رَجُل (رِجَال)	(rajul, rijāl) man
جَبَل (جِبَال)	(jabal, jibāl) mountain
جَمَل (جِمَال)	(jamal, jimāl) camel
بَحْر (بِحَار)	(baḥr, biḥār) sea
ريح (رِياح)	(rīḥ, riyāḥ) wind
حَال (أحوال)	(ḥāl, aḥwāl) state/condition
الطَّقْس	(aṭ-ṭaqs) the weather
دَرَجة الحَرارة	(darajat al-ḥarāra) temperature ('degree of heat')
حَارّ	(ḥārr) hot
مُعْتَدِل	(muɛtadil) mild/moderate
شَمْس	(shams) sun
مُشْمِس	(mushmis) sunny

غَيْم (غُيوم) (ghaym, ghuyūm) cloud

غائِم (ghā'im) cloudy/overcast

مَطَر (أَمْطار) (maṭar, amṭār) rain

مُمْطِر (mumṭir) rainy

شَديد (shadīd) strong/heavy (e.g. rain)

فَتْرة (فَتَرات) (fatra, fatarāt) period

سَماء صافِية (samā' ṣāfiya) clear sky

رِحْلة (رِحْلات) (riḥla, riḥlāt) trip/journey

مُمْتِع (mumtiع) enjoyable

لَذيذ (ladhīdh) tasty/delicious

يَوْم (أَيّام) (yawm, ayyām) day

آخِر يَوْم (ākhir yawm) the last day

دَيْر (أَدْيِرة) (dayr, adyira) monastery

صَديق (أَصْدِقاء) (ṣadīq, aṣdīqā) friend

فُنْدُق (فَنادِق) (funduq, fanādiq) hotel

مَسْبَح (مَسابِح) (masbaḥ, masābiḥ) swimming pool

شُروق الشَّمْس (shurūq ash-shams) sunrise

الأُسْبوع الماضي (al-usbūع al-māḍī) last week

نَزَل (nazal) stayed

دَرَس (daras) studied

شاهَد (shāhad) watched/witnessed

عَزيزي/عَزيزَتي (عazīzī/عazīzatī) Dear ... *(starting a letter)*

مَع تَحِيّاتي (maعa taḥiyyātī) Best wishes *(finishing a letter)*

كَيْفَ (kayfa) how

كَيْف حالَك/حالِك؟ (kayf ḥālak/ḥālik) How are you? *(masc./fem.)*

أحَد عَشَر (aḥad ʿashar) eleven

اثنا عَشَر (ithnā ʿashar) twelve

ثلاثة عَشَر (thalāthat ʿashar) thirteen

أربعة عَشَر (arbaʿat ʿashar) fourteen

خَمْسة عَشَر (khamsat ʿashar) fifteen

سِتّة عَشَر (sittat ʿashar) sixteen

سَبْعة عَشَر (sabʿat ʿashar) seventeen

ثَمانية عَشَر (thamānyat ʿashar) eighteen

تِسعَة عَشَر (tisʿat ʿashar) nineteen

عِشْرين (ʿishrīn) twenty

ثلاثين (thalāthīn) thirty

أربعين (arbaʿīn) forty

خَمسين (khamsīn) fifty

ستّين (sittīn) sixty

سَبْعين (sabʿīn) seventy

ثَمانين (thamānīn) eighty

تِسعين (tisʿīn) ninety

مائة (mi'a) a hundred

صِفر (ṣifr) zero

Structure notes

Higher numbers

The numbers 20, 30, 40, etc. have the same endings as the sound masculine plural: they end in ون (-ūn) in the nominative, and ين (-īn) in the accusative and genitive. Generally the nominative numbers are used only in more formal Standard Arabic. The -īn pronunciation is more practical for a learner to use.

On the website you can find links to interactive audio flashcards to help you review the key vocabulary in *Mastering Arabic 1*, Units 12–14.

15 Review

Exercise 1

Fill in the missing figures and words in the table below. Remember to start with the *right-hand* column.

٣٠	______	١١	أحد عشر	١	وَاحِد
__	أربعين	__	اثنا عشر	__	اِثْنَان
__	خمسين	١٣	ثَلاثَة ______	٣	ثَلاثَة
__	______	١٤	______ ______	٤	______
٧٠	______	__	خَمْسَة ______	__	خَمْسَة
__	ثمانين	١٦	______ ______	٦	______
٩٠	______	__	______ ______	٧	______
٩٥	______ وتسعين	__	______ عشر	__	ثَمَانية
__	ثلاثة وأربعين	__	تسعة ______	__	______
٣٤	______ و ______	__	عشرين	__	عَشَرَة

Exercise 2

CD2: 30

Now write down the numbers you hear on the audio. The first is an example.

١ ٩٤

Exercise 3

Can you finish these sequences of numbers?

٢ ٤ ٦ ٨ ١٠ ١٢ ___ ___ ___ ___ ___

٣ ٦ ٩ ١٢ ١٥ ١٨ ___ ___ ___ ___ ___

١١ ٢٢ ٣٣ ٤٤ ___ ___ ___ ___ ___ ___ ___

٧ ١٤ ٢١ ٢٨ ٣٥ ٤٢ ___ ___ ___ ___ ___

١ ١ ٢ ٣ ٥ ٨ ١٣ ___ ___ ___ ___

Exercise 4

Match the items to the material from which they are made, as in the example:

مائدة	ذَهب
قلادة	قُطْن
حقيبة	خَشَب
شُبَّاك	جلد
قَميص	زُجاج

Now request the items, like this:

أريد مائدة خشب، من فضلك.

(I'd like a wooden table, please.)

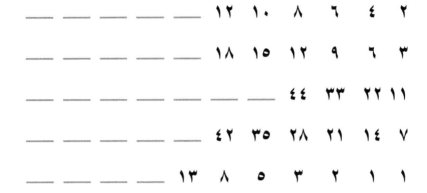

Exercise 5

So far you have met seven Arabic plural patterns:

ون/ين	(ūn/īn)	مُدَرِّس	←	مُدَرِّسون (teachers)
ات	(āt)	دَرّاجة	←	دَرّاجات (bicycles)
أَفعال	(afعāl)	قَلَم	←	أَقلام (pens)
فُعول	(fuعūl)	بَيت	←	بُيوت (houses)
فِعال	(fiعāl)	كَلب	←	كِلاب (dogs)
فُعَل	(fuعal)	دَولة	←	دُوَل (nations)
مَفاعِل	(mafāعil)	مَكتَب	←	مَكاتِب (offices)

Copy out the table below the box and then, in the correct columns, write the *plurals* of these words you know, with their meanings, as in the example:

~~وَلَد~~	شَمعة	مُهندس	فيلم	سوق
مُمرِّضة	جُنَيه	كوب	لِصّ	مَطعَم
سيّارة	عُلبة	مَسجِد	رِحلة	بَنك
خَبّاز	لُعبة	سَلَطة	قَلب	رَجُل
غَيم	جَبَل	صورة	جَمَل	تِليفون
بَحر	شَيخ	ريح	مَلِك	مَتحَف
فَترة	كيس	مَطَر	مُحاسِب	طَبَق

ون/ين	ات	أفعال	فُعول	فِعال	فُعَل	مَفاعِل
		أولاد boys				

Exercise 6

Now make questions and answers for each picture, as in the example.

١

كم كلباً في الصورة؟

هناك ثلاثة كلاب في الصورة.

٢

٣

٤

٥

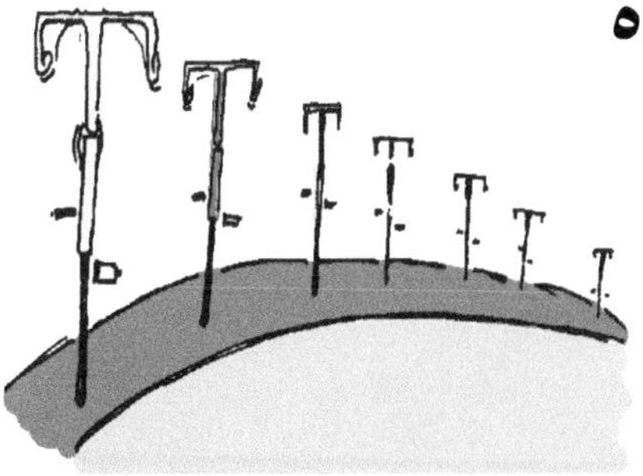

٦

٧

٨

Exercise 7

Nadia is at Ismail's grocery. Fill in the missing words, and then put the conversation in the correct order:

- ☐ ونصف ______ جبنة بيضاء من فضلَك. كم ______؟
- ☐ ______ النور يا مَدام نادية.
- ☐ تحت ______ ... تَفَضَّلي.
- ☐ ______ فضلَك، أعطني كيس سُكَّر و ______ عصير تُفَّاح.
- ☐ صباح ______. يا إسماعيل.
- ☐ ______ يسلِّمَك.
- ☐ ١٣ جنيه من ______.
- ☐ تفَضَّل. شكراً يا إسماعيل. مع السَلامَة.

Exercise 8

CD2: 31

Listen to Salwa and Ahmad in a restaurant. Fill in the chart below according to what they decide to order, as in the example.

	المشروبات	الطبق الأوّل	الطبق الرئيسي	الحلويات
سلوى	عصير منجة			
أحمد				

كوب عصير ليمون
kūb ع asīr laymūn
A glass of lemon juice

Exercise 9

Look back at the menu on page 158 and choose a meal, a dessert and a drink for a vegetarian customer.

Then make up a conversation similar to that on page 158 between the waiter and a male customer ordering the vegetarian meal. Write down the conversation and try to record both parts. If you're learning by yourself, indulge in some role-play acting!

Finally, complete the bill below for your vegetarian customer.

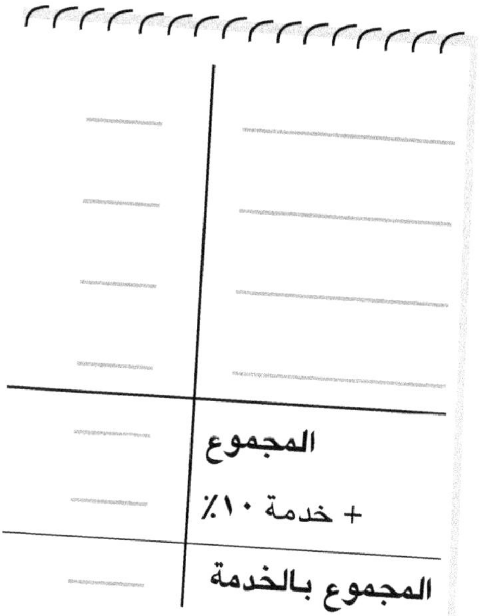

Exercise 10

Complete this table, as in the example:

Feminine	Masculine
خَضراء	أخضَر

Exercise 11

From the table on page 207, choose a colour word to fill each gap in the sentences below.

Remember: Always use the *feminine singular* for non-human plurals.

١ هذا الكرسي ______ .

٢ هذه المائدة ______ .

٣ هذه الأقلام ______ .

٤ هذا الباب ______ .

باب بيتي ______ . (colour of your front door)

٥ هذه السيّارات ______ و______ .

سيّارتي ______ . (colour of your family car)

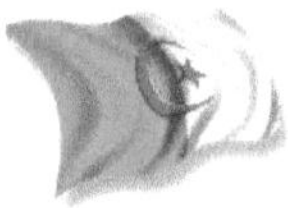

٦ عَلَم الجَزائِر ______ و______ و______ .

٧ عَلَم ألمانيا ______ و______ و______ .

٨ وجدتُ هذه الأطباق ______ في السوق.

Exercise 12

Jamila lives in Beirut with her husband Badr. Together they went to Cairo for three days last week with a German friend, Klara (كلارا). Read Jamila's account of the trip and write the correct form of the verb in brackets to complete the story. (See the table of past verbs on page 197.)

في الأسبوع الماضي، ــــــ (ذهب) مع بدر زوجي
وصديقتي الألمانيّة كلارا إلى القاهرة لِثلاثة أيّام.
ــــــ (نزل) في غُرفَتَين في فندق صغير هناك.
في أَوَّل يوم ــــــ (خرج) كُلّنا صباحاً و ــــــ (ذهب)
إلى المتحف المصري في وسط المدينة. بعد ذلك ــــــ
(وجد) مطعماً كبيراً بجانب المتحف. أنا ــــــ (أكل) سمكاً
لذيذاً من البحر الأحمر، ولكن بدر ــــــ (أكل) الكباب
وكلارا ــــــ (جرّب) الكشري.
في آخِر يوم أنا ــــــ (شاهد) الفيلم المصري الجديد في
السينما مع زوجي، ولكن كلارا ــــــ (جلس) في شُرفة
غُرفتها في الفندق و ــــــ (كتب) خطابًا لأُمّها في ألمانيا.
أخيرًا، ــــــ (رجع) كُلّنا إلى بَيروت مساءً.

Can you find all the time phrases in the passage? Underline these phrases.

Now write out the account again, this time as if you were relating what Jamila did to another friend. Start like this:

في الأسبوع الماضي، ذهبَت جميلة مع زوجها بدر
وصديقتها الألمانيّة كلارا إلى القاهرة لِثلاثة أيّام. هم...

CD2: 32

Conversation

Review

You're going to take part in two conversations which review some of the conversational language connected to shopping.

Below you will find some indicators as to what you want to buy. Prepare what you think you'll need to say.

Conversation 1

- you'd like a bag (حقيبة)
- you'd prefer a leather bag
- you like black, but you don't like blue
- your budget is 40 pounds

Conversation 2

- you'd like half a kilo of apples
- you'd prefer the red apples
- you also want a box of figs
- you want a plastic bag

Now join in the conversations on the audio, speaking when prompted. You could also practise with a native speaker, another learner or a teacher, with one of you playing the part of the storekeeper.

web

You'll find a full transcript of the conversations on the website.

16 Every day

What's the time? كم الساعة؟

Look at the clocks and listen to the times on the audio:

CD2: 33

كم الساعة؟

الساعة السابِعة.

كم الساعة؟

الساعة الواحِدة.

كم الساعة؟

الساعة الثالِثة.

كم الساعة؟

الساعة العاشِرة.

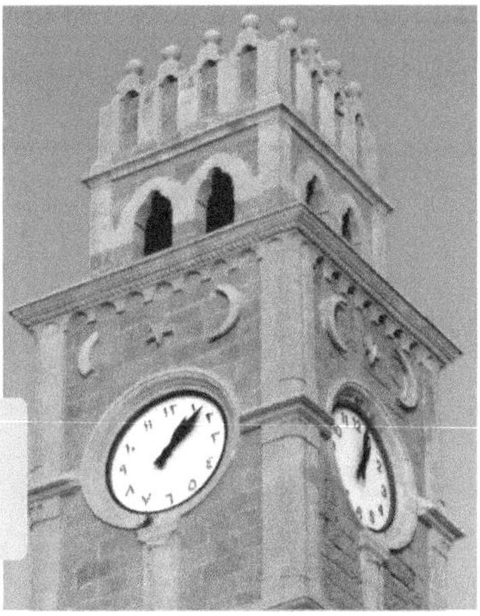

ساعة خان العمدان، عكّا

sāɛat khān al-ɛumdān, ɛakkā

Clock of 'Inn of the columns', Acre

(as-sāɛa al-wāḥida)	الساعة الواحدة	one o'clock
(as-sāɛa ath-thānya)	الساعة الثانية	two o'clock
(as-sāɛa ath-thālitha)	الساعة الثالثة	three o'clock
(as-sāɛa ar-rābiɛa)	الساعة الرابعة	four o'clock
(as-sāɛa al-khāmisa)	الساعة الخامسة	five o'clock
(as-sāɛa as-sādisa)	الساعة السادسة	six o'clock
(as-sāɛa as-sābiɛa)	السّاعة السابعة	seven o'clock
(as-sāɛa ath-thāmina)	الساعة الثامنة	eight o'clock
(as-sāɛa at-tāsiɛa)	الساعة التاسعة	nine o'clock
(as-sāɛa al-ɛāshira)	الساعة العاشرة	ten o'clock
(as-sāɛa al-ḥādya ɛashara)	الساعة الحادية عشرة	eleven o'clock
(as-sāɛa ath-thānya ɛashara)	الساعة الثانية عشرة	twelve o'clock

as-sāɛa athānya/ath-thālitha, etc. literally means 'the second/third hour'. In spoken Arabic you will often hear the regular (cardinal) numbers used with time, for example as-sāɛa ithnayn/thalātha, two/three o'clock.

Tip: ساعة (sāɛa) can also mean 'clock' or 'watch' as well as 'hour'.

Exercise 1

Say and write questions and answers for these times:

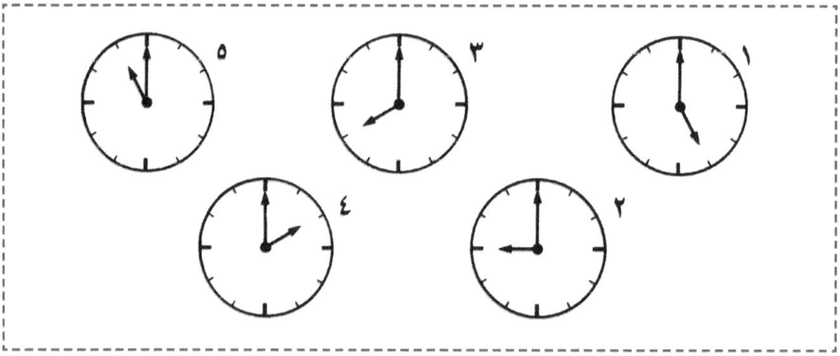

More about time

quarter past ...	الساعة ... والرُبع	(as-sāعa ... war-rubع)
twenty past ...	الساعة ... والثُلث	(as-sāعa ... wath-thulth)
half past ...	الساعة ... والنِصف	(as-sāعa ... wan-niṣf)
twenty to ...	الساعة ... إلا ثُلثاً	(as-sāعa ... illā thulthan)
quarter to ...	الساعة ... إلا رُبعاً	(as-sāعa ... illā rubعan)

Arabic uses the words niṣf, half, and rubع, quarter, to describe 30 and 15 minutes, as English does. In addition, the word thulth, third, is used to describe 20 minutes (a third of an hour).

CD2: 34

Look at the following clocks and listen to the times on the audio:

الساعة الثالثة والنصف .

الساعة السادسة والثلث .

الساعة الخامسة والربع .

الساعة الخامسة إلّا رُبْعًا .

الساعة الثانية عشرة إلّا ثُلْثًا .

الساعة العاشرة وخمس دَقَائِق .

الساعة الواحدة وعشر دَقَائِق .

الساعة السادسة إلّا خمسة وعشرين دَقِيقَة .

الساعة الثانية عشرة والثلث في تونس.
as-sāʿa ath-thānya ʿashara wath-thulth fī tūnis
It's twenty past twelve in Tunis.

Exercise 2

Now say and write questions and answers for these times:

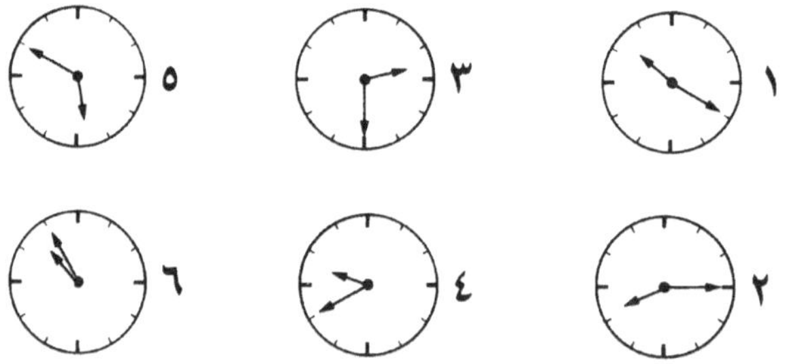

'At' plus time

Arabic doesn't have the equivalent of the English word 'at' when talking about time. Times are simply put directly after the event they describe:

متى الحفلة؟ (matā l-ḥafla?)	When's the party?
الحفلة السَاعة الثالثة. (al-ḥafla as-sāʿa ath-thālitha)	The party's at three o'clock.
متى أكلتم؟ (matā akaltum?)	When did you *(pl.)* eat?
أكلنا الساعة الثامنة والنصف. (akalnā as-sāʿa ath-thāmina wan-niṣf)	We ate at half past eight.

Exercise 3

Answer the questions using the clock prompts, as in the example:

متى الحفلة؟

الحفلة الساعة العاشرة.

١ متى الفيلم؟

٢ متى المَعرَض؟

٣ متى الباص؟

٤ متى ذهبتَ إلى السوق؟

٥ متى أكلَت جميلة؟

٦ متى رجع أبوك؟

٧ متى القطار؟

٨ متى سمعتُم عن السرقة؟

Every day كُلّ يوم

CD2: 35 Listen to what Mahmoud does every day (starting top right, page 217).

ويكتب دُروسهُ.

وبعد ذلك يَأْكُل العَشاء.

ويَشْرَب زجاجة كولا ولكن أُختهُ فاطمة
تَشْرَب فِنجان شاي.

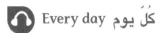

أخيراً يَلْبَس البيجاما الساعة التاسعة إلا ربعاً.

web PPT Download a PowerPoint presentation of Mahmoud's day to help you follow the sequence.

Start here

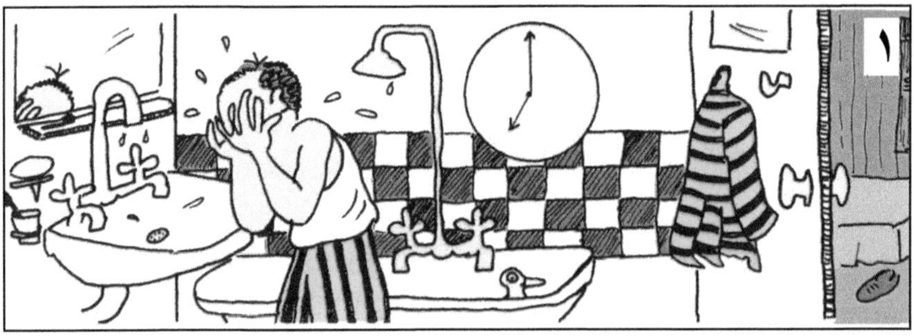

كُلّ يوم...

يَغْسِل مَحمود وَجْههُ الساعة السابعة.

وَيَأْكُل الإِفطار الساعة السابعة والنصف.

ثُمَّ يَخرُج من البيت الساعة الثامنة.

ويَذْهَب إلى المدرسة بالأوتوبيس.

يَرْجِع الساعة الثالثة والثلث.

العَشاء	الغَداء	الإفطار
dinner	lunch	breakfast

Means of transportation are preceded by بالـ (bil-, by [the]):

بالأوتوبيس
by bus

بالطائرة
by plane

بالسيّارة
by car

بالقِطار
by train

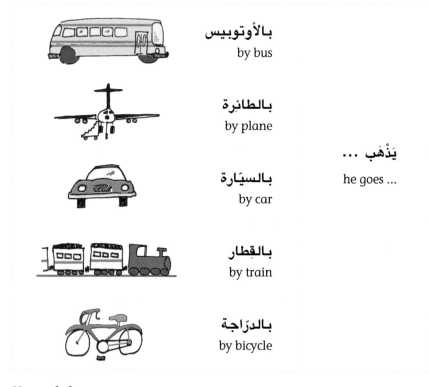

بالدرّاجة
by bicycle

يَذْهَب ...
he goes ...

He and she

Look at these sentences, taken from the picture story.

كلّ يوم يَشْرَب محمود زجاجة كولا. (kull yawm yashrab maḥmūd zujājat kūlā)	Every day Mahmoud drinks a bottle of cola.
كلّ يوم تَشْرَب فاطمة فنجان شاي. (kull yawm tashrab fāṭima finjān shāy)	Every day Fatima drinks a cup of tea.

Notice that the verb 'drinks' changes from <u>ya</u>shrab for Mahmoud ('he', huwa) to <u>ta</u>shrab for Fatima ('she', hiya):

(هُوَ) يَشْرَب

(هِيَ) تَشْرَب

Similarly the verb 'goes' changes from يَذهب (<u>ya</u>dhhab) to تَذهب (<u>ta</u>dhhab):

يذهب محمود إلى المدرسة بالأوتوبيس. (yadhhab maḥmūd ilā l-madrasa bil-ūtūbīs)	Mahmoud goes to school by bus.
تذهب فاطمة إلى المدرسة بالدراجة. (tadhhab fāṭima ilā l-madrasa bid-darrāja)	Fatima goes to school by bicycle.

Exercise 4

CD2: 36 Listen to what Mahmoud's sister, Fatima, does every day, and match the sentences to the times, as in the example. (One action and one time are not mentioned, but you can complete by process of elimination.)

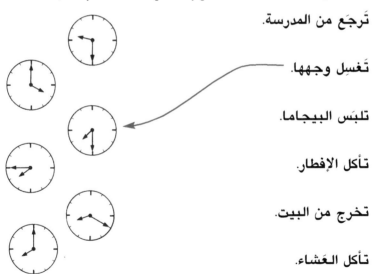

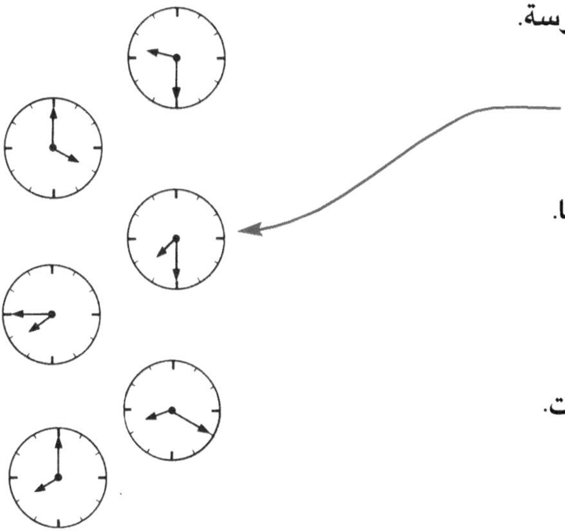

تَرجَع من المدرسة.

تَغسِل وجهها.

تلبَس البيجاما.

تأكل الإفطار.

تخرج من البيت.

تأكل العَشاء.

Now write a paragraph about what Fatima does every day. Use some of the words and phrases you know to join the sentences. Begin like this:

كلّ يوم تغسل فاطمة وجهها الساعة السابعة والنصف ثمّ...

Negative statements

CD2: 37

Listen to the audio and look at the pictures and sentences below:

لا يَذهَب مَحمود إلى المدرسة بالسيّارة، يذهب بالأوتوبيس.

لا تَشرَب فاطمة زجاجة كولا، تشرب فِنجان شاي.

لا يذهب

لا + *present verb* = *present negative*

Exercise 5

Make sentences for these pictures, following the model sentences above.

١

٢

٣

٤

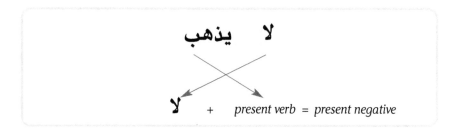

Asking questions about every day

CD2: 38

Listen to Mahmoud's and Fatima's teachers asking them about their everyday routines.

Present tense

In this unit you have met some verbs in the present tense, used when talking
about what happens routinely or what is happening now. In the past tense,
endings are added *after* the root letters to show the subject. The present tense
is mainly formed by adding prefixes *before* the root, although there are
sometimes also endings.

Here is an example of a present verb, using the verb 'drink'. The prefixes
and endings around the root are underlined.

English translation	Present tense
I drink	(<u>a</u>shrab) أَشْرَب
you *(masc.)* drink	(<u>ta</u>shrab) تَشْرَب
you *(fem.)* drink	(<u>ta</u>shrab<u>īn</u>) تَشْرَبِين
he drinks	(<u>ya</u>shrab) يَشْرَب
she drinks	(<u>ta</u>shrab) تَشْرَب
we drink	(<u>na</u>shrab) نَشْرَب
you *(pl.)* drink	(<u>ta</u>shrab<u>ūn</u>) تَشْرَبِون
they drink	(<u>ya</u>shrab<u>ūn</u>) يَشْرَبِون

'She' and the three words for 'you' all start with ta- in the present tense.
The feminine 'you' ends in -īn and the plural 'you' and 'they' end in -ūn
(sometimes shortened to -ī and -ū.)

Note that when two alifs combine in Arabic, they are written as one with a
wavy sign above called madda and pronounced ā. For example:

> I eat   (ākul) [أ + أَكل] آكل

Exercise 6

Think of three more questions and answers each for Mahmoud and Fatima,
following the examples on page 221.

You'll find more details about verbs in the present tense on the website and
further practice activities in *Mastering Arabic 1 Activity Book*.

What do you do everyday? ماذا تَفعل كلّ يوم؟

CD2: 39

Jamila lives in Beirut with her husband, Badr. Here she is telling us about what she does everyday. Listen to Jamila, following the text and taking note of the new vocabulary, and then try the exercises on page 224.

أنا اسمي جميلة وأسكن في بيروت مع بدر، زوجي.
أنا مهندسة وأعمل في مصنع كبير خارج المدينة.

كلّ يوم أَصحو الساعة السادسة والنصف صباحاً وأغسل وجهي. نأكل الإفطار الساعة السابعة. عادةً يشرب بدر فنجان قهوة ولكنّي لا أَشرب القهوة، أشرب عصير البرتقال.

أخرج من البيت الساعة الثامنة إلا ثُلثاً. أذهب إلى المصنع بالقطار. أنا لا أُحبّ الأوتوبيسات في الصباح.

أرجع من المصنع إلى البيت الساعة السادسة مساءً وعادةً أَطبُخ العشاء. بعد العشاء نَجلِس أنا وبدر مَعاً في غُرفة الجُلوس أو نذهب إلى النادي ونَلعَب كرة الريشة.

أخيراً أَنام الساعة العاشرة والنصف.

خارج (khārij)	outside
أَصحو (aṣḥū)	I wake up
عادةً (ɛādatan)	usually
أَطبُخ (aṭbukh)	I cook
غُرفة الجلوس (ghurfat al-julūs)	sitting room
النادي (an-nādī)	the club
نَلعَب (nalɛab)	we play
كُرة الريشة (kurat ar-rīsha)	badminton ('feather ball')
أَنام (anām)	I [go to] sleep

Tip: Some Arabic verbs, such as أَنام (anām, I sleep) and أَصحو (aṣḥū, I wake up), have long vowels in place of one of the root letters. You'll learn more about these verbs in Unit 17.

Exercise 7

Scan Jamila's routine for the following information:

1. What is Jamila's job and where does she work?
2. What time does she wake up?
3. Do Jamila and Badr usually have the same drink in the morning?
4. What time does she leave the house?
5. How does she travel to work? Why does she use this means of transport?
6. What does she usually do when she returns in the evening?
7. What do she and Badr do after dinner?
8. What time does Jamila go to sleep?

Exercise 8

See if you can make questions to ask Jamila about her daily routine, as in the example.

1. when/eat breakfast? متى تأكُلين الإفطار؟
2. what/drink/morning? ____________________
3. leave/house/7 o'clock? ____________________
4. how/go/factory? ____________________
5. when/return/house? ____________________
6. when/usually/cook/dinner? ____________________
7. and after dinner/what/do? ____________________
8. when/go to sleep? ____________________

Now imagine you are asking a male and a group the same questions. How would the questions change? Look at the table on page 222 to remind yourself. Here is the first question to a male and a group as an example:

1 *to a male:* متى تأكُل الإفطار؟

to a group: متى تأكُلون الإفطار؟

Exercise 9

Now talk about what *you* do everyday. Think about your daily routine. What time do you usually wake up? Eat your breakfast? Leave the house in the morning? How do you travel? When do you return from work, university (جامِعة jāmiɛa) or school? Have dinner? What do you do in the evening?

Use Jamila's routine as a model to write a paragraph about what you do every day.

web Practise talking about routine using the 'My day' questionnaire on the website.

Vocabulary learning

The *middle vowel* of the present tense changes from one verb to the next:

يشرَب (yashrab) drinks
يخرُج (yakhruj) goes out
يغسِل (yaghsil) washes

There is no automatic way of knowing which is the middle vowel, but the dictionary will show the present-tense vowel separately:

› غَسَلَ (v |i;) غَسْل | 1 [نَظَّفَ] to wash; to clean; to bathe; to rinse (out); غَسَلَ يَدَيْهِ to wash one's hands; غَسَلَ الغَسيلَ \ المَلابِسَ to do the wash/laundry; غَسَلَ الأَوانِيَ \ الصُحونَ to do/

Oxford Arabic Dictionary (Oxford University Press, 2014)

غسل *ǧasala* (*i*) (*ǧasl*) to wash (ه, ب ه s.o., s.th. with), launder (ه ب s.th. with); to cleanse, clean (ه s.th., e.g., the teeth); to purge, cleanse, clear, wash (ه s.th.,

A Dictionary of Modern Arabic (Hans Wehr, Otto Harrassowitz, 1993)

It is best to learn the past and present verbs together. If you are using the card system, write the middle vowel on the present verb:

غسل/يغسِل *to wash*

Video: *Abdou describes his daily routine*
Go to the *Mastering Arabic* website to play the video of Abdou talking about his daily routine. See if you can answer these questions:

1 Where is Abdou from?
2 At which university is he studying?
3 What time does he wake up?
4 What does he usually eat and drink for breakfast? Why is it different at the moment?
5 How does he travel to university?
6 What does he do when he gets home?

Try to pick out the key information.
You'll find a transcript, a translation and an extension activity on the website.

Structure notes

The present tense

Strictly speaking, verbs in the present tense end with a vowel, either ḍamma (u) or fatḥa (a), but this is generally only pronounced in more formal Arabic. The present verb with the full endings would be:

I drink	(ashrabu) أَشْرَبُ
you *(masc.)* drink	(tashrabu) تَشْرَبُ
you *(fem.)* drink	(tashrabīna) تَشْرَبينَ
he drinks	(yashrabu) يَشْرَبُ
she drinks	(tashrabu) تَشْرَبُ
we drink	(nashrabu) نَشْرَبُ
you *(pl.)* drink	(tashrabūna) تَشْرَبونَ
they drink	(yashrabūna) يَشْرَبونَ

Vocabulary in Unit 16

سَاعَة (سَاعَات) (sāعa, sāعāt) hour/watch/clock/o'clock

كَم السَاعة؟ (kam as-sāعa?) what's the time?

مَتى؟ (matā?) when?

دَقيقة (دَقائِق) (daqīqa, daqā'iq) minute

نِصْف (niṣf) half

ثُلْث (thulth) third

رُبْع (rubع) quarter

كُلّ (kull) every/all

كُلّ يَوم (kull yawm) every day

عادةً (عādatan) usually

إفْطار (ifṭār) breakfast

غَداء (ghadā') lunch

عَشاء (ʿashā') dinner/supper

أُوتوبيس (ـات) (ūtūbīs, ūtūbīsāt) bus

قِطار (قِطارات) (qiṭār, qiṭārāt) train

فَعَل/يَفْعَل (faʿal/yafʿal) to do/to make

ذَهَب/يَذْهَب (dhahab/yadhhab) to go

دَرَس/يَدْرُس (daras/yadrus) to study

غَسَل/يَغْسِل (ghasal/yaghsil) to wash

كَتَب/يَكْتُب (katab/yaktub) to write

خَرَج/يَخْرُج (kharaj/yakhruj) to go out/to leave

رَجَع/يَرْجِع (rajaʿ/yarjiʿ) to return

لَبِس/يَلبَس (labis/yalbas) to wear/to put on

شَرِب/يَشْرَب (sharib/yashrab) to drink

أَكَل/يأْكُل (akal/ya'kul) to eat

طَبَخ/يَطْبُخ (ṭabakh/yaṭbukh) to cook

صَحا/يَصْحو (ṣaḥā/yaṣḥū) to wake up

نام/يَنام (nām/yanām) to sleep

لَعِب/يَلْعَب (laʿib/yalʿab) to play

وَجْه (وجُوه) (wajh, wujūh) face

دَرْس (دُرُوس) (dars, durūs) lesson/class

غُرفة الجُلوس (ghurfat al-julūs) sitting room

النادي (an-nādī) the club

كُرة الريشة (kurat ar-rīsha) badminton ('feather ball')

خارِج (khārij) outside (of)

web You'll find links to interactive audio flashcards on the website to review the key vocabulary in *Mastering Arabic 1*, Unit 16.

17 Comparing things

The biggest in the world الأَكْبَر في العالَم

Look at the pictures and listen to the audio:

CD2: 40

هذا الولد طويل ...

ولكن هذه البنت أَطْوَل من الولد.
هي أَطْوَل بنت في المدرسة.

هذا البيت قديم ...

ولكن هذا القَصر أَقْدم.
هو أَقْدَم قَصر في الدولة.

هذه السيّارة سَريعة ...

ولكن هذه السيّارة أَسْرَع.
هي أَسْرَع سيّارة في العالم.

برج خليفة (دبي)، أطول بناء في العالم
burj khalīfa (dubay), aṭwal binā’ fil-عālam
Khalifa Tower (Dubai), the tallest building in the world

البنت.	من	أَطْوَل	هو
(al-bint)	(min)	(aṭwal)	(huwa)
the girl	than	taller	he (is)
القَصر.	من	أَقْدَم	هو
(al-qaṣr)	(min)	(aqdam)	(huwa)
the palace	than	older	it (is)
هذه السيّارة	من	أَسْرَع	هي
(hādhihi s-sayyāra)	(min)	(asraع)	(hiya)
this car	than	faster	it (is)

المدرسة.	في	أَطْوَل ولد	هو
(al-madrasa)	(fī)	(aṭwal walad)	(huwa)
the school	in	the tallest boy	he (is)
الدولة.	في	أَقْدَم قَصر	هو
(ad-dawla)	(fī)	(aqdam qaṣr)	(huwa)
the country	in	the oldest palace	it (is)
العالَم	في	أَسْرَع سيّارة	هي
(al-عālam)	(fī)	(asraع sayyāra)	(hiya)
the world	in	the fastest car	it (is)

Comparatives and superlatives

Both *comparatives* (taller, older, etc.) and *superlatives* (tallest, oldest, etc.) are formed in Arabic using the following pattern:

أَفْعَل (afعal)

taller/tallest أَطْوَل ← *(root letters)* ط/و/ل ← tall/long طويل

older/oldest أَقْدَم ← *(root letters)* ق/د/م ← old قديم

faster/fastest أَسْرَع ← *(root letters)* س/ر/ع ← fast سريع

Comparatives do not usually change according to whether they are describing something that is masculine, feminine or plural. The pattern remains the same:

هو أقدَم قَصر في الدولة. (huwa aqdam qaṣr fī d-dawla)	It's the oldest palace in the country.
هي أطوَل بنت في المَدرَسة. (hiya aṭwal bint fī l-madrasa)	She's the tallest girl in the school.
سيّارتنا أقدَم من هذه السيّارة. (sayyārat(u)nā aqdam min hādhihi s-sayyāra)	Our car is older than this car.
هُم أسرَع من هؤلاء الأولاد. (hum asraع min hā'ulā'i l-awlād)	They're faster than these boys.

If the second and third root letters of an adjective are the same, they are written together with a shadda (ـّ) in the comparative, and a fatḥa (ـَ) over the first root letter instead of the usual sukūn (ـْ).

lighter/lightest أَخَفّ ← *(root letters)* خ/ف/ف ← light خَفيف

If the third root letter is wāw or yā', this changes to alif maqṣūra (see page 78) in the comparative:

sweeter/sweetest أَحلَى ← *(root letters)* ح/ل/و ← sweet حِلو

Exercise 1

Complete this table, as in the example. The first ten adjectives should be familiar; the last five are new.

Pronunciation	Comparative/ superlative	Meaning	Adjective
akbar	أَكبَر	big/large	كبير
			قديم
			جميل
			قبيح
			صغير
			طويل
			جديد
			شديد
			سريع
			كثير
		good	فاضِل
		inexpensive / cheap	رَخيص
		rich	غَنيّ
		poor	فَقير
		important	هامّ

Exercise 2

Now choose one of the comparatives you formed in Exercise 1 to complete each sentence:

١ النيل ______ نهر في العالم.

٢ القاهرة ______ مدينة في أفريقيا.

٣ آسيا ______ قارّة (continent) في العالم.

٤ الفضّة ______ من الذهب.

٥ السيّارة ______ من الدرّاجة.

٦ اللوزة ______ من البطيخة.

web PPT Download a PowerPoint presentation to help you remember the comparatives.

Days of the week أيَّام الأُسبوع

Listen to the audio and look at the days of the week:

CD2: 41

يَوْم السَّبْت	Saturday
يَوْم الأَحَد	Sunday
يَوْم الاثْنَيْن	Monday
يَوْم الثُلاثاء	Tuesday
يَوْم الأَربِعاء	Wednesday
يَوْم الخَميس	Thursday
يَوْم الجُمعة	Friday

Tip: It is possible to shorten the days of the week, omitting the word يَوم (yawm, day) to make السبت (as-sabt, Saturday), etc.

Listen to these sentences:

CD2: 42

يَوْم الأَربِعَاء بعدَ يَوْم الثُلاثاء. Wednesday is after Tuesday.
(yawm il-arbaعā' baعda yawm ath-thulāthā')

يَوْم الأَثْنَيْن قبل يَوْم الثُلاثاء. Monday is before Tuesday.
(yawm il-ithnayn qabla yawm ath-thulāthā')

(qabla) قَبلَ = before (baعda) بَعدَ = after

Exercise 3

Now complete these sentences, as in the example:

١ يَوْم الجُمعَة قبل يَوْم السَّبْت.

٢ يَوْم الخَميس ______ يَوْم الأَربِعَاء.

٣ ______ الأحَد ______ يَوْم الاِثْنَيْن.

٤ ______ الثُلاثاء قبل يَوْم ______.

٥ ______ السَّبْت بعد ______ ______.

(Make four more similar sentences of your own.)

CD2: 43

Exercise 4

Murad is 16 years old and the oldest child. He has been allocated various tasks by his parents to help the family. Look at the list of tasks below. Then listen to Murad's weekly schedule and put a tick under the day of the week he performs each task, as in the example.

	Sat.	Sun.	Mon.	Tue.	Wed.	Thu.	Fri.
play with little sister							
sit with grandmother (جَدّة)							
go to bakery at 6AM	✔						
no tasks this day							
go out with the dog to the river							
write today's lessons with brother							
wash mother's car after school							

Exercise 5

Now imagine you are Murad. Look at your schedule and try to say what weekly tasks you perform. You can listen to the audio again to remind yourself of each day's task. Start like this:

يوم السبت أَذهَب إلى المَخبَز الساعة السادسة صباحاً.

يوم السبت أذهب إلى المخبز.
yawm as-sabt adh-hab ilā l-makhbaz
On Saturday I go to the bakery.

At the car rental office عند مكتب استئجار السيّارات

Bashir wants to rent a car and has gone to a car rental office to enquire.

Exercise 6

Before you listen to the conversation, decide what comparisons you might need to make between different aspects of the cars available.

In the table below, make some notes of the Arabic adjectives and comparatives.

Tip: غالٍ/غالية (ghāli/ghālya) = expensive *(masc./fem.)*
أغلى (aghlā) = more expensive

Comparative(s)	Adjective(s)	Aspect
		price
		size
		speed
		age

Exercise 7

CD2: 44

Listen once to the dialogue between Bashir and the employee of the car rental company and see whether you can answer the following questions:

Tip: أجدّ (ajadd), newer, is often pronounced 'ajdad' in casual conversation.

1. For how long does Bashir want the car?
2. What day of the week does he want the car rental to start/to end?
3. How many cars is he offered in total?
4. What colour is the car Bashir thinks is expensive? How much is the rental?
5. What is the colour and size of the car he decides to rent?

Exercise 8

CD2: 44 (replay)

Listen to the dialogue in Exercise 7 for a second time. Complete the chart below which compares the cars offered to Bashir, as in the example.

	سيّارة ١	سيّارة ٢	سيّارة ٣
أكبر	✔		
أصغر			
أسرع			
أجدّ			
أغلَى			
أرخص			

Exercise 9

Put the phrases in the order you heard them in the dialogue between Bashir and the assistant, as in the example. Then listen again to check your answer.

__ عندنا هذه السيّارة الكبيرة الجميلة.	__ بمائة وثمانين في اليوم.
__ الحمراء أجدّ وأسرع سيّارة عندنا.	__ نعم. هذا أفضل. آخذ البيضاء.
__ الاسم، من فضلك...	__ من متى يا سيّدي؟
__ البيضاء أرخص وأصغر.	__ بكم الحمراء؟
__ من يوم السبت حتّى الخميس.	__ غالية! هل هناك أرخص منها؟
١ مساء الخير. أريد سيّارة لخمسة أيّام.	__ ولكنّها قديمة. ممكن أجدّ منها؟

web

If you're learning in a group or with a friend, practise renting a car with the 'Car hire' role-play on the website.

Comparing past and present

مُنذُ عشرين سنة ... ← الآن ...

Fawzi and Fawzia have fallen on hard times. Look at the pictures of them now (الآن, al-ān) and twenty years ago (منذ عشرين سنة, mundhu ɛishrīn sana).

Now listen to the description and follow the text below.

CD2: 45

مُنْذُ عِشرين سَنَة كان فَوْزي غَنِيًّا. كان أَغْنَى رجُل في المَدينة...

ولَكنّه الآن فَقير وضَعيف.

في الماضي، كانَت زوجَتُه فَوْزيّة مُمَثِّلَة في الأفْلام السينمائيّة.

كان لَها أكبَر سيّارة في الشارِع... ولكِنَّها الآن فقيرة وليس لها سيّارة،

لها دَرَّاجة مكسورَة.

now الآن	←	the past الماضي
he is rich هو غَنيّ		he *was* rich كانَ غَنيًّا
she is an actress هي مُمَثِّلَة		she *was* an actress كانَت مُمَثِّلَة
she has a car لها سيّارة		she *had* a car كانَ لها سيّارة
له بيت جَميل he has a beautiful house		كانَ له بيت جَميل he *had* a beautiful house

Tip: Arabic expresses the concept of 'ago' using the word مُنذُ (mundhu) which literally means 'since': منذ عشرين سنة (mundhu ɛishrīn sana, twenty years ago), منذ يومين (mundhu yawmayn, two days ago), etc.

lākin + *attached pronoun*

If you want to follow the word لكن (lākin, but) with a pronoun (huwa, hiya, āna, etc.), then you should use the *attached pronouns* (see pages 60 and 129). In addition, the pronunciation before the pronoun will become lākinn(a). For example:

لكن (lākin) + هو (huwa) = لكنّهُ (lākinnahu)

لكن (lākin) + هي (hiya) = لكنّها (lākinnahā)

لكن (lākin) + أنا (āna) = لكنّي (lākinnī)

Exercise 10

Complete the following paragraphs about Fawzi and Fawzia, using the words in the box. (You may only use each word once.)

ولكنّها	دجاجة	كان	جميلة	ليس
كانَت	بيت	المدينة	أبيض	مُنذُ

______ عِشرين سَنَة ______ فَوْزي غَنِيّاً. كان له

______ جميل وكبير في وسط ______ ، ولَكنّه الآن

فَقير و ______ له بيت.

في الماضي، ______ زوجَتُه فَوْزيّة غَنيَّة، وكان لها

سيّارة ______ وكبيرة وكلب ______ وصغير،

______ الآن فقيرة وليس لها كلب، لها ______ .

CD2: 46

Now listen to Fawzi telling us about how things used to be:

Was/were (kān)

Many sentences do not need the verb ‘to be’ in the present. However, it *is* required in the past. The verb كان (kān) is used.

kān is a little different from the other verbs you have met so far as it seems to have only two root letters. The root is actually ك/و/ن, but the wāw can change into a long or short vowel. In the past tense, the parts of the verb for huwa (he), hiya (she) and hum (they) have a long ā in the middle, but the other parts of the verb have a short u. However, the endings indicating the subject are still the same as other verbs:

Translation	Arabic
I was	(أنا) كُنْتُ (kuntu)
you *(masc.)* were	(أنتَ) كُنْتَ (kunta)
you *(fem.)* were	(أنتِ) كُنْتِ (kunti)
he was	(هو) كانَ (kāna)
she was	(هي) كانَت (kānat)
we were	(نحن) كُنّا (kunnā)
you *(pl.)* were	(أنتم) كُنْتُم (kuntum)
they were	(هم) كانُوا (kānū)

Tip: kān is an important verb to learn. Try covering one of the two columns and testing yourself until you can remember all the different parts.

When the information that follows the verb kān (the *predicate*) is a noun or an adjective *without* tā' marbūṭa, you need to add the additional alif tanwīn (اً), as explained on page 148:

في الماضي كان فَوْزي غَنيًّا. (fī l-māḍī kāna fawzī ghanīyan)	In the past Fawzi was rich.
هل كُنتَ مدرّساً؟ (hal kunta mudarrisan)	Were you a teacher?

Exercise 11

Say and write the sentences and questions below in Arabic.
Tip: You can put كان (kān) in front of هناك (hunāka) to produce 'there was/were': كان هناك (kān hunāka)

1. In the past Ahmed was an engineer.
2. Twenty years ago there was a school in this street.
3. The weather was hot yesterday.
4. Two weeks ago they were in Cairo.
5. I was in the office on Saturday.
6. The tree was taller than my house.
7. Where were you *(pl.)* at 9 o'clock on Wednesday?
8. There were a lot of restaurants here.

Exercise 12

Fill in the gaps in the sentences using the correct form of kān, as in the example:

١ مُنْذُ عِشرين سَنَة كُنتُ غَنيًّا. الآن أنا فقير.

٢ منذ ثلاثين سَنَة ______ أحمد في الجيش. الآن هو محاسب في بنك.

٣ منذ نصف ساعة ______ في المدرسة. الآن هم في بيوتهم.

٤ منذ تِسْعين سَنَة ______ الرياض مدينة صغيرة. الآن هي أكبر مدينة في السعوديّة.

٥ في الماضي ______ مُدَرِّساً. الآن أنتَ ممثّل غنيّ.

٦ منذ دقيقتين ______ في البنك. الآن نحن عند البقّال.

Exercise 13

Now join the sentences in Exercise 12 using ولكن (wa-lākin). For example:

١ منذ عشرين سنة كُنتُ غنيّاً ولكني الآن فقير.

Can you make two or three comparisons in Arabic like this about *your* life now and in the past?

Weak verbs

Verbs like kān that have either wāw (و) or yā' (ي) as one of the root letters are called weak verbs. This is because wāw and yā' are 'weak' letters that can be pronounced as consonants (w or y) or as vowels.

Most irregularities in Arabic verbs are due to wāw or yā' being one of the root letters, particularly the second or third root. The main consequence is that the root sound is often replaced by a long or short vowel, leaving only two obvious root consonants. The precise rules as to how weak verbs behave take time and practice to absorb. However, there are some general principles that will help you begin to get a feel for them.

Hollow verbs

Weak verbs with wāw (و) or yā' (ي) as the *second* root letter are called 'hollow' verbs since the middle root letter often disappears. كان kān is a hollow verb, as are many other common verbs. Their main charactistics are:

In the past

Verbs for huwa, hiya and hum have a long ā in the middle:
كانَ (kāna), he/it was; نامَت (nāmat), she slept; باعوا (bā´ū), they sold.

The other parts of the verb have a short u or i vowel in the middle:
كُنْتُ (kuntu), I was; نِمْتِ (nimti), you *(fem.)* slept; بِعْنا (biɛnā), we sold.

In the present

Hollow verbs almost always have a long vowel in the middle, usually a long ū or ī, but sometimes a long ā: أزور (azūr), I visit; ينام (yanām), he sleeps; يبيعون (yabīɛūn), they sell.

Defective verbs

Weak verbs with wāw (و) or yā' (ي) as the *third* root letter are called 'defective' verbs. They are characterised by a long vowel at the end (مَشَى/يَمشي (mashā/yamshī), to walk; صَحا/يَصحو (ṣaḥā/yaṣḥū, to wake up).

Defective verbs include a number of different patterns. For the moment, just try to recognise the general type.

Weak verbs in the dictionary

You will need to look up weak verbs in a dictionary using the root letters. If you see the past of a hollow verb written like this – طار – or like this without vowels – طرت – you will not be able to tell whether the middle root letter is wāw or yā'. You may have to look in the dictionary under both roots. When you find the correct root you will see an entry like this:

> **(طير) طار *ṭāra* i (طيران *ṭayarān*) to fly; to fly away, fly off, take to the wing; to hasten, hurry, rush, fly (الى to); to be in a state of commotion, be jubilant, exult, rejoice; طار ب to snatch away**

Exercise 14 Dictionary work

Here are some common weak verbs. Complete the table using your dictionary, as in the example:

Past الماضي	Present المُضارِع	Root الجَذر	Meaning
طارَ (طِرْتُ)	يَطير	ط/ي/ر	to fly
زارَ ______	______	ز/و/ر	______
جرى ______	______	______	______
باع ______	______	______	______
عاد ______	يَعود	______	______
دعا	______	______	______
زاد ______	______	______	______
______ ______	______	ق/و/ل	______
______	______	ش/ك/و	______

You'll find details of *Mastering Arabic 2* on the companion website. This second level course will expand your knowledge of irregular verbs and cover more detail of how they work.

منذ أربعين سنة كان هناك حقول وصحراء.
mundhu arbaع‍īn sana kāna hunāka ḥuqūl wa-ṣaḥrā'
Forty years ago there were fields and desert.

Exercise 15

Write an email or letter to a friend telling him or her about a day trip you took a week ago to an historic town near you. Look back at page 196 to remind yourself of some useful general opening and closing phrases. Follow this plan:

- open with some greetings
- say where you were a week ago
- you were with your friends, Nadia and Anwar
- you travelled by train because it's faster than the bus
- the weather was very cold, but the town was beautiful
- there were many old houses
- you visited the museum
- in the past, the museum was a palace (the oldest in the country)
- there was a large market in the middle of town
- they sold many cheap leather bags and wooden boxes
- you walked to a small restaurant ('I walked' = مَشَيْتُ mashaytu)
- the food was cheaper than the hotel but it was delicious
- sign off with some closing phrases

This exercise is a chance for you to create your own email or letter. There's no definitive correct answer, but it is a good idea to show your writing to a teacher or an Arabic-speaking friend if possible.

web

Video: *Mahmoud talks about the Egypt of his youth*

Go to the *Mastering Arabic* website to play the video of Mahmoud talking about his memories of Egypt. See if you can answer these questions:

1 What was Mahmoud doing 30 years ago?
2 How does he compare the Cairo streets now and 30 years ago?
3 What could you see 30 years ago on the way to the pyramids (الأهرام al-ahrām)?
4 What can you see now?
5 What did Mahmoud cycle along by bicycle, and where used he to go?

Try to pick out the key information. You'll find a transcript, a translation and an extension activity on the website.

Vocabulary in Unit 17

العالَم (al-ءālam) the world

قـارّة (قـارّات) (qārra, qārrāt) continent

أفريقيا (afrīqyā) Africa

آسيا (āsyā) Asia

بُرْج (أَبْراج) (burj, abrāj) tower

حَقْل (حُقول) (ḥaql, ḥuqūl) field

بِناء (binā') building/structure

صَحْراء (ṣaḥrā') desert

سَريع (sarīع) fast

حِلْو (ḥilw) sweet

غَنيّ (ghanīy) rich

فَقير (faqīr) poor

هَامّ (hāmm) important

رَخيص (rakhīṣ) inexpensive/cheap

غالٍ، غالية (ghālin, ghālya) expensive *(masc., fem.)*

كَثير (kathīr) many/a lot

أَكْثَر (akthar) more/most

أَفْضَل (afḍal) better/best

اِسْتِئْجار السيّارات (isti'jār as-sayyārāt) car rental

مُمَثِّل (مُمَثِّلون) (mumaththil, mumaththilūn) actor

مُمَثِّلة (مُمَثِّلات) (mumaththila, mumaththilāt) actress

جَدّ/جَدّة (jadd/jadda) grandfather/grandmother

أُسْبُوع (usbūع) week

(يَوْم) السَّبْت (yawm as-sabt) Saturday

(يَوْم) الأَحَد (yawm al-aḥad) Sunday

(يَوْم) الاِثْنَيْن (yawm al-ithnayn) Monday

(يَوْم) الثُلاثَاء (yawm ath-thulāthā’) Tuesday

(يَوْم) الأَربِعَاء (yawm al-arbiع ā’) Wednesday

(يَوْم) الخَميس (yawm al-khamīs) Thursday

(يَوْم) الجُمعَة (yawm al-jumعa) Friday

بَعْدَ (baعda) after

قَبْلَ (qabla) before

الماضي (al-māḍī) the past

مُنْذُ (mundhu) since/ago

سَنَة (سَنوات) (sana, sanawāt) year

مُنْذُ عشرين سنة (mundhu عishrīn sana) 20 years ago

اليَوْم (al-yawm) today

الآن (al-ān) now

كان / يكون (kān/yakūn) to be

طار / يطير (ṭār/yaṭīr) to fly

باع / يبيع (bāع, yabīع) to sell

قال / يقول (qāl/yaqūl) to say

زار / يزور (zār/yazūr) to visit

عاد / يَعود (عād/yaعūd) to go back/return

زاد / يَزيد (zād/yazīd) to increase/go up (in price, etc.)

مَشى / يَمشي (mashā/yamshī) to walk

رَمى / يَرمي (ramā/yarmī) to throw

جَرى / يَجري (jarā/yajrī) to run

شَكا / يَشكو (shakā/yashku) to complain

web You’ll find links to interactive audio flashcards on the website to review the key vocabulary in *Mastering Arabic 1*, Unit 17.

18 Education and business

Education: at school التعليم: في المدرسة

 Look at the different school subjects and listen to the audio.

CD2: 47

الجُغرافيا

التَّربِيَة الدينيّة

التّاريخ

العَرَبيّة

الإنجِليزيّة

الكيمياء

الرِّياضيّات

الموسيقَى

الرَّسم

الرِّياضة

Tip: Take care to distinguish between the similar words used for sport and mathematics/arithmetic:

sport = الرياضة (ar-riyāḍa)

mathematics/arithmetic = الرياضيّات (ar-riyāḍiyyāt)

Look at the timetable and try to remember the names of the subjects.

الخميس	الأربعاء	الثلاثاء	الاثنين	الأحد	السبت	
	ابت	٢+٢=٤				٨:٣٠
٢+٢=٤		abc	ابت	٢+٢=٤	ابت	١٠:٠٠
الغَداء						١٢:٠٠
					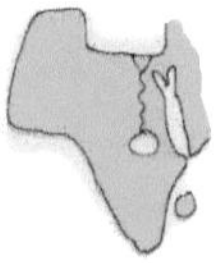	١٣:٣٠ – ١٥:٠٠

CD2: 48

What does the class study? Listen to the headteacher asking the class teacher what her class studies on Saturday morning:

(min ... hattā ...) مِن ... حَتَّى ... from ... until ...

Exercise 1

Look at the school timetable and make up more questions and answers between the head and the teacher for the following, following the model on page 246:

١ يوم الثلاثاء ظهراً

٢ يوم الثلاثاء صباحاً

٣ يوم الاثنين ظهراً

٤ يوم الخميس صباحاً

٥ يوم السبت ظهراً

٦ يوم الأحد ظهراً

٧ يوم الاثنين صباحاً

Exercise 2

Now complete this paragraph about the children's school day, as in the example.

كلّ يوم يخرجون من بُيوتهم الساعة الثامنة إلا ربعاً

و________ إلى المدرسة بالأوتوبيس. يدرسون حتّى الساعة

________ ________ وبعد ذلك ________ الغداء.

بعد الغداء يدرسون من ________ الواحدة والنصف ________

الساعة الثالثة ثم ________ من المدرسة إلى بيوتهم.

Download a PowerPoint presentation of the different school subjects to help you remember them.

Education: at university التعليم: في الجامعة

Here is some other useful words for talking about university life:

(muḥāḍara) مُحاضرة	lecture
(kulliyya) كُلِّيّة	faculty/college
(maktaba) مَكتَبة	library
(ustādh) أُستاذ	professor/lecturer
(al-ɛulūm) العُلوم	science
(al-lughāt) اللُغات	languages
(aṭ-ṭibb) الطِّبّ	medicine
(al-handasa) الهَندَسة	engineering
(al-ḥuqūq) الحُقوق	law

Exercise 3

CD2: 49

Listen to Hisham talking about a typical day at university.
Make notes in English about the following:

- the name of his university
- his degree subject
- his daily routine.

web

Video: *Cyrine talks about her studies*
Go to the *Mastering Arabic* website to play the video of Cyrine talking about her life as a student. See if you can answer these questions:

1 Where does Cyrine study?
2 What time does she leave and return?
3 What does she do when she gets back?
4 What subjects does she like and not like?
5 What does she want to study at university?

You'll find a transcript, a translation and an extension activity on the website.

Arabic words in English

English words have commonly been adopted into Arabic, especially in the realm of new technology. However, there are also a number of words that have come the other way, usually making their way into English via Arabic literature and science or from contact between Arabic-speakers and Europeans, through trade for example, .

You have already met the word قطن (quṭn), from which we get the word 'cotton', and the word جمل (jamal), from which we get 'camel'.

Exercise 4

Here are some more English words derived from Arabic. See whether you can match them to the Arabic words on the right, as in the example.

algebra	زَعْفَران
emir (prince)	الكُحول
saffron	وَزير
alkali	الجَبْر
vizier (minister)	تَمْر هِنْدي*
tamarind	أَمير
alcohol	القِلي

* *Literally, 'Indian dates'.*

Plural pattern 5

CD2: 50

Here are two of the words from Exercise 4. Listen and repeat them with their plurals several times until you can hear the pattern.

Plural	Singular	
(wuzarā') وُزَراء	(wazīr) وَزير	minister
(umarā') أُمَراء	(amīr) أَمير	emir (prince)

فُعَلاء (fuعalā')

This plural pattern is used for most words referring to male humans when the singular has the pattern فعيل (faعīl). It is a plural pattern that is only used for people. It cannot be used for words that are not male humans.

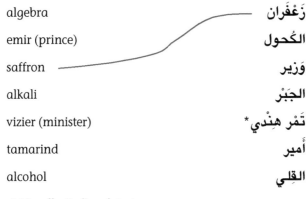

Exercise 5

CD2: 51 Listen to these words, pausing after each one. (They can all be made plural by using pattern 5.) Say the plural, following the same pattern, and then release the pause button to check your answer.

سَفير	ambassador
رَئيس	president/chairman
مُدير	manager
زَعيم	leader
وَكيل	agent
زَميل	colleague/associate

Repeat this exercise orally until you are confident of the pattern. Read the box below and then write down the plurals.

Hamza as a root letter

Notice that أمير and رَئيس both have hamza as one of their root letters.

In the case of أمير, hamza is the first root letter, and in the case of رَئيس it is the second root letter.

The fact that hamza is one of the root letters makes no difference to the patterns except that how the hamza is written may change. At the beginning of a word, hamza is written on an alif, but in the middle or at the end of a word you may also find it sitting on a yā' (with no dots), on a wāw, or by itself on the line:

رؤساء (ru'asā')   رئيس (ra'īs)

Hamza is listed in the dictionary under alif. So for رئيس (ra'īs) you would look under راس, and for أمير under امر.

The feminine

Note that a female minister, ambassador, etc. will have a tā' marbūṭa in the singular, with the plural made by using the sound feminine plural (-āt):

Plural	Singular	
(wazīrāt) وَزيرات	(wazīra) وَزيرة	*(female)* minister
(amīrāt) أَميرات	(amīra) أَميرة	princess

Exercise 6

Write out the feminine singulars and plurals for the words in Exercise 5.

fiɛāla *nouns*

Words with the فعيل (faɛīl) pattern referring to male people can often be made into general nouns from the same root letters using the pattern فِعالة (fiɛāla), or sometimes فَعالة (faɛāla). For example وزير (wazīr, minister) is changed to وِزارة (wizāra, ministry).

Exercise 7

Complete the table below, as in the example. The pattern is فِعالة (fiɛāla), unless marked with an asterisk, in which case the pattern is فَعالة (faɛāla).

Meaning	General noun	Root letters
ministry	وِزارة	و ز ر
embassy		
emirate		
agency*		
leadership*		
presidency/chairing		
colleagueship*		

web

You'll find more activities to help you practise these word patterns in the companion *Mastering Arabic 1 Activity Book.*

الإمارات العربيّة المتّحدة
al-imārāt al-ɛarabīya al-muttaḥida
The United Arab Emirates (UAE)

(Emblem of the UAE with seven stars representing the seven emirates: Abu Dhabi, Dubai, Ajman, Sharjah, Fujairah, Ras al-Khaimah and Umm al-Qaiwain.)

Talking about business and politics

CD2: 52 You can combine many of the words you have learnt using the iḍāfa construction (see pages 85–6) to talk about people and places specific to business and politics. Listen to some examples:

(amīr ash-shāriqa) أمير الشارِقة	the Emir of Sharjah
(sifārat al-ɛirāq) سفارة العراق	the embassy of Iraq
(safīr qatar) سفير قَطَر	the ambassador of Qatar
(mudīr ash-sharika) مُدير الشَرِكة	the manager of the company
(ijtimāɛ az-zuɛamā') اجتماع الزعماء	the meeting of the leaders
مُؤتَمَر المدرّسين (mu'tamar al-mudarrisīn)	the teachers' conference ('conference of the teachers')
(ra'īs al-wuzarā') رئيس الوزراء	the prime minister ('head of the ministers')
(wakālat al-iɛlān) وكالة الإعلان	the advertising agency
(wazīrat aṣ-ṣiḥḥa) وزيرة الصِحّة	the *(female)* minister of health
(wizārat aṣ-ṣināɛa) وزارة الصِناعة	the ministry of industry
(imārat ɛajmān) إمارة عجمان	the emirate of Ajman

Exercise 8

Now say and write these in Arabic, using the examples above as models:

1. the Emir of Kuwait
2. the agents of the company
3. the president of Egypt
4. the ambassador of China
5. the ministry of health
6. the meeting of the managers
7. the *(female)* minister of education
8. the *(male)* minister of industry
9. the council of ministers (i.e. the cabinet)
10. the leaders of Africa
11. the engineers' conference ('conference of the engineers')
12. the chairing of the meeting

You could use your dictionary and the patterns above to create a list of people and places particularly relevant to you.

A new life حَياة جديدة

The prime minister is concerned that his ministers are becoming out of touch with the people. He wants them to get out and see how the people really live and work. He called a meeting of his cabinet last week and now his ministers have a new routine to their working lives.

لا تعرفون الشارع ولا تسمعون الشعب.
lā taɛrafūn ash-shāriɛ wa lā tasmaɛūn ash-shaɛb
You don't know the street or hear the people.

This is how the new routine came about.

CD2: 53

خاصّ	(khāṣṣ)	private
مُختَلِف	(mukhtalif)	different
بِداية	(bidāya)	beginning
حَياة	(ḥayāh)	life
بَدَأ/يَبدَأ	(bada'/yabda')	to begin
عَرَف/يَعرِف	(ɛaraf/yaɛrif)	to know
الشَعب	(ash-shaɛb)	the people

صباح كلّ يوم، يجلس الوزراء في سيّارات خاصّة ويذهبون إلى مكاتبهم في الوزارات.

ولكن يوم الخميس الماضي كان يوماً مختلفاً وبداية لحياة جديدة.

بدأت هذه الحياة الجديدة بعد اجتماع مجلس الوزراء في الأسبوع الماضي. قال رئيس الوزراء في هذا الاجتماع: «أنتم تجلسون في مكاتبكم ولا تَعرَفون الشارع ولا تسمعون الشَعب.»

Exercise 9

Can you answer these questions about the ministers' new life.

1 How do the ministers usually travel to their offices every morning?
2 Which day was the beginning of a new life for them?
3 After what event did their new life begin?
4 Who told them they were out of touch?
5 What do you think he wants them to do to rectify the situation?

Word order and verbs

There are two key principles to remember about word order and Arabic verbs. You will build on both principles as you develop your fluency.

1 Verb and subject

The verb usually comes first in Arabic, *before* the subject (the person or thing that carries out the action), or the rest of the sentence. This is in contrast to English where we usually put the verb *after* the subject:

قال رئيس الوزراء ...	The prime minister said ...
qāla ra'īs al-wuzarā'	('said the prime minister')
بدأت هذه الحياة الجديدة ...	This new life began ...
bada'at hādhihi l-ḥayāt al-jadīda	('began this new life')

However, the word order is flexible and you will sometimes find the subject before the verb. This is especially true of less formal Arabic as it reflects what happens in spoken dialects.

2 Singular and plural verbs

Look at the first sentence from the text on page 253:

يجلس الوزراء في سيّارات خاصّة ويذهبون إلى مكاتبهم ...

The ministers sit in private cars and go to their offices ...

The ministers are the subject of the sentence. Now look at the verbs.

- The first verb is singular: يجلس (yajlis, *sit*).
- The second verb is plural: يذهبون (yadhhabūn, *go*).

If a verb comes *before* its subject it will always be singular, even if the subject is plural. The verb will change according to whether the subject is masculine or feminine, but not according to whether it is singular or plural.

Verbs that come *after* the subject will be singular for a singular subject and plural for a plural subject.

Exercise 10

Choose a past or present verb from the box to fill each gap in the sentences. Use the masculine, feminine, singular or plural as appropriate. You can use a verb more than once or not at all. The first is an example.

قال/يقول	كتَب/يكتب	ذهب/يذهَب	سمِع/يسمَع
أكَل/يأكُل	جلَس/يجلِس	فعل/يفعَل	رجَع/يرجِع
شرِب/يشرَب	خرَج/يخرُج	زار/يزور	عرَف/يعرِف

١ أمس خرج السفراء من السفارات وذهبوا إلى القصر الملكيّ.

٢ كلّ أسبوع ______ الوُكَلاء مكاتب الشركة و______ القهوة مع الرئيس.

٣ الأسبوع الماضي ______ الزُّعَماء إلى المصنع و______ عن السيارة الجديدة.

٤ كلّ صباح ______ المديرة على مكتبها و______ خطابات.

٥ كلّ يوم ______ الرِجال سمكاً في المطعم، وبعد ذلك ______ زجاجات كولا.

٦ منذ يومَين ______ وزيرة التعليم مع المدرّسات.

٧ لا ______ الوزراء الشارع ولا ______ من الشّعب.

٨ ماذا ______ الملكة يوم الثلاثاء الماضي ومتى ______ إلى القصر؟

You'll expand your knowledge of verb variations by using our second-level course, *Mastering Arabic 2*. Details are on the companion website.

Last Thursday يوم الخميس الماضي

On the Thursday following the cabinet meeting, all the ministers changed their routine to get out amongst the people. What did the ministers for health, education and industry do? Find out about their different days.

Listen, following the text. Don't worry about understanding every word initially. Exercises 11, 12 and 13 will help you to gradually decode the text.

CD2: 54

يوم الخميس الماضي لَمْ يذهب وزير الصحّة إلى الوزارة بالسيّارة، ولكنّه رَكِبَ الأوتوبيس وذهب إلى مستشفى صغير في مدينة بَعيدة. عادةً يجلس الوزير مع زوجته في الشُّرفة ويأكل الغداء في الشمس كلّ يوم خميس، ولكن يوم الخميس الماضي أكل الغداء مع الممرّضات والممرّضين في كافيتريا المستشفى.

ذهبَت وزيرة التعليم بالقطار إلى مدرسة صغيرة خارِج المدينة يوم الخميس الماضي. لَمْ تكتب الوزيرة خطابات على الكمبيوتر في مكتبها، بَلْ سمعَت من المدرّسين والمدرّسات عن حَياتهم وعَمَلهم.

ويوم الخميس الماضي أيضاً لبس وزير الصناعة قبّعة بلاستيكية صفراء وذهب إلى مصنع أَسمَنت مع العُمّال والمهندسين في أوتوبيس المصنع. عادةً يلعب الوزير التِّنِس كلّ يوم خميس ولكن يوم الخميس الماضي لَمْ يلعب التنس، بَلْ جلس مع العمّال في المصنع وشرب الشاي مَعَهُم.

Exercise 11

First listen to and scan the text on page 256 for general information. Tick the boxes matching each minister with the statements that apply to him or her, as in the example.

	Health	Education	Industry
went to a small school outside the city		✔	
went to a cement factory			
travelled by train			
usually has lunch on the balcony			
drank tea			
listened to the teachers			
usually plays tennis every Thursday			
ate lunch in a cafeteria			
put on a yellow plastic hat			
went to a distant town			
usually writes letters on the computer			

Past negative

There are *two* ways of making a past verb negative:

ما with *past verb*	ما شَرِبَ الشاي	He didn't drink tea.
لَمْ with *present verb*	لَمْ يَشرَب الشاي	

لَمْ is more common in Modern Standard Arabic and ما is more common in spoken Arabic, but both are acceptable.

It can seem confusing that the *past* negative can be made with لَمْ and a *present* verb, but you can draw analogies with English – we say 'He *drank* tea' but 'He didn't *drink* tea'.

Tip: When لم is put in front of the present verb parts for أنتِ (anti, you *fem.*), أنتم (antum, you *pl.*) and هم (hum, they), the verb loses the nūn on the end. An extra, silent alif is written after the final wāw.

you *(fem.)* didn't drink (lam tashabī) لم + تشربين = لم تشربي

you *(pl.)* didn't drink (lam tashabū) لم + تشربون = لم تشربوا

they didn't drink (lam tashabū) لم + يشربون = لم يشربوا

web Practise being negative! Play the 'Contradictions' game on the website.

Exercise 12

Underline all the verbs in the text on page 256, including the negative verbs. Decide what they mean. If you're not sure of the meaning, check the verb by looking it up under its root.

Exercise 13

You should now be able to understand most of the passages on page 256. See if you can find these expressions and decide the meaning from the context and familiar vocabulary, as in the example:

١ رَكِبَ الأوتوبيس — he rode the bus

٢ مدينة بَعيدة — ________

٣ الممرّضات والممرّضين — ________

٤ خارِج المدينة — ________

٥ بَلْ سمعَت — ________

٦ عن حَياتهم وعَمَلهم — ________

٧ مصنع أَسمَنت — ________

٨ مع العُمّال — ________

٩ قبّعة بلاستيكية صفراء — ________

١٠ لَمْ يلعب التنس — ________

مكتب الشركة السعوديّة
maktab ash-sharika as-saعūdīya
The office of the Saudi company

Structure notes

More about iḍāfa

Look at these two phrases:

السفير الألمانيّ the German Ambassador

سفير ألمانيا the Ambassador of Germany

These are two different phrases expressing the same meaning. (The English translations are also different ways of expressing the same meaning.)

The first phrase uses an adjective to describe the nationality of the ambassador. The adjective 'al-almānīy' comes after the noun 'as-safīr' in Arabic, and both have the article 'al-' as the adjective describes a definite noun.

The second phrase is an iḍāfa construction (two or more nouns together). Remember that only the last noun in an iḍāfa can have 'al-' (although it does not have to). So, in the second phrase above, the word 'safīr' does not have 'al-', even though it means 'the ambassador'.

If you want to use an adjective to describe an iḍāfa, the adjective must come after the *whole* iḍāfa. You cannot put an adjective in the middle of the nouns in an iḍāfa:

مؤتمر الوكلاء القادم the next conference of the agents

You can form an iḍāfa with three nouns:

مؤتمر وكلاء الشركة the conference of the agents of the company

Notice that the word wukalā' doesn't have 'al-' as it is no longer the *last* word in the iḍāfa.

Vocabulary in Unit 18

التَّعْليم (at-taعlīm) education

الرِّياضَة (ar-riyāḍa) sport

التاريخ (at-tārikh) history

التَّرِبية الدينيّة (at-tarbīyya ad-dīnīyya) religious education

الجُغرافيا (al-jughrāfyā) geography

الكيمياء (al-kīmiyā') chemistry

الموسيقى (al-mūsīqā) music

الرَسْم (ar-rasm) drawing/art

العَرَبيّة (al-ɛarabīyya) Arabic (language)

الإنجليزية (al-injilīzīyya) English (language)

الرياضيَّات (ar-riyāḍiyyāt) mathematics

مُحاضَرة (ات) (muḥāḍara, muḥāḍarāt) lecture

كُلِّيّة (كُلِّيّات) (kulliyya, kulliyyāt) faculty/college

مَكتَبة (مَكتَبات) (maktaba, maktabāt) library/bookshop

أُستاذ (أَساتِذة) (ustādh, asātidha) professor/lecturer

العُلوم (al-ɛulūm) science

اللُّغات (al-lughāt) languages

الطِّبّ (aṭ-ṭibb) medicine

الهَندَسة (al-handasa) engineering

الحُقوق (al-ḥuqūq) law (academic study)

وَزير (وُزَرَاء) (wazīr, wuzarā') minister

وِزارة (وِزارات) (wizāra, wizārāt) ministry

أَمير (أُمَراء) (amīr, umarā') emir, prince

إمارَة (إمارات) (imāra, imārāt) emirate

سَفير (سُفَرَاء) (safīr, sufarā') ambassador

سِفارة (سِفَارات) (sifāra, sifārāt) embassy

رَئيس (رُؤَسَاء) (ra'īs, ru'asā') president/chairman

رِئاسَة (رِئَاسات) (ri'āsa, ri'āsāt) presidency/chair

زَعيم (زُعَماء) (zaɛīm, zuɛamā') leader

زَعامة (زَعامات) (zaɛāma, zaɛāmāt) leadership

وَكيل (وُكَلاء) (wakīl, wukalā') agent

وَكالة (وَكالات) (wakāla, wikālāt) agency

زَميل (زُمَلاء) (zamīl, zumalā') colleague/associate

زَمالة (زَمالات) (zamāla, zamālāt) colleagueship

مُدير (مُدَراء) (mudīr, mudarā') manager

رَئيس الوُزَراء (ra'īs al-wuzarā') the prime minister

مَجْلِس الوُزَراء (majlis al-wuzarā') the Cabinet (council of ministers)

الإمارات العربيّة المتّحدة (al-imārāt al-عarabīya al-muttaḥida) the United Arab Emirates (UAE)

الإعْلان (al-iعlān) advertising

شَرِكة (شَرِكات) (sharika, sharikāt) company (business)

اِجْتِمَاع (اِجْتِمَاعات) (ijtimāع, ijtimāعāt) meeting

مُؤتَمَر (مُؤتَمَرات) (mu'tamar, mu'tamarāt) conference

الصِناعة (aṣ-ṣināعa) industry

الصِحَّة (aṣ-ṣiḥḥa) health

خاصّ (khāṣṣ) private

مُخْتَلِف (mukhtalif) different

حَياة (ḥayāh) life

بِداية (bidāya) beginning

الشَّعْب (ash-shaعb) the people

عامِل (عُمّال) (عāmil, عummāl) worker

بَدَأَ / يَبْدَأ (bada'/yabda') to begin

عَرَف / يَعْرِف (عaraf/yaعrif) to know

رَكِب / يَرْكَب (rakib/yarkab) to ride (on)

حَتَّى (ḥattā) until

خارِج (khārij) outside of

بَلْ (bal) but rather, instead

On the website you'll find a link to flashcards to revise vocabulary in Unit 18.

19 Future plans

Months of the year أَشْهُر السَنَة

Look at the months and listen to the audio:

CD2: 55

١	يناير	٧	يوليو
٢	فَبراير	٨	أَغُسْطُس
٣	مارِس	٩	سِبتَمبِر
٤	أَبريل	١٠	أُكتوبِر
٥	مايو	١١	نوفَمبِر
٦	يونيو	١٢	ديسَمْبِر

Exercise 1

Listen to the audio and write down the month *after* each of the eight months you hear. For example, the first answer is: مارس (March)

CD2: 56

Now for each of your eight answers, make sentences as follows:

١ شَهر مارس بَعدَ فبراير وقَبلَ أبريل.

The month of March is after February and before April.

Exercise 2

'Birthday' in Arabic is عيد ميلاد (ع‍īd mīlād), literally 'festival of birth'. Say in which months your birthday and those of your family or friends are, like this:

عيد ميلادي في شهر ... (ع‍īd mīlādī fī shahr ...)
My birthday is in the month of ...

عيد ميلاد أختي في شهر ... (ع‍īd mīlād ukhtī fī shahr ...)
My sister's birthday is in the month of ...

If you look at the top of an Arabic newspaper or website, you may well see two dates: one in the Western calendar and the other in the Islamic calendar. The most famous month of the Islamic calendar is Ramadan, the month of fasting. The Islamic date will have the letter hā' (ـه) after it, which stands for hijra (هجرة) or 'flight', as the calendar starts with the Prophet Muhammad's flight from Mecca to Medina in 622AD. The Western date is followed by a mīm (م), which stands for mīlādīyya (ميلاديّة) or 'Christian'. Can you work out the two dates shown on the newspaper above?

There are also alternative names for the months of the Western calendar, which are used in some Arab countries. The more international names are used here, but the alternatives and the months of the Islamic calendar appear on page 288 for reference.

In the future في المُستَقبَل

Today is 22 February. Look at the Minister for Health's diary for this week and see whether you can work out what he is scheduled to do today.

Tip:
زيارة (ziyāra) = visit(ing)
نائب (nā'ib) = deputy
الاقتصاد (al-iqtiṣād) = the economy

الظهر	الصباح	
←	زيارة الكويت	٢٠ فبراير
٦ نائب وزير الصحة في مكتبي	٩,٣٠ مؤتمر للممرضات في فندق ماريوت	٢١ فبراير
٥ زيارة المستشفى الجديد	١٠,٣٠ اجتماع مع وزير الاقتصاد	٢٢ فبراير (اليوم)
٤,٤٥ أستاذة من كلّية الطبّ في مكتبي	١١ اجتماع مع رئيس الوزراء	٢٣ فبراير
←	زيارة عمّان	٢٤ فبراير

CD2: 57

It's 11AM. What is the Minister doing today and what did he do yesterday?

اليوم فِبرايِر ٢٢ والآن الساعة الحادية عشرة صباحاً.

الآن يَحضُر وزير الصحّة اجتماعاً مع وزير الاقتصاد، وسَيَزور المستشفى الجديد الساعة الخامسة مساءً.

أمس، فِبرايِر ٢١ صباحًا، حَضَرَ الوزير مؤتمراً للممرضات في فندق ماريوت، وبعد ذلك اِستَقبَلَ نائب وزير الصحّة الساعة السادسة.

To express the future, you can simply add سَـ (sa-) in front of a present verb:

يحضُر الوزير اجتماعًا. (yaḥḍur al-wazīr ijtimāɛan)	The minister is attending a meeting.
سيحضُر الوزير اجتماعًا. (sa-yaḥḍur al-wazīr ijtimāɛan)	The minister will attend a meeting.
يزور المستشفى الجديد. (yazūr al-mustashfā l-jadīd)	He is visiting the new hospital.
سيزور المستشفى الجديد. (sa-yazūr al-mustashfā l-jadīd)	He will visit the new hospital.
اِستَقبَلَ الأستاذ أمس. (istaqbala al-ustādh ams)	He received the professor yesterday.
سَيَستَقبِل الأستاذ غداً. (sa-yastaqbil al-ustādh ghadan)	He will receive the professor tomorrow.

Notice that all Arabic words and particles that consist of only one letter with a short vowel, such as سَـ (sa-), are written together with the next word:

س	+	يَزوُر	=	سيزور he will visit (sa-yazūr)
وَ	+	بنت	=	وبنت and a girl (wa-bint)
لِ	+	جيهان	=	لجيهان to Jihan/Jihan has (li-jīhān)
بِ	+	السيّارة	=	بالسيّارة by car (bis-sayyāra)
فَ	+	رَجَعَت	=	فرَجَعَت so she returned (fa-rajaɛat)
كَ	+	مدرّس	=	كَمدرّس as a teacher (ka-mudarris)

web PPT Download a PowerPoint presentation to help you remember how to spell the months of the year in Arabic.

Exercise 3

(ghadan) غَدًا	tomorrow
(baɛda ghad) بَعدَ غد	the day after tomorrow
(ams) أمس	yesterday
(awwal ams) أَوَّل أمس	the day before yesterday

Using the diary on page 263, fill in the gaps in this description of the minister's schedule tomorrow, 23 February:

غَداً، فبراير ٢٣، سيحضُر الوزير ______ مع ______ الوزراء الساعة

الحادية ______ صباحاً. و______ ذلك سيَستَقبِل ______ من

______ الطبّ في مكتبه الساعة ______ إلا ربعاً.

Now write a similar description for his schedule on 20 February and 24 February, using the time phrases above and taking care to use the correct tense.

Exercise 4

Think of something on your agenda today. It could be anything – going to school, university or work, going to a restaurant, attending a meeting or an exhibition, and so on. In addition, think of at least one other thing that you did yesterday and the day before yesterday, and that you will do tomorrow and likewise the day after tomorrow.

Firstly, try to write each event for the five days in note form in Arabic as if in a diary. Then write a description of your schedule for each day. For example, if today you're going to the centre of town with your mother to eat fish and tomorrow morning you'll attend a meeting in the office, you could start something like this:

اليوم أبريل ١٤ والآن الساعة السادسة مساءً. سأذهب إلى وسط المدينة مع أمّي وسنأكل سمكاً في مطعم.

غَداً، أبريل ١٥، سأحضر اجتماعاً في المكتب صباحاً.

Talking about your plans التَكَلُّم عَن خِطَطك

You can use future verbs to talk about your plans.

سأطير إلى تونس. (sa-aṭīr ilā tūnis)	I will fly to Tunis.
سنذهب إلى النادي. (sa-nadhhab ilā n-nādī)	We will go to the club.

You may want to add some more detail about the reasons for your plans. You can use the Arabic wordp لـ (li) meaning 'to' or 'in order that' and add a second verb. Notice that the second verb must also agree with the subject:

سأطير إلى تونس لأزور جدّي. (sa-aṭīr ilā tūnis li-azūr jaddī)	I will fly to Tunis to visit ('in order that I visit') my grandfather.
سنذهب إلى النادي لنلعب التنس. (sa-nadhhab ilā n-nādī li-nalع ab at-tinis)	We will go to the club to play ('in order that we play') tennis.

Two other useful expressions for talking about future plans are آمل أن (āmal an) 'I hope to' and أريد أن (urīd an) 'I'd like to'. Again the second verb must also agree with the subject:

آمل أن أدرس العربيّة في الجامعة. (āmal an adrus al-عarabīya fīl-jāmiعa)	I hope to study ('that I study') Arabic at university.
في المستقبل أريد أن أعمل كمدرّس. (fīl-mustaqbal urīd an aعmal ka-mudarris)	In the future I'd like to work ('that I work') as a teacher.

آمل أن أدرس العربيّة في الجامعة.
āmal an adrus al-عarabīya fīl-jāmiعa
I hope to study Arabic at university.

More detail	Second verb	Plan	Time phrase
jaddī جدّي (my grandfather)	لأزور li-azūr (in order to visit)	سأذهب إلى ... sa-adhhab ilā ... (I'll go to ...)	في شهر ... fī shahr ... (in the month of ...)
ṣadīqī صديقي (my friend)		سأسافر إلى ... sa-usāfir ilā ... (I'll travel to ...)	في الصيف fīṣ-ṣayf (in the summer)
dirāsatī دراستي (my studies)	لأبدأ li-abda' (in order to begin)	سأرجع من ... sa-arjiɛ min ... (I'll return from ...)	
ɛamalī عملي (my work)			في العطلة fīl-ɛuṭla (in the holiday)
al-ɛarabīya العربيّة (Arabic)	أدرس adrus (study)	آمل أن āmal an (I hope to)	في المستقبل fīl-mustaqbal (in the future)
aṭ-ṭibb الطبّ (medicine)			
mudarris مدرّس (teacher)	أعمل كـ... aɛmal ka- (work as a ...)	أريد أن urīd an (I'd like to)	بعد الامتحانات baɛda l-imtiḥānāt (after the exams)
ṭabīb طبيب (doctor)			

Exercise 5

Select elements from the table above to talk about your future plans. Follow the sequence from right to left. The table is a template and you can use it as is or adapt it to your personal circumstances. Make an oral and a written presentation. Try to record the oral presentation and play it to a native speaker, or post it online in an appropriate language-learning forum for comments if you're feeling brave.

CD2: 58

Listen to this example to help you before you start.

في الصيف سأذهب إلى بيروت لأزور صديقي بِلال. في شهر أغسطس سأرجع من لبنان لأبدأ دِراستي. آمل أن أدرس الطبّ في الجامعة. في المستقبل أريد أن أعمل كَطَبيب أطفال وآمل أن أسافر إلى أمريكا.

Forms of the verb: an introduction

You may have noticed that some verbs have additional features, in contrast to the basic verbs that are based only on the three root letters.

In English you can sometimes find verbs that all which have different, but related, meanings. For example, 'liquefy', 'liquidate' and 'liquidise' are all related, but not interchangeable.

Arabic takes this concept much further. The root letters of a verb can be put into a number of patterns to give different, but connected, meanings. These variations are called *forms of the verb*.

One common form doubles the middle root letter with a shadda (ـّ):

فَضَّل/يُفَضِّل (faḍḍal/yufaḍḍil) to prefer; root = **فضل**

Another form adds a long ā *after the first root letter*:

سافَر/يُسافِر (sāfar/yusāfir) to travel; root = **سفر**

And yet another form puts (i)sta- *before the first root letter*:

اِسْتَقْبَل/يَسْتَقْبِل (istaqbal/yastaqbil) to receive; root = **قبل**

There are eight significant forms. At the outset the most important thing is to understand the principle of the forms of the verb. As you expand your knowledge of Arabic you will become familiar wih the individual forms and the general meanings connected with them. You will still need to remember each individual verb, but understanding the patterns will help you with this.

The variations in the forms of the verb do not affect the endings and prefixes used to show the subject. These remain the same as those you have already learnt – see pages 197 and 222. The exception is that the first vowel of the present verb sometimes changes to 'u' rather than 'a'.

سافرنا إلى أسبانيا الصيف الماضي. (sāfarnā ilā isbānyā aṣ-ṣayf al-māḍī)	We travelled to Spain last summer.
أُفضّل الأكل اللبنانيّ. (ufaḍḍil al-akl al-lubnānī)	I prefer Lebanese food.
يستقبل الأمير ضيوفاً كلّ يوم جمعة. (yastaqbil al-amīr ḍuyūfan kull yawm jumع a)	The emir receives guests every Friday.
سيقابلون زينة في المكتبة. (sa-yuqābilūn zayna fīl-maktaba)	They will meet Zeinah in the library.

web The second-level course *Mastering Arabic 2* covers the detailed patterns for the various forms of the verb.

Forms of the verb in the dictionary

To look up forms of the verb in the dictionary you will need to identify the root letters. In the *Oxford Arabic Dictionary,* you will find the forms written out as separate entries under the root in the past tense with alternative meanings and examples. In Wehr's dictionary, you will find the forms referred to only by Roman numerals. For example, doubling the middle root letter is form II, adding a long ā is form III, adding an initial alif is form IV and adding ista- is form X. (There is a complete list of the forms on page 286 for your reference.) Compare the dictionary entries below for verbs with the root letters سخن.

> سَخُنَ *v* |u; سُخْنة, سَخانة, سُخونة| to warm up, to be/become warm/hot
>
> سَخَّنَ *v* to heat, to warm/heat up; سَخَّنَ الماءَ to heat water
>
> أَسْخَنَ *v* to heat, to warm (up)

Oxford Arabic Dictionary (Oxford University Press, 2014)

> سخن *sakuna u, sakana u* and *sakina a* (سخونة *sukūna,* سخانة *sakāna,* سخنة *sukna*) to be or become hot or warm; to warm (up); to be feverish **II** to make hot, to heat, warm (ه s.th.) **IV** = **II**

A Dictionary of Modern Arabic (Hans Wehr, Otto Harrassowitz, 1993)

Exercise 6

Following the information above and the vowelling patterns on page 268, have a go at creating these verbs using the root and the appropriate form. You may already recognise the root from other related words.

Meaning	*Present*	*Past*	*Form*	*Root*
to heat	يُسَخِّن	سَخَّن	II	سخن
to meet	______	______	III	قبل
to teach	______	______	II	درس
to clean	______	______	II	نظف
to try	______	______	III	حول
to use	______	______	X	خدم
to mend/fix	______	______	II	صلح
to enquire	______	______	X	علم

Zeinah's plans خِطَط زينة

CD2: 59

Zeinah is in her last year of school. A couple of weeks ago I met her in the library. This is what Zeinah said about her plans.

قابَلتُ زينة في المكتبة منذ أسبوعَين وسَأَلتُها عن خِطَطها للمستقبل.

فقالَت زينة، "سأدرس في المدرسة حتّى شهر مايو. شهر يونيو هو شهر الاِمتِحانات. وفي الصيف سأكون مَشغولة. في شهر يوليو، سأُسافِر إلى بيت جدّي وجدّتي في الريف، ثمّ سأطير إلى بيروت في شهر أغسطس لأزور صديقتي في لبنان. سأرجع في سبتمبر لأبدأ الدراسة في الجامعة."

سأل/يسأل (sa'al/yas'al)	to ask
خِطّة/خِطَط (khiṭṭa/khiṭaṭ)	plan/plans
اِمتِحان/اِمتِحانات (imtiḥān/imtiḥānāt)	exam/ exams
مَشغول (mashghūl)	busy
ريف (rīf)	countryside
في الحَقيقة (fīl-ḥaqīqa)	actually, in truth
رَسميّ (rasmī)	official *(adj.)*

سألتُها، "هل تَعرِفين في أيّة جامعة ستدرُسين؟"

قالت زينة، "في الحَقيقة أنا لا أعرف الآن، ولكنّي سأعرف في آخر أسبوع من أغسطس. ستَبعَث الجامعة خطاباً رسميّاً. آمُل أن يكون الخطاب من جامعة أكسفورد أو كمبريدج!"

Exercise 7

Write the correct month next to Zeinah's plans, as in the example.

الشهر	
مايو	الدراسة في المدرسة
	الامتحانات
	بيت الجدّ والجدّة
	لبنان
	الدراسة في الجامعة

Exercise 8

Below is a translation of the text on page 270. Fill in the missing words in English, referring to the Arabic.

I met Zeinah in the ________ two weeks ago and I asked her about her ________ for the future.

Zeinah said: 'I will ________ in ________ until [the month of] May. The month of ________ is the month of exams. And in the summer I will be ________. In [the month of] July I will ________ to the ________ of my grandfather and my ________ in the countryside. Then I'll fly to ________ in August in order to ________ my ________ in Lebanon. I'll return in ________ to ________ the studies in ________.'

I asked her, 'Do you know in which ________ you'll ________?'

Zeinah said, 'Actually I don't know ________, but I will know in the last week of ________. The ________ will send an ________ letter. I hope that the letter is from the university of Oxford or ________!'

Exercise 9

Imagine you are telling another friend about Zeinah's summer plans. Start like this:

سَتَدرُس زينة في المدرسة حتّى شهر مايو.
شهر يونيو...

Video: *Abdou talks about his future plans*

Go to the *Mastering Arabic* website to play the video of Abdou talking about his plans for the future. See if you can answer these questions:

1 Where does Abdou plan to travel after his exams?
2 Whom will he visit there?
3 When will he return and why?
4 What would Abdou like to achieve in the future?
5 What is his other hope for the future?

Try to pick out the key information. You'll find a transcript, a translation and an extension activity on the website.

Vocabulary in Unit 19

شَهْر (أَشْهُر/شُهور) (shahr, ash-hur/shuhūr) month
يـنَـايِر (yanāyir) January
فِبرايِر (fibrāyir) February
مَـارِس (māris) March
أبريل (abrīl) April
مـايُو (māyū) May
يونيو (yūniyū) June
يُوليو (yūliyū) July
أَغُسْطُس (aghustus) August
سِبتَمبِر (sibtambir) September
أُكتُوبَر (uktūbir) October
نوفَمبِر (nūfambir) November
ديسَمْبِر (dīsambir) December
المُسْتَقْبَل (al-mustaqbal) the future
غَداً (ghadan) tomorrow
بَعْدَ غد (baعda ghad) the day after tomorrow
أَوَّل أَمْس (awwal ams) the day before yesterday

عيد ميلاد (ɛīd mīlād) birthday

زِيارة (زِيارات) (ziyāra, ziyārāt) visit *(noun)*

نائِب (نُوّاب) (nā'ib, nuwwāb) deputy

الاِقْتِصاد (al-iqtiṣād) the economy

عُطْلة (عُطَل) (ɛuṭla, ɛuṭal) holiday

دِراسة (دِراسات) (dirāsa, dirāsāt) study *(noun)*

اِمْتِحان (اِمْتِحانات) (imtiḥān/imtiḥānāt) exam

خِطّة (خِطَط) (khiṭṭa/khiṭaṭ) plan

حَضَر/يَحْضُر (ḥaḍar/yaḥḍur) to attend

أَمَل/يَأْمَل (amal/ya'mal) to hope

سَأَل/يَسْأَل (sa'al/yas'al) to ask

فَضَّل/يُفَضِّل (faḍḍal/yufaḍḍil) to prefer

سَخَّن/يُسَخِّن (sakhkhan/yusakhkhin) to heat

صَلَّح/يُصَلِّح (ṣallaḥ/yuṣalliḥ) to mend/to fix

نَظَّف/يُنَظِّف (naẓẓaf/yunaẓẓif) to clean

دَرَّس/يُدَرِّس (darras/yudarris) to teach

سافَر/يُسافِر (sāfar/yusāfir) to travel

قابَل/يُقابِل (qābal/yuqābil) to meet

حاوَل/يُحاوِل (ḥāwal/yuḥāwil) to try/to attempt

اِسْتَقْبَل/يَسْتَقْبِل (istaqbal/yastaqbil) to receive *(guests, etc.)*

اِستَخدَم/يَسْتَخْدِم (istakhdam/yastakhdim) to use

اِسْتَعْلَم/يَسْتَعْلِم (istaɛlam/yastaɛlim) to enquire

مَشْغول (mashghūl) busy

رَسْميّ (rasmī) official

الريف (ar-rīf) the countryside

في الحَقيقة (fīl-ḥaqīqa) actually/in truth

web

On the website, you'll find a link to flashcards to review vocabulary in Unit 19.

20 Review and further study

Exercise 1

CD2: 60

Salwa and her friend Nabil want to go to the cinema and they're discussing what films are showing. Listen and fill in the days and times below.

	Arabic film	American film	French film
Thursday showing times			
Friday showing times			
Saturday showing times			

Exercise 2

Look at the clocks and give the time and date in Arabic, as in the example.

الساعة الثانية ظهرًا، يوم يناير ١٤	14:00 14 JAN	١
	06:30 23 OCT	٢
	20:00 10 JUL	٣
	16:45 15 DEC	٤
	07:20 6 MAR	٥
	10:55 11 APRIL	٦

Exercise 3

Fill in the table below with the past, present and future verbs according to the subject, as in the example.

Future	Present	Past	Subject	Meaning
سَأَذهَب	أَذهَب	ذَهَبتُ	أنا	to go
			هي	to drink
			أنتَ	to prefer
			هو	to attend
			هم	to say
			أنتِ	to take
			نحن	to enquire
			أنتم	to visit
			هي	to clean
			أنا	to know
			هو	to run
			نحن	to travel
			هم	to use
			أنتِ	to return
			أنا	to play
			أنتَ	to meet

Exercise 4

CD2: 61 Last year, Fatima went on a seven-month tour of the world. Listen to her talking about where she went, and write the countries next to the months in which she visited them.

March	France/Belgium
April	....
May	....
June	....
July	....
August	....
September	....

Exercise 5

Look at the two photos of the city of Dubai, seventy years ago and today. Make as many comparisons as you can. Try to write up your comparisons in a paragraph. You could start like this:

منذ سبعين سنة كانَت مدينة دبي صغيرة
ولكن الآن هي كبيرة جدّاً. كان هناك...

Can you make a similar comparison for a town or an area you know well, comparing how it is now to how it was in the past?

Exercise 6

Rewrite these sentences, starting with the phrase in brackets, as in the example.

١ حَضَرَ الوزير أمس اجتماعاً. (كلّ يوم...) كلّ يوم يَحضُر الوزير اجتماعاً.

٢ ذهبَت زينب أمس إلى البنك. (كلّ يوم...)

٣ زُرْنا أوَّل أمس المتحف في وسط المدينة. (غداً...)

٤ كل صباح أُنظِّف المطبخ بعد الإفطار. (أمس...)

٥ أخذوا القطار إلى المدرسة. (يوم الخميس القادِم...)

٦ سيذهب الأصدقاء الآن إلى المدينة وسيشربون القهوة. (السبت الماضي...)

٧ نسافر كلّ سنة إلى الريف ولكنّنا لا نركب الخيل. (السنة الماضي....)

٨ يوم الجمعة اِستَقبَلَ الأمير رئيس الوزراء. (كلّ أسبوع...)

٩ الصيف الماضي سافَرنا إلى لبنان. (الصيف القادم...)

١٠ لا يلعَبون كُرة الريشة في النادي. (أمس...)

Exercise 7

Look at Nadia's to-do list. She has ticked off what she has done so far. Nadia is telling her friend what she has achieved today and what she has left until tomorrow. She begins like this:

صلّحتُ الكرسيّ المكسور.

I mended the broken chair.

لم أُصلّح/ما صلّحتُ الدرّاجة المكسورة. سأُصلّحها غداً.

I didn't mend the broken bicycle. I'll mend it tomorrow.

What else could Nadia say? Continue the summary of her tasks. (There may be more than one correct answer.)

Finally, write about some tasks you have completed today and some you have left until tomorrow.

CD2: 62

Conversation

Review

In your final review, you're going to speak about yourself, your job or studies, and what you did for your holiday last year.

Firstly, prepare the following information in Arabic. Look back at the relevant units if you need to remind yourself of the language you'll need.

- your name
- where you're from
- your occupation (job/student – look in a dictionary if necessary)
- where you went for your holiday last year
- what month it was
- how you travelled
- what the weather was like
- one thing you did on holiday and one thing you ate
- one thing you *didn't* do

Now join in the conversation on the audio. You'll be asked questions which will prompt the information you have prepared. There is no single correct answer – the reply is up to you. Replay the conversation as many times as you like, making up different answers every time.

Good luck! حَظّ سَعيد!

You'll find a full transcript of the conversation on the website.

Further study

You have now come to the end of this level and we hope that it has encouraged you to continue your study of Arabic. *Mastering Arabic 1* has given you a solid foundation in the Arabic script and informal standard Arabic, as used throughout the Middle East.

You are now in a position to decide in which direction to go, and this depends on your particular needs and interests. Your main options are:

- to continue to study Modern Standard Arabic in more depth
- to study a particular spoken dialect
- to branch into the classical language.

The following notes are intended to help you decide how you would like to continue your studies. You will probably want to concentrate on one of the above options. However, they are not mutually exclusive, so you can keep going and sample them all.

Modern Standard Arabic

If you have an interest in understanding Arabic in the context of TV and radio programmes, internet sites, newspapers, comics, books, signs, advertisements, correspondence, conference proceedings, formal speeches, and the like, then you should continue to expand your knowledge of Modern Standard Arabic (MSA).

Mastering Arabic 1: Activity Book can either be used alongside *Mastering Arabic 1* or as a review when you have completed the course.

Mastering Arabic 2 follows on directly from the first level, employing a similarly accessible and engaging method of learning. There is a particular emphasis in the second-level course on developing your ability to understand and produce more extended and sophisticated language, as well as on regional and cultural features.

There are also a number of other programmes for MSA that will take you beyond the scope of *Mastering Arabic*. Make sure you choose one that matches your needs. Some, for example, are designed for use in a classroom and are difficult to follow if you're working by yourself. Others may use more traditional methods of teaching. In addition, a number of organisations offer online tuition, some better organised than others. Try to sign up for a sample lesson before you commit yourself.

If you are interested in continuing to study MSA, you should make sure you have good reference books and dictionaries for grammar, verbs and vocabulary. Again, choose carefully. It's better to take your time and browse than to choose a title blind and find that it doesn't suit your style of learning or your level. If you don't already own them, we would suggest you also consider the companion books *Mastering Arabic Grammar* and *Mastering Arabic Script* (published in the US as *Easy Arabic Grammar* and *Easy Arabic Script*).

Arabic media

There is a wealth of other material for you to use to improve your knowledge of Modern Standard Arabic. The era of Arabic TV satellite stations and the internet has triggered a renaissance and revitalisation of 'standard' Arabic. Pan-Arab communication has become much more common and immediate. Politicians, leading personalities and members of the public from different parts of the Middle East now routinely take part in interviews and chat shows intended for a pan-Arab audience. It is possible to hear a wide range of Arabic accents and levels of formality all within the same programme, and sometimes within the same sentence! Arabic-speakers from all walks of life are now used to adjusting their language to make themselves understood outside their local area.

Arabic websites and many Arabic satellite stations are available outside the Middle East. Arab newspapers, magazines and broadcast media almost always have related websites, and a few have areas especially for learners of Arabic.

Literature

In 1988 Naguib Mahfouz, an Egyptian writer, won the Nobel prize for literature. He died in 2006 at the age of 94. The prize created international interest in modern Arabic literature. Mahfouz himself wrote many novels which can be found outside the Arab World both in the original Arabic and in translation, as can the work of other modern Arab writers. However, Arabic literary style can be difficult for a beginner and it is better to start with graded readers designed for learners, such as *Easy Arabic Reader,* and then progress to authors who use a simpler style, such as Taha Hussein or Jibran Khalil Jibran. Children's books and fables are a good way of introducing yourself to Arabic stories. *Mastering Arabic 2* also contains some introductory samples of Arabic poetry and literature.

Look around you

If you go to a part of a town where there are a lot of Arabic-speakers, you can look at the signs, posters, labels on imported food, etc. (A word of warning: other languages are also written in Arabic script, for example, Farsi and Urdu, so don't be put off if you come across material in which many of the words look unfamiliar and the script has some strange additions.) You will also find ingredients and instructions written in Arabic on many food packages and household products.

Spoken dialects

Native speakers are not as aware as learners of the differences between spoken dialects and Modern Standard, and will slip in and out of them quite easily when they speak. So, in informal talk and chat you may suddenly hear a word or an expression which is unfamiliar.

If your main interest is in talking to Arabic-speakers in everyday informal situations, you should acquire a knowledge of the appropriate spoken dialect. These vary from region to region but are all more or less related to MSA, so your present knowledge will be very useful. In this course we have tried to point out where there are variations from MSA which are common to many spoken dialects, but to gain fluency you will need either access to native speakers or a course in your chosen dialect, or ideally both.

There are many programmes designed to teach you the dialect of a particular country or region. If possible, choose one that includes Arabic script as well as transliteration (English letters). Having mastered the script, you will find it useful to be able to compare dialect written in Arabic as well as transliteration. If you are interested in travelling to more than one region of the Arab world, then it is best to concentrate on the dialect of Egypt or the Levant (Syria, Jordan, etc.), as these are the most widely understood.

Classical Arabic

Classical Arabic, as used in the Qur'an and other religious and classical literature, is structurally not that different from MSA. It is the use of vocabulary and the style of the language that varies, just as Shakespearian English varies from English in *The Times* newspaper.

There are specialist dictionaries and reference books for classical Arabic. They are not always very user-friendly, however, and may be old and difficult to follow. You may find it easier to continue to study Modern Standard and to combine this with reading classical texts that have translations alongside the Arabic, so that you acquire a feel for the vocabulary and style.

CD2: 63

It only remains to wish you luck, and to hope that this course has given you the foundation you need to continue to master Arabic.

Reference material

Quick reference

The Arabic alphabet

Final	Medial	Initial	Isolated	Letter
ـا	ـا	ا	ا	ألف (alif)
ـب	ـبـ	بـ	ب	باء (bā’)
ـت	ـتـ	تـ	ت	تاء (tā’)
ـث	ـثـ	ثـ	ث	ثاء (thā’)
ـج	ـجـ	جـ	ج	جيم (jīm)
ـح	ـحـ	حـ	ح	حاء (ḥā’)
ـخ	ـخـ	خـ	خ	خاء (khā’)
ـد	ـد	د	د	دال (dāl)
ـذ	ـذ	ذ	ذ	ذال (dhāl)
ـر	ـر	ر	ر	راء (rā’)
ـز	ـز	ز	ز	زاى (zāy)
ـس	ـسـ	سـ	س	سين (sīn)
ـش	ـشـ	شـ	ش	شين (shīn)
ـص	ـصـ	صـ	ص	صاد (ṣād)
ـض	ـضـ	ضـ	ض	ضاد (ḍād)
ـط	ـطـ	طـ	ط	طاء (ṭā’)
ـظ	ـظـ	ظـ	ظ	ظاء (ẓā’)
ـع	ـعـ	عـ	ع	عين (ʿayn)
ـغ	ـغـ	غـ	غ	غين (ghayn)

Final	Medial	Initial	Isolated	Letter
ـف	ـفـ	فـ	ف	فاء (fā’)
ـق	ـقـ	قـ	ق	قاف (qāf)
ـك	ـكـ	كـ	ك	كاف (kāf)
ـل	ـلـ	لـ	ل	لم (lām)
ـم	ـمـ	مـ	م	ميم (mīm)
ـن	ـنـ	نـ	ن	نون (nūn)
ـه	ـهـ	هـ	ه	هاء (hā’)
ـو	ـو	و	و	واو (wāw)
ـي	ـيـ	يـ	ي	ياء (yā’)

فتحة (fatḥa) a dash above the letter, pronounced as a short ‘a’ after the letter, e.g. بَـ... (ba)

ضمّة (ḍamma) a comma-shape above, pronounced as a short ‘u’ after the letter, e.g. بُـ... (bu)

كسرة (kasra) a dash below, pronounced as a short ‘i’ after the letter, e.g. بِـ... (bi)

سكون (sukūn) a small circle above, showing that *no vowel* follows the letter, e.g. بِنْت (bint, girl)

شدّة (shadda) a small ‘w’ shape above, showing that the letter is *doubled*, e.g. بُنّ (bunn, coffee beans)

مدّة (madda) a wavy symbol written over an alif and pronounced ā, e.g. آنسة (ānisa, young woman)

(Note: These symbols are not generally included in modern written Arabic. *Mastering Arabic* uses them where necessary for clarity.)

web

You’ll find a table showing the handwritten Arabic alphabet on the companion website.

Isolated Arabic letters on a computer keyboard. Arabic software automatically changes the letters in a word to the correct form.

The Arabic verb

Past tense

The feminine plural verbs are relatively uncommon and so have not been taught. They are included here for your reference.

Example	Ending	Subject
I opened (fataḥtu) فَتَحتُ	(-tu) ـتُ	أنا
you *(masc.)* opened (fataḥta) فَتَحتَ	(-ta) ـتَ	أنتَ
you *(fem.)* opened (fataḥti) فَتَحتِ	(-ti) ـتِ	أنتِ
he/it opened (fataḥa) فَتَحَ	(-a) ـَ	هو
she/it opened (fataḥat) فَتَحَت	(-at) ـَت	هي
we opened (fataḥnā) فَتَحنا	(-nā) ـنا	نَحنُ
you *(masc. pl.)* opened (fataḥtum) فَتَحتُم	(-tum) ـتُم	أنتُم
you *(fem. pl.)* opened (fataḥtunna) فَتَحتُنَّ	(-tunna) ـتُنَّ	أنتُنَّ
they *(masc.)* opened (fataḥū) فَتَحوا	(-ū) ـوا	هُم
they *(fem.)* opened (fataḥna) فَتَحنَ	(-na) ـنَ	هُنَّ

Present/future tense

The feminine plural verbs are again included for your reference.

Example	Suffix (ending)	Prefix	Subject
I open (aftaḥ[u]) أفتَح		(a-) أ	أنا
you *(masc.)* open (taftaḥ[u]) تَفتَح		(ta-) تَـ	أنتَ
you *(fem.)* open (taftaḥīn[a]) تَفتَحين	(-īn) ين	(ta-) تَـ	أنتِ
he/it opens (yaftaḥ[u]) يَفتَح		(ya-) يَـ	هو
she/it opens (taftaḥ[u]) تَفتَح		(ta-) تَـ	هي
we open (naftaḥ[u]) نَفتَح		(na-) نَـ	نَحنُ
you *(masc. pl.)* open (taftaḥūn[a]) تَفتَحون	(-ūn) ون	(ta-) تَـ	أنتُم
you *(fem. pl.)* open (taftaḥna) تَفتَحن	(-na) نَ	(ta-) تَـ	أنتُنَّ
they *(masc.)* open (yaftaḥūn[a]) يَفتَحون	(-ūn) ون	(ya-) يَـ	هُم
they *(fem.)* open (yaftaḥna) يَفتَحنَ	(-na) نَ	(ya-) يَـ	هُنَّ

* *The full pronunciation includes the final vowels in square brackets, but these are more common in formal standard Arabic.*

Dual verbs

There are also special verb endings for 'they' and 'you' when the subject is dual. ا (-ā) is added to past verbs and ان (-ān) to present verbs:

they both attended حَضَرا (ḥaḍarā)

you both drank شَرِبتُما (sharibtumā)

they both travel يُسافِران (yusāfirān)

you both use تَستَخدِمان (tastakhdimān)

Forms of the verb
Here is a full list of the forms of the verb for your information.

Present المضارع	Past الماضي	Form
(yufaعّil) يُفَعِّل	(faعّal) فَعَّل	Form II
(yufāعil) يُفاعِل	(fāعal) فاعَل	Form III
(yufعil) يُفْعِل	(afعal) أَفْعَل	Form IV
(yatafaعّal) يَتَفَعَّل	(tafaعّal) تَفَعَّل	Form V
(yatafāعal) يَتَفاعَل	(tafāعal) تَفاعَل	Form VI
(yanfaعil) يَنفَعِل	(infaعal) اِنفَعَل	Form VII
(yaftaعil) يَفتَعِل	(iftaعal) اِفتَعَل	Form VIII
(yastafعil) يَستَفعِل	(istafعal) اِستَفعَل	Form X

You'll find details of *Mastering Arabic 2* on the companion website. This second level course covers forms of the verb in more detail.

Active and passive participles
You can form active and passive participles from verbs. An *active participle* will show the 'doer', or subject, of the action; a *passive participle* will show the 'receiver', or object, of the action.

Basic verbs
Active participles are formed using the pattern فاعِل (fāعil):

player/(someone) playing (lāعib) لاعِب ← to play لَعِبَ/يلْعَب

Passive participles are formed using the pattern مَفعول (mafعūl):

(something) broken (maksūr) مكسور ← to break كَسَرَ/يَكسِر

Forms of the verb

Active and passive participles are made from forms of the verb by taking the present verb and:

- replacing the initial يُـ (yu-) or يَـ (ya-) with مُـ (mu-)
- vowelling with a final kasra (i) for the active participle and a final fatḥa (a) for the passive participle:

trainer (mudarrib) مُدَرِّب ← trains (yudarrib) يُدَرِّب
trained (person) (mudarrab) مُدَرَّب ← trains (yudarrib) يُدَرِّب

user (mustakhdim) مُستَخدِم ← uses (yastakhdim) يُستَخدِم
used (item) (mustakhdam) مُستَخدَم ← uses (yastakhdim) يُستَخدِم

Broken plurals

Example	Plural pattern
(kilāb) كِلاب ← dog (kalb) كَلب	(fiعāl) فِعال
(aṣḥāb) أصحاب ← friend/owner (ṣāḥib) صاحِب	(afعāl) أَفعال
(عulab) عُلَب ← box/packet (عulba) عُلبة	(fuعal) فُعَل
(buyūt) بُيوت ← house (bayt) بَيت	(fuعūl) فُعول
(kutub) كُتُب ← book (kitāb) كِتاب	(fuعul) فُعُل
(ash-hur) أشهُر ← month (shahr) شَهر	(afعul) أَفعُل
(shawāriع) شَوارِع ← street (shāriع) شارِع	(fawāعil) فَواعِل
(wuzarā') وُزَراء ← minister (wazīr) وَزير	(fuعalā') فُعَلاء
(qumṣān) قُمصان ← shirt (qamīṣ) قَميص	(fuعlān) فُعلان
(mawā'id) مَوائِد ← table (mā'ida) مائِدة	(fuعā'il) فَعائِل
(fanādiq) فَنادِق ← hotel (funduq) فُندُق	(faعālil) فَعالِل
(mafātīḥ) مَفاتيح ← key (miftāḥ) مِفتاح	(faعālīl) فَعاليل

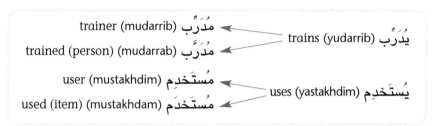

Months of the year

(See page 263 for further information.)

Islamic lunar calendar

١ المُحَرَّم

٢ صَفَر

٣ رَبيع الأول

٤ رَبيع الثاني

٥ جَمادَى الأولى

٦ جَمادَى الآخِرة

٧ رَجَب

٨ شَعْبان

٩ رَمَضان

١٠ شَوَّال

١١ ذُو القِعْدَة

١٢ ذُو الحِجَّة

Alternative names for Western months

كانُون الثّاني January

شُباط February

آذار March

نيسان April

آيّار May

حَزيران June

تَمُّوز July

آب August

أيلول September

تِشرين الأوَّل October

تِشرين الثّاني November

كانُون الأوَّل December

Answers to exercises

Unit 1

Exercise 1

1 tā'
2 thā'
3 nūn
4 tā'
5 yā'
6 bā'
7 yā'
8 bā'
9 nūn

Exercise 2

1 بَ
2 نِ
3 تُ
4 ثِ
5 يَ
6 تِ
7 بُ
8 ثَ

Exercise 3

1 bi
2 na
3 ya
4 tu
5 ba
6 ti
7 nu
8 thu

Exercise 4

اتصالات ناجحة أعادت الأمور إلى
طبيعتها بين السعودية ولبنان

Exercise 5

1 ت + ي + ن = تين
2 ن + ي = ني
3 ت + ب + ن = تبن
4 ن + ب + ت = نبت
5 ي + ب + ن + ي = يبني
6 ب + ي + ت + ي = بيتي

Exercise 6

1 بَيْت
2 ثَبَتَت
3 تِبْن
4 ثَبَتَ
5 يَثِبُ
6 ثُبَن

Exercise 7

1 بَ + ت + ت = بَتّ (batt)
2 بَ + ي + يِ + ن = بَيِّن (bayyin)
3 تُ + ن + ن = تُنّ (tunn)
4 نَ + ي + ي = نَيّ (nayy)

Exercise 8

A4 (tibn, hay) **B3** (bayt, house) **C1** (bint, girl/daughter)
D2 (bunn, coffee beans) **E5** (bayna, between)

Unit 2

Exercise 1

See the table on page 13.

Exercise 2

1	بَ (ba)	+	ر (r)	+	د (d)	=	بَرْد (bard)
2	وَ (wa)	+	ر (r)	+	د (d)	=	وَرْد (ward)
3	رَ (ra)	+	ب (b)	+	و (w)	=	رَبْو (rabw)
4	بَ (ba)	+	ذ (dh)	+	ر (r)	=	بَذْر (badhr)
5	بِ (bi)	+	ر (r)	+	ر (r)	=	بِرّ (birr)
6	يَ (ya)	+	ثِ (thi)	+	بُ (bu)	=	يَثِبُ (yathibu)
7	ثَ (tha)	+	و (w)	+	ب (b)	=	ثَوْب (thawb)
8	دَ (da)	+	رَ (ra)	+	ز (z)	=	دَرَز (daraz)

Exercise 3

1 وَزير
2 دين
3 دَيْن
4 بَيْت
5 يُريد
6 بَريد
7 بَيْنَ
8 بَيِّن
9 زَيْن
10 وارِد

Exercise 4

1 بَدْر
2 نور
3 رَدّ
4 نادِر
5 نار
6 دار
7 بَرْد
8 يَزيد

Exercise 5

zayn **1**
dīnā **2**
badr **3**
zaynab **4**
nādir **5**
zayd **6**

A4 **B3** **C1** **D3**

Exercise 6

1 أنا زينب.
2 أنا زين.
3 أنا دينا.
4 أنا بدر.

Exercise 7

1 أنا زينب وأنتَ؟ أنا نادر.
2 أنا زين وأنتِ؟ أنا دينا.

Unit 3

Exercise 1

1 خ **ح** ه
2 **خ** ح ه
3 خ **ح** ه
4 خ ح **ه**
5 **خ** ح ه
6 خ ح **ه**
7 خ ح **ه**
8 **خ** ح ه
9 خ **ح** ه
10 خ ح **ه**

Exercise 2

(midḥat) **5A**	(aḥmad) **1G**
(ukht) **6H**	(najjār) **2D**
(akh) **7B**	(baḥḥār) **3F**
(najāḥ) **8E**	(mawj) **4C**

Exercise 3

1 ن + ح + ت = نحت
2 ب + ه + ي = بهي
3 ج + م + د = جمد
4 ي + ت + ي + ه = يتيه
5 ب + ح + ر = بحر
6 أ + م + ه = أمه
7 ه + ا + م + د = هامد
8 ن + ج + ز = نجز

Exercise 4

1 feminine
2 feminine
3 masculine
4 feminine
5 feminine
6 feminine
7 masculine
8 masculine

Exercise 5

1 هذا حمار.
2 هذه دجاجة.
3 هذا نهر.
4 هذه خيمة.
5 هذه زجاجة.
6 هذه بنت.

Exercise 6

sister	أُخت
daughter	بِنْت
mother	أُمّ
husband	زَوْج
brother	أَخ
wife	زَوْجَة
son	ابْن
father	أَب

Exercise 7

1 مدحت هو ابن أحمد.

2 وردة هي أخت مدحت.

3 أحمد هو زوج جيهان.

4 وردة هي بنت/اِبنة جيهان.

5 جيهان هي أمّ وردة.

6 جيهان هي زوجة أحمد.

Exercise 8

There are many possibilities for different sentences using this family tree. Use Exercise 7 as a guide.

Tip: Take care with أب (ab, father) and أخ (akh, brother). When they are put in front of another name, a long ū is added, making abū and akhū:

أنور هو أبو زينب. (anwar huwa abū zaynab) Anwar is Zaynab's father.

بدر هو أخو زينب. (badr huwa akhū zaynab) Badr is Zaynab's brother.

Unit 4

Exercise 1

1 (س) ص

2 د (ض)

3 ه (ح)

4 (د) ض

5 س (ص)

6 (ه) ح

7 د (ض)

8 (د) ض

9 (س) ص

10 س (ص)

11 ه (ح)

12 (س) ص

Exercise 2

E6 5D B4 F3 A2 C1

Exercise 3

1 هي ممرّضة.

2 هو مهندس.

3 هي خبّازة.

4 هو محاسب.

5 هو نجّار.

6 هي مهندسة.

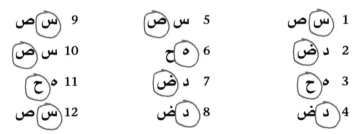

Exercise 4

Family member	Name	Occupation
me	Anwar	photographer
wife	Nur	engineer
father	Hassan	carpenter
mother	Shadya	accountant
brother	Badr	accountant

Exercise 5

Feminine plural	*Masculine plural*
خبّازات	خبّازون
محاسبات	محاسبون
ممرّضات	ممرّضون
مهندسات	مهندسون
نجّارات	نجّارون

Exercise 6

1 نحن ممرّضات.
هنّ ممرّضات.

2 نحن مهندسون.
هم مهندسون.

3 نحن مصوّرات.
هنّ مصوّرات.

4 نحن محاسبون.
هم محاسبون.

5 نحن مهندسون.
هم مهندسون.

6 نحن نجّارون.
هم نجّارون.

Optional exercise (Structure notes)

1 هي ممرّضةٌ (mumarrida<u>tun</u>).

2 هو مهندسٌ (muhandis<u>un</u>).

3 هي خبّازةٌ (khabbāza<u>tun</u>).

4 هو محاسبٌ (muḥāsib<u>un</u>).

5 هو نجّارٌ (najjār<u>un</u>).

6 هي مهندسةٌ (muhandisa<u>tun</u>).

Unit 5

Exercise 1

1 same
2 same
3 different
4 same
5 different
6 different
7 same
8 different

Exercise 2

كلمات أمير قطر الصادقة

تعكس عمق علاقات الشعبين الشقيقين

Exercise 3

1 هذا كتاب.
2 هذا مفتاح.
3 هذا قلم.
4 هذه حقيبة.
5 هذا قميص.
6 هذا كلب.
7 هذه درّاجة.
8 هذه سيّارة.
9 هذا خاتم.

Exercise 4

ة	م	ي	[1] خ	■	■
■	■	■	ا	■	■
■	[3] ب	ا	ت	[2] ك	■
■	ي	■	م	ل	[4] ق
■	ت	■	■	ب	■

Exercise 5

جميل ... قبيح

ثقيل ... خفيف

أبيض ... أسود

مكسور ... سليم

جديد ... قديم

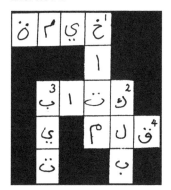

Exercise 6

1 هذا القميص أبيض.
2 وهذا القميص أسود.
3 هذه المدينة جميلة.
4 وهذه المدينة قبيحة.
5 هذه السيّارة قديمة.
6 وهذه السيّارة جديدة.

Exercise 7

(Model answers: yours may vary slightly.)

هذا مفتاح محمّد وهو أسود.

هذه درّاجة محمّد وهي مكسورة وقديمة.

هذا قميص محمّد وهو أبيض. قميصه قديم.

هذا كلب محمّد وهو أسود. كلبه جميل وخفيف.

هذا قلم محمّد وهو أبيض. قلمه جديد.

هذا مفتاح جيهان وهو أبيض.

هذه سيّارة جيهان. سيّارتها جديدة وجميلة.

هذه حقيبة جيهان وهي قديمة.

هذا خاتم جيهان وهو جميل.

Exercise 8

Try to check your descriptions with an Arabic-speaker.

Unit 6

Exercise 1

1 ط
2 ت
3 ظ
4 ذ
5 ص
6 س
7 ض
8 د

Exercise 2

1 ✔
2 ✘
3 ✘
4 ✔
5 ✔
6 ✘
7 ✘
8 ✔

Exercise 3

Name	Printed	Handwritten	Name	Printed	Handwritten
alif	ا	ا	ḍād	ض	ض
bā'	ب	ب	ṭā'	ط	ط
tā'	ت	ت	ẓā'	ظ	ظ
thā'	ث	ث	ʿayn	ع	ع
jīm	ج	ج	ghayn	غ	غ
ḥā'	ح	ح	fā'	ف	ف
khā'	خ	خ	qāf	ق	ق
dāl	د	د	kāf	ك	ك
dhāl	ذ	ذ	lām	ل	ل
rā'	ر	ر	mīm	م	م
zāy	ز	ز	nūn	ن	ن
sīn	س	س	hā'	ه	ه
shīn	ش	ش	wāw	و	و
ṣād	ص	ص	yā'	ي	ي

Exercise 4

j12 f11 c10 b9 g8 i7 e6 l5 k4 h3 a2 d1

Exercise 5

1 ع + ل + ي = علي

2 ج + م + ع = جمع

3 غ + ط + س = غطس

4 ظ + ل + م = ظلم

5 ط + ي + ن = طين

6 ن + ع + م = نعم

7 ب + غ + د + ا + د = بغداد

8 م + س + ق + ط = مسقط

Exercise 6

Sun letter?	Initial letter	Word
✗	ب	البنت
✔	ت	التبن
✔	ث	الثوب
✔	ن	النهر
✗	ي	الياسمين
✔	د	الدجاجة
✔	ذ	الذباب
✔	ر	الراديو
✔	ز	الزجاجة
✗	و	الولد
✗	ف	الفيلم
✗	ق	القميص
✗	ك	الكتاب
✔	ل	الليمون
✔	ط	الطين
✔	ظ	الظاهر
✗	ع	العرب
✗	غ	الغرب

Exercise 7

1 هذا كرسي. d

2 هذه خزانة. c

3 هذه مائدة. f

4 هذا باب. h

5 هذا شبّاك. b

6 هذا تليفزيون. g

7 هذا سرير. a

8 هذه صورة. e

Exercise 8

1 هل هذه خزانة؟
لا هي مائدة.

2 هل هذا كتاب؟
لا، هو قلم.

3 هل هذا مفتاح؟
لا، هو خاتم.

4 هل هذا كلب؟
نعم، هو كلب.

5 هل هذه درّاجة؟
لا، هي سيّارة.

6 هل هذا شبّاك؟
نعم، هو شبّاك.

Exercise 9

1 الزجاجة تحت المائدة.
2 الجريدة على الكرسيّ.
3 الحمار بين الخيمة والسيّارة.
4 الصورة بجانب الشبّاك.
5 الكلب في الحقيبة.
6 الصورة فوق التليفزيون.

Exercise 10

1 نعم، هو بجانب المائدة.
2 التليفزيون على المائدة.
3 المائدة بين الخزانة والكرسيّ.
4 نعم، هي بجانب الشبّاك.
5 الخزانة بجانب الباب.
6 لا، هو على المائدة.
7 السرير تحت الشبّاك.
8 لا، هو بجانب الخزانة.
9 هي على الخزانة.
10 نعم، هي بين الكرسي والخزانة.

Exercise 11

1 On the River Nile between Luxor and Aswan. **2** In the morning. **3** Large and beautiful. **4** The bed is large and beside the window, the table is small and the cupboard is also small. **5** The television is above the cupboard; it's new and unbroken.

Exercise 12

1 على المَركَب	5 بين الأُقصُر وأسوان
2 في الصَّباح	6 كَذلِك
3 بِجانِب الشُّبّاك	7 جَديد وسَليم
4 فوق الخِزانة	8 نَهر النيل

Unit 7

Exercise 1

A2 B4 C1 D3

1 بدر محاسب وهو في البنك.

2 زينب ممرّضة وهي في المستشفى.

3 زين مدرّسة وهي في المدرسة.

4 أحمد مهندس وهو في المصنع.

Exercise 2

1	✔	6	✘
2	✔	7	✔
3	✘	8	✘
4	✔	9	✔
5	✘	10	✘

Exercise 3

1 هناك تليفزيون على المائدة ولكن ليس هناك زجاجة.

2 هناك سيّارة في الشارع ولكن ليس هناك درّاجة.

3 هناك ولد بجانب الكرسي ولكن ليس هناك بنت.

4 هناك كلب تحت الشجرة ولكن ليس هناك حمار.

Exercise 4

1 هناك سيّارة جديدة أمام المصنع.

2 هناك قلم مكسور على المائدة.

3 أنا في سيّارتي الجديدة الجميلة.

4 ليس هناك شجر بجانب المستشفى.

5 هناك مدرّس جديد في المدرسة.

6 بدر محاسب في البنك الجديد.

Exercise 5

1 هذه الدرّاجة كبيرة.

2 هذا الولد طويل.

3 هذه الدرّاجة صغيرة.

4 هذه البنت قويّة.

5 هذه البنت قصيرة.

6 هذا الولد ضعيف.

Exercise 6

Here is a translation of the advertisement:

A large and beautiful apartment!

- In the town of Marrakesh
- Sharif Street
- Near the hospital
- Between the university and Ibn Sina school
- There are beautiful palm trees in front of the house and a large balcony

Telephone: 442 137891

Exercise 7

Your drawing should feature the following:

- a street
- a hospital in the middle of the picture, with a tall nurse standing by the door
- a new white factory on the right of the hospital, with big beautiful trees in front of it
- an ugly black dog under the trees and some pigeons above it
- a small school to the left of the hospital, with an old bicycle next to the school gate/door.

Unit 8

Exercise 1

1 م + ص + ر = مِصر

2 ع + م + ا + ن = عُمان

3 د + م + ش + ق = دِمَشق

4 م + س + ق + ط = مَسقَط

5 ل + ب + ن + ا + ن = لُبنان

6 ب + ي + ر + و + ت = بَيروت

7 ب + غ + د + ا + د = بَغداد

Exercise 2

Word with الـ	Meaning	Sun letter?	Initial letter	Word
(al-bayt) اَلْبَيْت	house	✘	ب	بيت
(an-nahr) اَلنَّهْر	river	✔	ن	نهر
(al-khayma) اَلْخَيْمة	tent	✘	خ	خيمة
(al-madīna) اَلْمَدينة	town/city	✘	م	مدينة
(az-zujāja) اَلزُّجاجة	bottle	✔	ز	زجاجة
(ash-shaqqa) اَلشَّقّة	apartment	✔	ش	شقّة
(at-tīn) اَلتّين	figs	✔	ت	تين
(al-kitāb) اَلْكتاب	book	✘	ك	كتاب
(as-sayyāra) اَلسَّيّارة	car	✔	س	سيّارة
(ad-darrāja) اَلدَّرّاجة	bicycle	✔	د	درّاجة
(al-qamīṣ) اَلْقميص	shirt	✘	ق	قميص
(al-ḥaqība) اَلْحقيبة	bag	✘	ح	حقيبة
(al-yamīn) اَلْيَمين	right (side)	✘	ي	يَمين
(aṣ-ṣūra) اَلصّورة	picture	✔	ص	صورة
(al-ghurfa) اَلْغُرفة	room	✘	غ	غُرفة
(al-jarīda) اَلْجَريدة	newspaper	✘	ج	جَريدة
(aṭ-ṭālib) اَلطّالِب	student	✔	ط	طالِب
(al-walad) اَلْوَلَد	boy	✘	و	وَلَد

Exercise 3

أحمد/زيد/أنور/حسين/محمّد/مدحت/بدر	male
زينب/جيهان/دينا	female
نور/زين	both

Exercise 4

father حسين mother جيهان

son أحمد elder daughter زينب younger daughter دينا

Exercise 5

ق	ا	ف	و	ن
م	ث	ظ	م	ي
م	ص	ش	ه	ح
ر	ا	ج	ن	س
ض	ذ	ض	د	ق
ة	م	ت	س	ش
ي	د	خ	ط	ر
و	ر	ب	ه	ن
ب	س	ا	ح	م
ا	ل	ز	ج	و
خ	ط	ت	م	ش

Feminine pl.	Feminine sing.	Masculine pl.	Masculine sing.
مدرّسات	مدرّسة	مدرّسون	مدرّس
مهندسات	مهندسة	مهندسون	مهندس
نجّارات	نجّارة	نجّارون	نجّار
خبّازات	خبّازة	خبّازون	خبّاز
ممرّضات	ممرّضة	ممرّضون	ممرّض
محاسبات	محاسبة	محاسبون	محاسب

Exercise 6

1 جريدة　3 زينب　5 مصنع　7 كتاب

2 هل　4 هناك　6 أُخت　8 باب

Exercise 7

1 هذه سيّارة.　5 هذا سرير.　9 هذه حقيبة.

2 هذا مفتاح.　6 هذا باب.　10 هذا كرسيّ.

3 هذا كتاب.　7 هذا تليفزيون.　11 هذا كلب.

4 هذه درّاجة.　8 هذا شبّاك.　12 هذا قلم.

Exercise 8

The answer to this depends on where you put the objects. Try to check your answer with an Arabic-speaker.

Exercise 9

مكسور ... سليم　جديد ... قديم　كبير ... صغير

طويل ... قصير　قويّ ... ضعيف　أسود ... أبيض

قبيح ... جميل　ثقيل ... خفيف

(Model answer: yours may vary slightly.)

هذه صورة بيت جميل، وعلى يمين البيت هناك شجرة طويلة . لَون هذا البيت الجميل أبيض، ولكن الباب أسود. أمام البيت هناك سيّارة جديدة ولكن على يسار السيّارة هناك درّاجة مكسورة، والدرّاجة أمام الشجرة الطويلة.

هناك دجاجة صغيرة تحت السيّارة. على يمين الصورة هناك حمار جميل، وبين الحمار الجميل والسيارة هناك كلب أبيض وقبيح .

Exercise 10

1 هل الحمار قبيح؟ لا، هو جميل.

2 هل السيّارة أمام البيت؟ نعم، هي أمام البيت.

3 هل الكلب جميل؟ لا، هو قبيح.

4 هل الدرّاجة سليمة؟ لا، هي مكسورة.

5 هل الدجاجة على السيّارة؟ لا، هي تحت السيّارة.

6 هل باب البيت أبيض؟ لا، هو أسود.

7 هل الشجرة طويلة؟ نعم، هي طويلة.

8 هل الكلب بين الحمار والسيّارة؟ نعم، هو بين الحمار والسيّارة.

Exercise 11

1 هذا قلمي.
هذا قلم زينب. هذا قلمُها.

2 هذا بيتي.
هذا بيت نادر. هذا بيتُهُ.

3 هذه درّاجتي.
هذه درّاجة زين. هذه درّاجتُها.

4 هذه سيّارتي.
هذه سيّارة زيد. هذه سيّارتُهُ.

Unit 9

Exercise 1

1 لا، هي في مصر.

2 لا، هي في العراق.

3 نعم، هي في السعوديّة.

4 هي في الأردنّ.

5 نعم، هي بين السعوديّة وسوريا.

6 هي في عُمان.

7 لا، هي بجانب مصر.

8 نعم، هي بجانب عُمان.

Exercise 2

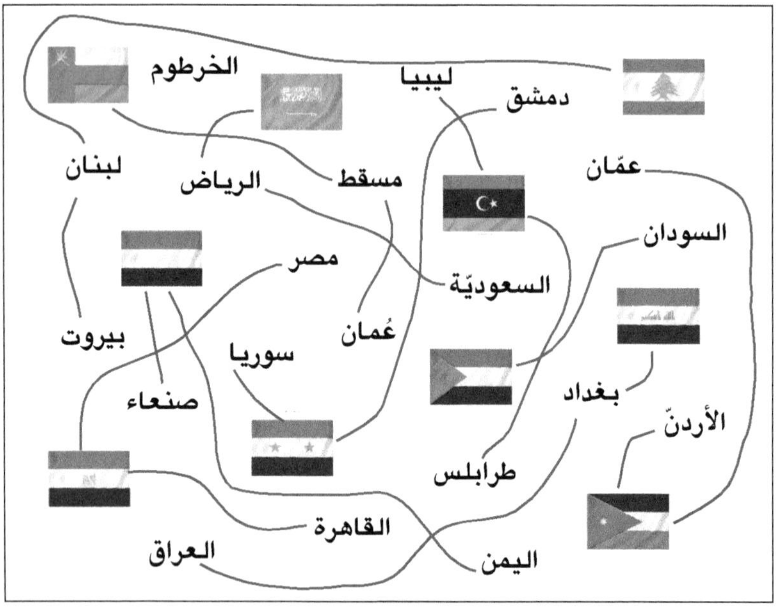

Exercise 3

1 القاهرة في مصر وهي عاصمة مصر.

2 الخرطوم في السودان وهي عاصمة السودان.

3 طرابلس في ليبيا وهي عاصمة ليبيا.

4 عمّان في الأردنّ وهي عاصمة الأردنّ.

5 بيروت في لبنان وهي عاصمة لبنان.

6 دمشق في سوريا وهي عاصمة سوريا.

7 بغداد في العراق وهي عاصمة العراق.

8 الرياض في السعوديّة وهي عاصمة السعوديّة.

9 مسقط في عُمان وهي عاصمة عُمان.

10 صنعاء في اليمن وهي عاصمة اليمن.

Exercise 4

1 أسوان في جنوب مصر.

2 سيوة في غرب مصر.

3 الإسكندرية في شمال مصر.

4 بور سعيد في شرق مصر.

Exercise 5

1C 2A 3F 4E 5G 6H 7I 8B 9D

Exercise 6

Country الدّوْلة	*Nationality* الجنْسيّة
الأردنّ	أردنيّ
العراق	عراقيّ
اليابان	يابانيّ
أمريكا	أمريكيّ
أسبانيا	أسبانيّ
روسيا	روسيّ
الصين	صينيّ
عُمان	عُمانيّ
إيطاليا	إيطاليّ
سوريا	سوريّ
لبنان	لبنانيّ
مصْر	مصْريّ
السعوديّة	سعوديّ
فرنسا	فرنسيّ
ألمانيا	ألمانيّ
إنجلترا	إنجليزي

Exercise 7

1 هو من الأردنّ. هو أردنيّ.

2 هو من روسيا. هو روسيّ.

3 هي من مصر. هي مصريّة.

4 هي من إيطاليا. هي إيطاليّة.

5 هو من السعوديّة. هو سعوديّ.

6 هي من لبنان. هي لبنانيّة.

7 هو من أمريكا. هو أمريكيّ.

8 هي من ليبيا. هي ليبيّة.

Exercise 8

A3 B1 C5 D2 E4

A هو من نيو يورك. هو أمريكيّ.   D هم من موسكو. هم روس.

B هي من طوكيو. هي يابانيّة.   E هنّ من مدريد. هنّ أسبانيّات.

C هم من الرياض. هم سعوديّون.

Exercise 9

9 نحن إنجليز.	1 هو سوريّ.
10 هل هو صينيّ؟	2 هل أنتِ أمريكيّة؟
11 هم عراقيّون.	3 هم لبنانيّون.
12 نحن أسبانيّات.	4 نحن فرسنيّون.
13 هي أردنّيّة.	5 هي سعوديّة.
14 هل هنّ سودانيّا؟	6 هل أنتُم عُمانيّون؟
15 هل أنتُم روس؟	7 هل أنتَ ألمانيّ؟
	8 هنّ يابانيّات.

Exercise 10

الاسم ..... أحمد حسين ....

الجِنسِيّة ... سعوديّ ....

المِهنة ... مهندس (في الرياض)

اسم الزوجة ... دينا حسين ....

جنسية الزوجة .. مصريّة ....

مهنة الزوجة .. مدرّسة ....

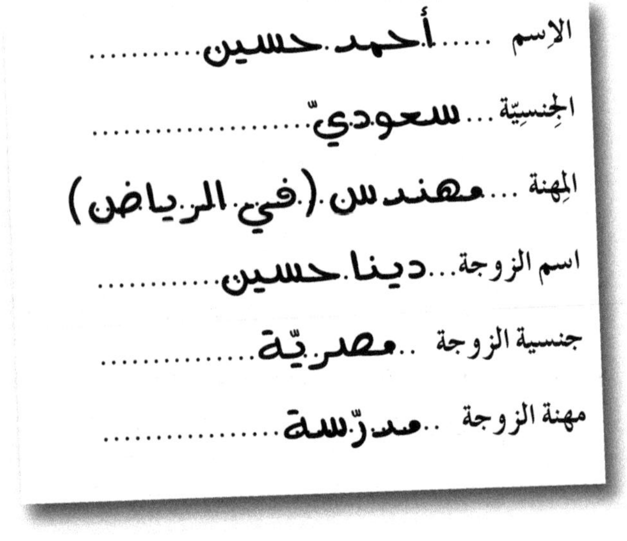

Exercise 11

(Model description: yours may vary slightly.)

محمد نور طبيب في دمشق. محمد سوريّ ولكن زوجته زينب يمنيّة. زينب ممرّضة في دمشق.

Unit 10

Exercise 1

See pages 118–19.

Exercise 2

١ كتابان/ين 2 books

٢ مفتاحان/ين 2 keys

٣ مدرستان/ين 2 schools

٤ نهران/ين 2 rivers

٥ جريدتان/ين 2 newspapers

٦ دولتان/ين 2 nations

Exercise 3

١ ثلاثة تليفونات

٢ ستّ زُجاجات

٣ نجّاران/نجّارَين

٤ خمسة بالونات

٥ حقيبتان/حقيبتَين

٦ عشر ممرّضات

Exercise 4

١ هناك كم سيّارة في الصورة؟ هناك خمس سيّارات.

٢ هناك كم شجرة في الصورة؟ هناك ستّ شجرات.

٣ هناك كم ممرّضة في الصورة؟ هناك ثلاث ممرّضات.

٤ هناك كم كلبًا في الصورة؟ هناك كلبان.

٥ هناك كم مهندسًا في الصورة؟ هناك أربعة مهندسين.

٦ هناك كم زجاجة في الصورة؟ هناك زجاجتان.

Exercise 5

– بكم كيلو التفاح؟ كيلو التفاح بثمانية جنيهات.

– بكم كيلو البطاطس؟ كيلو البطاطس بثلاثة جنيهات.

– بكم كيلو البرتقال؟ كيلو البرتقال بستّة جنيهات.

– بكم كيلو الطماطم؟ كيلو الطماطم بأربعة جنيهات.

– بكم كيلو المنجة؟ كيلو المنجة بعشرة جنيهات.

Exercise 6

Your conversations will vary depending on which fruit you choose and how many kilos you want. Try to check your answer with an Arabic-speaking friend or teacher.

Exercise 7

– بكم الصندل من فضلك؟

– بكم الطبلة من فضلك؟

– بكم القلادة من فضلك؟

– بكم السلّة من فضلك؟

– بكم التي-شيرت من فضلك؟

– بكم الطبق من فضلك؟

Exercise 8

I'd like a gold/silver necklace, please.	أريد قلادة ذهب/فضّة من فضلك.
I'd like a gold/silver ring, please.	أريد خاتم ذهب/فضّة من فضلك.
I'd like some leather sandals, please.	أريد صندل جلد من فضلك.
I'd like a cotton T-shirt, please.	أريد تي-شيرت قطن من فضلك.
I'd like a silk/cotton shirt, please.	أريد قميص حرير/قطن من فضلك.
I'd like a glass bottle, please.	أريد زجاجة زجاج من فضلك.
I'd like a wooden chair, please.	أريد كرسي خشب من فضلك.
I'd like a leather bag, please.	أريد حقيبة جلد من فضلك.
I'd like a copper/silver plate, please.	أريد طبق نحاس/فضّة من فضلك.

Exercise 9

(Model answers: yours may vary slightly.)

١ عِندَ سارة سيّارة كبيرة.

٢ لي أُخت في المَغرِب.

٣ لمُحمّد حقيبة جديدة.

٤ عِندَنا طبق فضّة جميل.

٥ عِندَهُم ثلاثة تليفزيونات.

٦ لأَنور كلب أسود صغير.

٧ مَعي مِفتاحان.

٨ هل عِندَكم بُرتُقال؟

٩ هل مَعَك قلم؟

١٠ هل عندِك سيّارة؟

Unit 11

Exercise 1

General meaning	Root	Word
calculating	ح/س/ب	محاسب
bigness	ك/ ب/ ر	كبير
carving (wood)	ن/ج/ر	نجّار
opening	ف/ت/ح	مفتاح
sealing (a letter)	خ/ت/م	خاتم
moving along	د/ ر/ ج	درّاجة
producing	ص/ ن/ ع	مصنع
falling sick	م/ ر/ ض	ممرّضة
studying	د/ ر/س	مُدرّس + مَدرَسة

Exercise 2

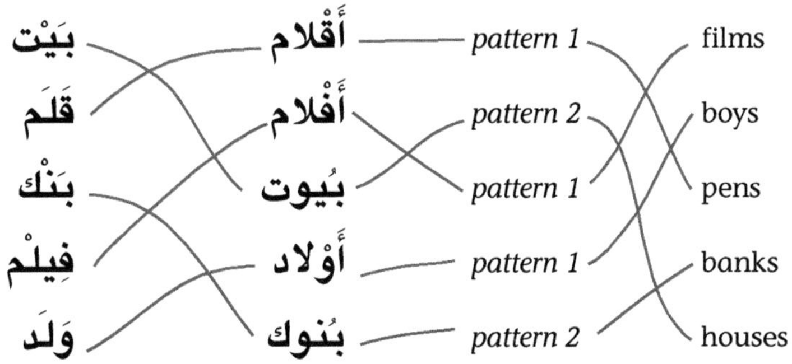

Exercise 3

ألوان لَوْن (lawn) colour

أطباق طَبَق (ṭabaq) plate

أصحاب صَاحِب (ṣāḥib) owner/friend

أشكال شَكل (shakl) shape

أوقات وَقْت (waqt) time

أسعار سعْر (siɛr) price

أعلام عَلَم (ɛalam) flag

Exercise 3 (continued)

أكواب	كُوب (kūb) glass/tumbler
أعوام	عام (ɛām) year
سُيوف	سَيْف (sayf) sword
قُلوب	قَلْب (qalb) heart
مُلوك	مَلِك (malik) king
شُموع	شَمعة (shamɛa) candle
شُيوخ	شَيْخ (shaykh) sheikh

Exercise 4

١ هذه قلوب. ٢ هذه بيوت. ٣ هؤلاء أولاد.

٤ هذه أطباق. ٥ هذه أشكال. ٦ هؤلاء شيوخ.

Exercise 5

١ هذه بيوت.
٢ هؤلاء أولاد.
٣ هل هذه سيوف؟
٤ هذه الأكواب مكسورة.
٥ هذه الشموع جميلة.
٦ أين البنوك؟
٧ الدرّاجات خفيفة.
٨ هذه الأعلام من أين؟
٩ هل هؤلاء مدرّسون؟
١٠ لا، هم محاسبون.

Exercise 6

أريد ستّة أطباق ورق، من فضلك.
أريد عشرة أكواب بلاستيك، من فضلك.
أريد ستّ قبّعات، من فضلك.
أريد سبع زجاجات كولا، من فضلك.
أريد خمس شموع، من فضلك.
أريد تسعة أكياس بلاستيك، من فضلك.

Exercise 7

Root letters	Feminine adj.	Masculine adj.	Colour
خ/ض/ر	خَضراء	أخضَر	green
ز/ر/ق	زَرقاء	أزرَق	blue
س/و/د	سَوداء	أسوَد	black
ص/ف/ر	صَفراء	أصفَر	yellow

Exercise 8

١ قميص أحْمَر

٢ سيّارة حَمْراء

٣ أطباق بَيْضاء

٤ زجاجات خَضْراء

٥ أكياس صَفْراء

٦ الكلب الأسْوَد

٧ الدرّاجة الزَرْقاء

٨ الشُموع الصَفراء

Exercise 9

1 8 Sudan Street (next to the hospital). **2** Do you have children at school? **3** 10 September. **4** Yes. **5** The shoes. **6** The black pens.

Exercise 10

pens (blue)	4.75
pens (black)	4.25
shirt	17.00
trousers	25.50
caps	12.50
shoes	34.00
big bag (green)	27.50
small bag (yellow)	16.25

Exercise 11

١ سِروال

٢ أَحذِية

٣ حَتّى

٤ أسعار رائعة

٥ للرِياضة

٦ للعام الجديد

٧ أفضل أسعار في المدينة

٨ مَوقِعنا على الإنترنت

Exercise 12

Your advertisement will vary depending on which items and prices you choose. Try to check your advertisement with an Arabic-speaking friend or teacher.

Unit 12

Exercise 1

biscuits بَسْكَوِيت   rice أَرُزّ   sugar سُكَّر
shampoo شَامْبو   cake كَعْك   macaroni مَكَرونَة

Exercise 2

(Sample answer – yours may vary.)

أنبوبة	قطعة	كيس	علبة	زجاجة
معجون الطماطم	كعك	أرز	حليب	عصير برتقال
	جبنة	سكّر	بيض	كولا
		تفّاح	طماطم	شامبو
			مكرونة	
			بنّ	
			تين	
			مسحوق الغسيل	

Exercise 3

1 In the morning. **2** Tomatoes. **3** Sugar. **4** White cheese: half a kilo. **5** Four and a half pounds.

Exercise 4

١ مساء الخير.
٢ مساء النور يا مدام ... تحت أمرك.
٣ أعطني من فضلك زجاجة زيت ...
٤ لتر؟
٥ لا نصف لتر من فضلك.
٦ تفضّلي.
٧ وعلبة مكرونة كبيرة وكيسين أرزّ.
٨ تفضّلي يا مدام.
٩ شكراً ... كم الحساب من فضلك؟
١٠ عشرة جنيهات.
١١ تفضّل.
١٢ شكرًا ... مع السلامة يا مدام.
١٣ الله يسلّمك.

Exercise 5

Name	Likes	Dislikes	Favourite dish
Jamal	chicken roast meat rice potatoes	cheese milk	grilled chicken with rice
Karima	fish vegetables	meat chicken	fish fried in oil with tomato salad
Mido	fried chicken chips cola	vegetables fruit	pizza

Exercise 6

١ تينة a fig

٢ وردة a rose

٣ حمامة a pigeon

٤ شجرة a tree

٥ لوزة an almond

٦ تفّاحة an apple

Exercise 7

كَباب	مَهَلَبيّة	كُشَري	
✔			دجاج / لحم
		✔	مكرونة / أرزّ
	✔		حليب
		✔	بَصَل
✔			بطاطس
	✔		سكّر

Exercise 8

الطبق الأوّل

✔ سلطة طماطم بالبيض ٣٠ ريالاً

سلطة دجاج بالمايونيز ٥٠ ريالاً

الطبق الرئيسي

لحم بالبطاطس ٦٠ ريالاً

✔ سمك بالأرز ٧٠ ريالاً

مكرونة بالطماطم والجبنة ٤٥ ريالاً

الحلويات

✔ آيس كريم ٢٥ ريالاً

كعك باللوز ٢٨ ريالاً

المشروبات

قهوة ١٣ ريالاً — شاي بالحليب ١٧ ريالاً

شاي ١٥ ريالاً — عصير برتقال ١٨ ريالاً

كولا ١٤ ريالاً — ✔ عصير تفاح ٢٠ ريالاً

Exercise 9

سلطة طماطم	٣٠
سمك بالأرز	٧٠
آيس كريم	٢٥
عصير تفاح	٢٠
المجموع	١٤٥
+ خدمة ١٠٪	١٤,٥٠
المجموع بالخدمة	١٥٩,٥٠

Exercise 10

سلطة دجاج	٥٠
لحم بالبطاطس	٦٠
كعك باللوز	٢٨
شاي بالحليب	١٨
المجموع	١٥٦
+ خدمة ١٠٪	١٥,٦٠
المجموع بالخدمة	١٧٣,٦٠

Exercise 11

Plural	Noun of place meaning	Root meaning
ملاعب	ملعب playground/court	لعب playing
معارض	معرض exhibition	عرض showing
مداخل	مدخل entrance	دخل coming in
مخارج	مخرج exit	خرج going out
مخابز	مخبز bakery	خبز baking
مطابخ	مطبخ kitchen	طبخ cooking
مغاسل	مغسلة laundry	غسل washing
مساجد	مسجد mosque	سجد kneeling in prayer

Unit 13

Exercise 1

thief لصّ — with مَعَ

dollar دولار — investigation تَحْقيق

yesterday أَمْس — Kuwaiti كُوَيتيّ

theft/robbery سَرِقة

1 In Amman. **2** A million dollars. **3** Yesterday. **4** The Kuwaiti Bank. **5** Two.

Exercise 2

١ هل كَتَبْتَ خِطابات في مكتبك؟ نعم، كَتَبْتُ خِطابات في مكتبي.

٢ هل ذهبتَ إلى مطعم أمريكيّ؟ لا، ذهبتُ إلى مطعم عربيّ.

٣ هل أكلتَ سمكاً في المطعم؟ نعم، أكلتُ سمكاً في المطعم.

٤ هل رجعتَ إلى البيت (بيتك) مساءً؟ نعم، رجعتُ إلى البيت (بيتي) مساءً.

٥ هل سمعتَ عن السرقة في الراديو؟ لا، سمعتُ عن السرقة في التليفزيون.

Exercise 3

١ أنا زينب شَوْقي وبيتي في وسط مدينة عمّان.

٢ أمس ... ذهبتُ إلى البنك صباحًا،

٣ وشربتُ فنجان شاي.

٤ فتحتُ الخزانة ...

٥ وجلستُ على مكتبي.

٦ ذهبتُ إلى مطعم صيني...

٧ وفي المطعم سمعتُ عن السرقة في الراديو.

٨ رجعتُ من المطعم إلى البنك ...

٩ ووجدتُ الشبّاك المكسور.

Exercise 4

١ ماذا شَرِبْتَ؟

٢ أين شَرِبْتَ القهوة؟

٣ هل ذهبتَ إلى مطعم عربي؟

٤ ماذا أكلتَ في المطعم؟

٥ ماذا فعَلتَ في مكتبِك؟

٦ ما اسمَك؟

٧ متى سَمَعتَ عن السرقة؟

Exercise 5

١ أمس، خرَجْتُ من البيت صباحًا.

٢ ذَهَبَتْ إلى البنك.

٣ هل أَكَلْتَ التُفَّاحة؟

٤ أوّلاً، كَتَبَ خطابات.

٥ أين سَمِعْتِ عن السرقة؟

٦ ذَهَبْتُ إلى البيت وجَلَسْتُ على كرسيّ.

٧ شَرِبَتْ فنجان قهوة مع أُختها.

٨ ماذا فَعَلْتَ أمس؟

Exercise 6

اسمها زينب شوقي
وبيتها في وسط مدينة عمّان .
أمس ذهبَت إلى البنك الكويتي صباحًا .
أوّلاً شربَت فنجان شاي . . .
وفتحت الخزانة .
ثمّ جلسَت على مكتبها .
وبعد ذلك ذهبَت إلى المطعم
وسمعَت عن السرقة في الراديو .
فرجعَت إلى البنك .
أخيراً وجدَت الشبّاك المكسور .

Exercise 7

أكلتُ سمكاً في المطعم أمس.

شَرِبَت دينا زجاجة كولا.

وَجَدْتُ ولداً صغيراً بجانب باب المدرسة.

أولاً، فتحَت زينب خزانة البنك الكويتي صباحاً.

جلسَت على كرسيّ خشبيّ.

أخيراً، رَجَعتُ إلى بيتي مساءً.

Exercise 8

٢ ذهب إلى مصنع السيّارات في جنوب المدينة.

٥ ذهب إلى مدرسة كبيرة في وسط المدينة.

٣ شرب فنجان قهوة مع المهندسين في المصنع.

١ خرج من القصر الملكي.

٧ رجع إلى القصر الملكي.

٦ جلس مع الأولاد والبنات والمدرّسين.

٤ سمع من المهندسين عن السيّارة الجديدة.

Unit 14

Exercise 1

Plural	Pattern	Singular	
جِبال	فِعال	جَبَل	mountain
جِمال	فِعال	جَمَل	camel
لُعَب	فُعَل	لُعْبَة	toy/game
بِحار	فِعال	بَحْر	sea
تُحَف	فُعَل	تُحْفَة	masterpiece/artefact
دُوَل	فُعَل	دَوْلَة	nation/state
رِياح	فِعال	ريح	wind

Exercise 2

١ كم كلباً في الصورة؟ هناك أربعة كِلاب.

٢ كم جملاً في الصورة؟ هناك خمسة جِمال.

٣ كم لُعبة في الصورة؟ هناك تسع لُعَب.

٤ كم جبلاً في الصورة؟ هناك ستّة جِبال.

٥ كم رَجُلاً في الصورة؟ هناك سبعة رِجال.

٦ كم عُلبة في الصورة؟ هناك ثماني عُلَب.

Exercise 3

See the number panel on page 188.

Exercise 4

See the number panels on pages 119 and 188.

Exercise 5

١٨٥	٧	٩٣	٥	٣٥	٣	٤٦	١
١٥٧	٨	٧٢	٦	١٢٤	٤	٨١	٢

Exercise 6

٦١ رجلاً (wāḥid wa-sittīn rajul)

٢٣ سيفاً (thalātha wa-ع ishrīn sayf)

٧٢ قلماً (ithnān wa-sabع īn qalam)

٥٨ كلباً (thamānya wa-khamsīn kalb)

٤٩ صورة (tisع wa-arbaع īn ṣūra)

٢٨ مفتاحاً (thamānya wa-ع ishrīn miftāḥ)

١٦ زجاجة (sitt ع ashar zujāja)

١٨ جملاً (thamanyat ع ashar jamal)

٩٣ خيمة (thalāth wa-tis ع īn khayma)

Exercise 7

١ ما هي دَرَجَة الحَرارة؟ دَرَجَة الحرارة ١٥. الطَّقس بارد.

٢ ما هي دَرَجَة الحَرارة؟ دَرَجَة الحرارة ٤٠. الطَّقس حارّ.

٣ ما هي دَرَجَة الحَرارة؟ دَرَجَة الحرارة ٢٥. الطَّقس مُعْتَدِل.

٤ ما هي دَرَجَة الحَرارة؟ دَرَجَة الحرارة ٥. الطَّقس بارد جدًّا.

٥ ما هي دَرَجَة الحَرارة؟ دَرَجَة الحرارة ٥٠. الطَّقس حارّ جدًّا.

٦ ما هي دَرَجَة الحَرارة؟ دَرَجَة الحرارة ١٠. الطَّقس بارد.

Exercise 8

✓					✓	١
	✓		✓			٢
		✓		✓		٣
✓					✓	٤

Exercise 9

City	Temperature	Weather
Cairo	23°	light rain
Baghdad	25°	sunny
Abu Dhabi	31°	sunny periods
Rabat	18°	heavy rain(s)
Damascus	19°	black clouds
Beirut	20°	strong wind(s)
Khartoum	40°	sunny
Riyadh	34°	sunny periods
Kuwait City	29°	white clouds

Exercise 10

مدينة الكويت:
الطقس مُعتَدِل. درجة الحرارة
٢٩ وهناك غُيوم بيضاء.

مدينة الخرطوم:
الطقس حارّ جدّاً. درجة الحرارة
٤٠ والطقس مشمس.

Exercise 11

١ ✔ ٣ ✘ ٥ ✔ ٧ ✘
٢ ✘ ٤ ✔ ٦ ✘ ٨ ✔

Exercise 12

١ في آخِر يوم
٢ شُروق الشمس
٣ أطباق مصريّة لَذيذة
٤ لِثلاثة أيّام
٥ جبل موسَى
٦ رِحلة مُمتِعة

Exercise 13

1 Ahmad. **2** London. **3** Cold and cloudy. **4** Centre of town. **5** Japanese. **6** To a museum. **7** Went back to the hotel. **8** Have you written a letter to me?

Exercise 14

عزيزتي سارة،
كيف حالِك؟ نحن في باريس والطقس حارّ ومشمس. ذهبنا أمس صباحاً
إلى متحف كبير. ثمّ أكلنا في مطعم فرنسي في وسط المدينة.
بعد ذلك أنا ذهبتُ إلى البنك ولكن نادر والأولاد ذهبوا إلى المتحف.
وأنتِ؟ هل كتبتِ لي خطاباً؟
مع تحياتي زينب

Unit 15

Exercise 1

وَاحِد	١	أحد عشر	١١	ثلاثين	٣٠
اِثْنَان	٢	اثنا عشر	١٢	أربعين	٤٠
ثَلاثَة	٣	ثَلاثَة عشر	١٣	خمسين	٥٠
أرْبَعة	٤	أرْبَعة عشر	١٤	سِتّين	٦٠
خَمْسَة	٥	خَمْسَة عشر	١٥	سَبعين	٧٠
سِتّة	٦	سِتّة عشر	١٦	ثَمانين	٨٠
سَبْعة	٧	سَبْعة عشر	١٧	تِسعين	٩٠
ثَمانية	٨	ثَمانية عشر	١٨	خَمْسَة وتسعين	٩٥
تِسْعة	٩	تسعة عشر	١٩	ثَلاثة وأربعين	٤٣
عَشرَة	١٠	عشرين	٢٠	أرْبَعة وثلاثين	٣٤

Exercise 2

١ ٩٤ ٣ ١٩ ٥ ٦١ ٧ ٤٣ ٩ ٣٨

٢ ٥٦ ٤ ٧٠ ٦ ٨٨ ٨ ١٤ ١٠ ٢٩

Exercise 3

٢	٤	٦	٨	١٠	١٢	١٤	١٦	١٨	٢٠	٢٢
٣	٦	٩	١٢	١٥	١٨	٢١	٢٤	٢٧	٣٠	٣٣
١١	٢٢	٣٣	٤٤	٥٥	٦٦	٧٧	٨٨	٩٩	١١٠	١٢١
٧	١٤	٢١	٢٨	٣٥	٤٢	٤٩	٥٦	٦٣	٧٠	٧٧
١	١	٢	٣	٥	٨	١٣	٢١	٣٤	٥٥	٨٩

(add together the previous two numbers)

Exercise 4

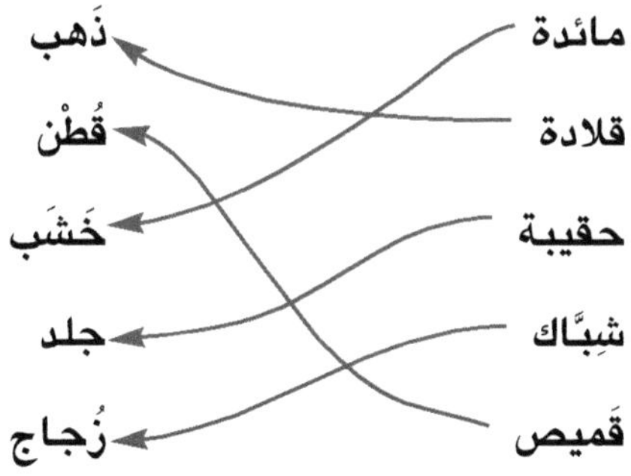

أريد مائدة خشب من فضلك.
أريد قلادة ذَهب من فضلك.
أريد حقيبة جلد من فضلك.
أريد شبّاك زُجاج من فضلك.
أريد قَميص قُطْن من فضلك.

Exercise 5

مَفاعِل	فُعَل	فِعال	فُعول	أفعال	ات	ون/ين
مَطاعِم *restaurants*	عُلَب *boxes*	رِجال *men*	شُموع *candles*	أولاد *boys*	ممرّضات *nurses*	مهندسون *engineers*
مَتاحِف *museums*	لُعَب *toys*	جِبال *mountains*	لُصوص *thieves*	أفلام *films*	جنيهات *pounds*	خبّازون *bakers*
مَساجِد *mosques*	صُوَر *pictures*	جِمال *camels*	بُنوك *banks*	أسواق *markets*	سيّارات *cars*	محاسبون *accountants*
		بِحار *seas*	قُلوب *hearts*	أكواب *glasses*	رِحلات *trips*	
		رِياح *winds*	غُيوم *clouds*	أكياس *bags/sacks*	سلطات *salads*	
			شُيوخ *sheikhs*	أمطار *rains*	تليفونات *telephones*	
			مُلوك *kings*	أطباق *plates*	فَترات *periods*	

Exercise 6

١ كم كلبًا في الصورة؟ هناك ثلاثة كلاب في الصورة.

٢ كم جملاً في الصورة؟ هناك أربعة جمال في الصورة.

٣ كم سيّارة في الصورة؟ هناك عشر سيّارات في الصورة.

٤ كم صورة في الصورة؟ هناك خمس صُوَر في الصورة.

٥ كم درّاجة في الصورة؟ هناك سبع درّاجات في الصورة.

٦ كم رجلاً في الصورة؟ هناك ستّة رجال في الصورة.

٧ كم علبة في الصورة؟ هناك ثلاث عُلَب في الصورة.

٨ كم لعبة في الصورة؟ هناك ثماني لُعَب في الصورة.

Exercise 7

٥ ونصف كيلو جبنة بيضاء من فضلَك. كم الحساب؟

٢ صباح النور يا مدام نادية.

٤ تحت أمرك ... تَفَضَّلي.

٣ من فضلَك، أعطني كيس سُكَّر وزجاجة (عُلبة) عصير تُفَّاح.

١ صباح الخير يا إسماعيل.

٨ اللّه يسلِّمَك.

٦ ١٣ جنيه من فضلِك.

٧ تفَضَّل. شكراً يا إسماعيل. مع السَلامَة.

Exercise 8

	المشروبات	الطبق الأوّل	الطبق الرئيسي	الحلويات
سلوى	عصير منجة	مكرونة	سمك بالأرزّ	–
أحمد	كولا	سلطة	دجاج بالبطاطس	كعك

Exercise 9

A vegetarian would probably choose the tomato salad and the macaroni with tomato. The final bill and conversation will depend on your choice of dessert and drink. Try to check them with an Arabic-speaker.

Exercise 10

Feminine	**Masculine**
خَضْراء	أَخْضَر
زَرْقاء	أَزْرَق
بَيْضاء	أَبْيَض
سَوْداء	أَسْوَد
صَفْراء	أَصْفَر
حَمْراء	أَحْمَر

Exercise 11

١ هذا الكرسي أحمر.

٢ هذه المائدة سوداء.

٣ هذه الأقلام زرقاء.

٤ هذا الباب أخضر. / باب بيتي [colour of your door *(masc.)*].

٥ هذه السيّارات بيضاء وصفراء.

سيّارتي [colour of your car *(fem.)*].

٦ عَلَم الجَزائِر أبيض وأخضر وأحمر.

٧ عَلَم ألمانيا أحمر وأصفر وأسود.

٨ وجدتُ هذه الأطباق الزرقاء في السوق.

Exercise 12

في الأسبوع الماضي، ذهبتُ مع بدر زوجي وصديقتي الألمانيّة كلارا إلى القاهرة لِثلاثة أيّام. نزلنا في غُرفَتَين في فندق صغير هناك.
في أوَّل يوم خرجنا كُلّنا صباحاً وذهبنا إلى المتحف المصري في وسط المدينة. بعد ذلك وجدنا مطعماً كبيراً بجانب المتحف. أنا أكلتُ سمكاً لذيذاً من البحر الأحمر، ولكن بدر أكلَ الكباب وكلارا جرّبَت الكشري.
في آخِر يوم أنا شاهدتُ الفيلم المصري الجديد في السينما مع زوجي، ولكن كلارا جلسَت في شُرفة غُرفتها في الفندق وكتبَت خطابًا لأُمّها في ألمانيا. أخيرًا، رجعنا كُلّنا إلى بَيروت مساءً.

في الأسبوع الماضي، ذهبَت جميلة مع بدر زوجها وصديقتها الألمانيّة كلارا إلى القاهرة لِثلاثة أيّام. نزلوا في غُرفَتَين في فندق صغير هناك.
في أوَّل يوم خرجوا كُلّهم صباحاً وذهبوا إلى المتحف المصري في وسط المدينة. بعد ذلك وجدوا مطعماً كبيراً بجانب المتحف. أكلَت جميلة سمكاً لذيذاً من البحر الأحمر، ولكن بدر أكلَ الكباب وكلارا جرّبَت الكشري.
في آخِر يوم شاهدَت جميلة الفيلم المصري الجديد في السينما مع زوجها، ولكن كلارا جلسَت في شُرفة غُرفتها في الفندق وكتبَت خطابًا لأُمّها في ألمانيا. أخيرًا، رجعوا كُلّهم إلى بَيروت مساءً.

Unit 16

Exercise 1

١ كم الساعة؟ الساعة الخامسة.

٢ كم الساعة؟ الساعة التاسعة.

٣ كم الساعة؟ الساعة الثامنة.

٤ كم الساعة؟ الساعة الثانية.

٥ كم الساعة؟ الساعة الحادية عشرة.

Exercise 2

١ كم الساعة؟ الساعة العاشرة والثُلث.

٢ كم الساعة؟ الساعة الثامنة والرُبع.

٣ كم الساعة؟ الساعة الثانية والنِصف.

٤ كم الساعة؟ الساعة العاشرة إلا ثُلثًا.

٥ كم الساعة؟ الساعة السادسة إلا عشر دَقائِق.

٦ كم الساعة؟ الساعة الحادية عشرة إلا خمس دَقائِق.

Exercise 3

١ الفيلم الساعة العاشرة وخمس دقائِق.

٢ المعرض الساعة السابعة.

٣ الباص الساعة التاسعة والثُلث.

٤ ذهبتُ إلى السوق الساعة الثالثة.

٥ أكلَت جميلة الساعة التاسعة والثلث.

٦ رجع أبي الساعة العاشرة والربع.

٧ القطار الساعة الواحدة إلا خمس دقائِق.

٨ سَمِعنا عن السرقة الساعة الحادية عشرة والنصف.

Exercise 4

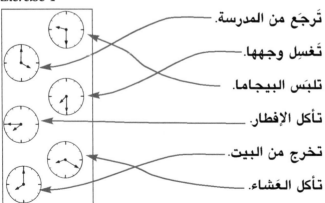

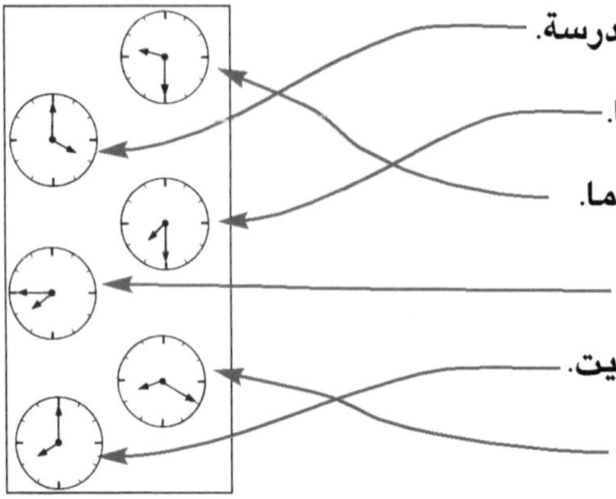

تَرجَع من المدرسة.

تَغسِل وجهها.

تلبَس البيجاما.

تأكل الإفطار.

تخرج من البيت.

تأكل العَشاء.

Try to check your paragraph with an Arabic-speaker.

Exercise 5

These are model answers: yours may vary slightly.

١ لا تذهب فاطمة إلى المدرسة بالحمار، تذهب بالدراجة.

٢ لا يذهب محمود إلى المدرسة الساعة السابعة والنصف، يذهب الساعة الثامنة.

٣ لا يشرب محمود فنجان شاي، يشرب زجاجة كولا.

٤ لا تغسل فاطمة وجهها الساعة الواحدة والثلث، تغسل وجهها الساعة السابعة والنصف.

Exercise 6

Try to check your answers with an Arabic-speaker.

Exercise 7

1 She's an engineer in a large factory in Beirut. **2** Half past six. **3** No. Jamila usually drinks tea and Badr coffee. **4** Twenty to eight. **5** By train, because she doesn't like buses in the morning. **6** Cooks dinner. **7** Sit together in the sitting room or go to the club and play badminton. **8** Half past ten.

Exercise 8

to Jamila:

١ متى تَأكُلينَ الإفطار؟

٢ ماذا تَشرَبينَ صباحاً؟

٣ هل تَخرُجينَ من البيت الساعة السابعة؟

٤ كيف تَذهبينَ إلى المصنع؟

٥ متى تَرجِعينَ إلى البيت؟

٦ متى تَطبُخينَ العشاء عادةً؟

٧ وبعد العشاء ماذا تفعلينَ؟

٨ متى تنامينَ؟

to a male:

١ متى تَأكُل الإفطار؟

٢ ماذا تَشرَب صباحاً؟

٣ هل تَخرُج من البيت الساعة السابعة؟

٤ كيف تَذهب إلى المصنع؟

٥ متى تَرجِع إلى البيت؟

٦ متى تَطبُخ العشاء عادةً؟

٧ وبعد العشاء ماذا تَفعَل؟

٨ متى تنام؟

to a group:

١ متى تَأكُلونَ الإفطار؟

٢ ماذا تَشرَبونَ صباحاً؟

٣ هل تَخرُجونَ من البيت الساعة السابعة؟

٤ كيف تَذهبونَ إلى المصنع؟

٥ متى تَرجِعونَ إلى البيت؟

٦ متى تَطبُخونَ العشاء عادةً؟

٧ وبعد العشاء ماذا تَفعَلونَ؟

٨ متى تنامونَ؟

Exercise 9
Try to check your paragraph with an Arabic-speaker.

Unit 17

Exercise 1

Pronunciation	Comparative /superlative	Meaning	Adjective
akbar	أكبَر	big/large	كبير
aqdam	أقدَم	old	قديم
ajmal	أجمَل	beautiful	جميل
aqbaḥ	أقبَح	ugly	قبيح
aṣghar	أصغَر	small	صغير
aṭwal	أطوَل	tall	طويل
ajadd	أجَدّ	new	جديد
ashdad	أشَدّ	strong	شديد
asraع	أسرَع	fast	سريع
akthar	أكثَر	many	كثير
afḍal	أفضَل	good	فاضِل
arkhaṣ	أرخَص	inexpensive/cheap	رَخيص
aghnā	أغنَى	rich	غَنيّ
afqar	أفقَر	poor	فَقير
ahamm	أهَمّ	important	هامّ

Exercise 2

١ النيل أطول نهر في العالم.
٢ القاهرة أكبر مدينة في أفريقيا.
٣ آسيا أكبر قارّة في العالم.
٤ الفضّة أرخص من الذهب.
٥ السيّارة أسرع من الدرّاجة.
٦ اللوزة أصغر من البطيخة.

Exercise 3

١ يَوْم الجُمعَة قَبلَ يَوْم السَّبْت.
٢ يَوْم الخَميس بَعدَ يَوْم الأَربِعَاء.
٣ يَوْم الأحَد قبل يَوْم الاِثْنَيْن.
٤ يَوْم الثُلاثاء قبل يَوْم الأربِعاء.
٥ يَوْم السَّبْت بعد يَوم الجُمعة.

Exercise 4

	Sat.	Sun.	Mon.	Tue.	Wed.	Thu.	Fri.
play with little sister						✔	
sit with grandmother				✔			
go to bakery at 6AM	✔						
no tasks this day							✔
go out with the dog to the river		✔					
write today's lessons with brother			✔				
wash mother's car after school					✔		

Exercise 5

يوم السبت أَذهَب إلى المخبز الساعة السادسة صباحاً.
يوم الأحد أَخرُج مع الكلب إلى النهر.
يوم الأثنين أَكتُب دروس اليوم مع أخي.
يوم الثلاثاء أَجلِس مع جَدّتي بعد الظهر.
يوم الأربعاء أَغسِل سيّارة أمّي بعد المدرسة.
يوم الخميس أَلعَب مع أختي الصغيرة.
يوم الجمعة لا أفعَل شيئاً!

Exercise 6

Model answer – yours may vary.

Comparative(s)	Adjective(s)	Aspect
أرخَص أغلَى	رخيص غالٍ	price
أكبَر أصغَر	كبير صغير	size
أسرَع	سريع	speed
أجَدّ أقدَم	جديد قديم	age

Exercise 7

1 6 days. **2** From Saturday to Thursday. **3** Three. **4** Red/180 per day. **5** White and small.

Exercise 8

	سيّارة ١	سيّارة ٢	سيّارة ٣
أكبر	✔		
أصغر			✔
أسرع		✔	
أجدّ		✔	
أغلَى		✔	
أرخص			✔

Exercise 9

٤ عندنا هذه السيّارة الكبيرة الجميلة.

٦ الحمراء أجدّ وأسرع سيّارة عندنا.

١٢ الاسم، من فضلك...

١٠ البيضاء أرخص وأصغر.

٣ من يوم السبت حتّى الخميس.

١ مساء الخير. أريد سيّارة لستّة أيّام.

٨ بمائة وثمانين في اليوم.

١١ نعم. هذا أفضل. آخذ البيضاء .

٢ من متى يا سيّدي؟

٧ بكم الحمراء؟

٩ غالية! هل هناك أرخص منها؟

٥ ولكنّها قديمة. ممكن أجدّ منها؟

Exercise 10

مُنذُ عِشرين سَنَة كان فَوْزي غَنِيًّا. كان له بيت جميل وكبير في وسط المدينة، ولَكنّه الآن فَقير وليس له بيت.

في الماضي، كانَت زوجَتُه فَوْزيّة غَنيَّة، وكان لها سيّارة جديدة وكبيرة وكلب جميل وصغير، ولَكنّها الآن فقيرة وليس لها كلب، لها دجاجة.

Exercise 11

١ كان أحمد مدرّساً في الماضي.

٢ منذ عشرين سنة كان هناك مدرسة في هذا الشارع.

٣ الطقس كان حاراً أمس.

٤ منذ أسبوعَين كانو في القاهرة.

٥ كُنتُ في المكتب يوم السبت.

٦ كانت الشجرة أطول من بيتي.

٧ أين كُنتُم يوم الأربعاء الساعة التاسعة.

٨ كان هناك مطاعم كثيرة هنا.

Exercise 12 & Exercise 13 (in brackets)

١ مُنْذُ عِشرين سَنَة كُنتُ غَنيًّا. الآن أنا (ولكنّي الآن) فقير.

٢ منذ ثلاثين سَنَة كان أحمد في الجيش. الآن هو (ولكنّه الآن) محاسب في بنك.

٣ منذ نصف ساعة كانوا في المدرسة. الآن هم (ولكنّهم الآن) في بيوتهم.

٤ منذ تِسْعين سَنَة كانَت الرياض مدينة صغيرة. الآن هي (ولكنّها الآن) أكبر مدينة في السعوديّة.

٥ في الماضي كُنتَ مدرّساً. الآن أنتَ (ولكنّك الآن) ممثّل غنيّ.

٦ منذ دقيقتين كُنّا في البنك. الآن نحن (ولكنّا الآن) عند البقّال.

Exercise 14

Past الماضي	Present المُضارِع	Root الجَذر	Meaning
طَارَ (طِرْتُ)	يَطير	ط/ي/ر	to fly
زَارَ (زُرْتُ)	يَزور	ز/و/ر	to visit
جرى (جَرَيْتُ)	يَجْري	ج/ر/ي	to run
باع (بِعْتُ)	يَبيع	ب/ي/ع	to sell
عاد (عُدْتُ)	يَعود	ع/و/د	to return
دعا (دَعَوْتُ)	يَدْعو	د/ع/و	to call/ to invite
زاد (زِدْتُ)	يَزيد	ز/ي/د	to increase
قال (قُلْتُ)	يَقول	ق/و/ل	to say
شَكا (شَكَوْتُ)	يَشكو	ش/ك/و	to complain

Exercise 15
Try to check your email or letter with an Arabic-speaker.

Unit 18

Exercise 1

١ ماذا تدرسون يوم الثلاثاء ظهرًا؟ ندرس الموسيقى من الساعة الواحدة والنصف حتّى الساعة الثالثة.

٢ ماذا تدرسون يوم الثلاثاء صباحًا؟ ندرس الرياضيّات من الساعة الثامنة والنصف حتّى الساعة العاشرة وبعد ذلك ندرس الانجليزية حتّى الساعة الثانية عشرة.

٣ ماذا تدرسون يوم الاثنين ظهرًا؟ ندرس الرسم من الساعة الواحدة والنصف حتّى الساعة الثالثة.

٤ ماذا تدرسون يوم الخميس صباحًا؟ ندرس الكيمياء من الساعة الثامنة والنصف حتّى الساعة العاشرة وبعد ذلك ندرس الرياضيّات حتّى الساعة الثانية عشرة.

٥ ماذا تدرسون يوم السبت ظهرًا؟ ندرس الجغرافيا من الساعة الواحدة والنصف حتّى الساعة الثالثة.

٦ ماذا تدرسون يوم الأحد ظهرًا؟ ندرس الرياضة من الساعة الواحدة والنصف حتّى الساعة الثالثة.

٧ ماذا تدرسون يوم الاثنين صباحًا؟ ندرس التربية الدينية من الساعة الثامنة والنصف حتّى الساعة العاشرة وبعد ذلك ندرس العربيّة حتّى الساعة الثانية عشرة.

Exercise 2

كلّ يوم يخرجون من بيوتهم الساعة الثامنة إلا ربعًا ويذهبون إلى المدرسة بالأوتوبيس. يدرسون حتّى الساعة الثانية عشرة وبعد ذلك يأكلون الغداء.

بعد الغداء يدرسون من الساعة الواحدة والنصف حتّى الساعة الثالثة ثم يرجعون من المدرسة إلى بيوتهم.

Exercise 3

- Damascus University • medicine • lectures on Sunday/Monday/Thursday
- eggs/tea for breakfast • leaves house 10 AM • university by train
- attends lectures/sits in library until 4 PM • returns home
- Friday goes to cinema with friends • eats in falafel restaurant

Exercise 4

algebra	الجَبْر
emir (prince)	أَمير
saffron	زَعْفَران
alkali	القِلي
vizier (minister)	وَزير
tamarind	تَمْر هِنْدي
alcohol	الكُحول

Exercise 5

سُفَراء	ambassadors
رُؤَساء	presidents/chairmen
مُدَراء	managers
زُعَماء	leaders
وُكَلاء	agents
زُمَلاء	colleagues/associates

Exercise 6

سَفيرة/سَفيرات	*(female)* ambassador/s
رَئيسة/رَئيسات	*(female)* president/s; chairwoman/women
مُديرة/مُديرات	*(female)* manager/s
زَعيمة/زَعيمات	*(female)* leader/s
وَكيلة/وَكيلات	*(female)* agent/s
زَميلة/زَميلات	*(female)* colleague/s; associate/s

Exercise 7

Meaning	General noun	Root letters
ministry	وِزارة	و ز ر
embassy	سِفارة	س ف ر
emirate	إِمارة	ء م ر
agency	وَكالة	و ك ل
leadership	زَعامة	ز ع م
presidency/chairing	رِئاسة	ر ء س
colleagueship	زَمالة	ز م ل

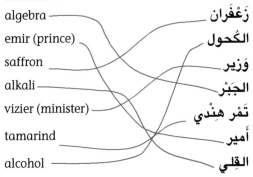

Exercise 8

١ أمير الكُوَيت
٢ وُكَلاء الشَرِكة
٣ رَئيس مصر
٤ سفير الصين
٥ وِزارة الصِّحّة
٦ اِجتِماع المُدَراء
٧ وزيرة التَّعليم
٨ وزير الصِّناعة
٩ مَجلِس الوُزَراء
١٠ زُعَماء أفريقيا
١١ مُؤتَمَر المهندسين
١٢ رِئاسة الاِجتِماع

Exercise 9

1 In private cars. **2** Last Thursday. **3** After a cabinet meeting last week. **4** The prime minister. **5** He wants them to know and listen to the people.

Exercise 10

١ أمس خرج السفراء من السفارات وذهبوا إلى القصر الملكيّ.

٢ كلّ أسبوع يَزور الوُكَلاء مكاتب الشركة ويَشرَبون القهوة مع الرئيس.

٣ الأسبوع الماضي ذَهَبَ الزُّعَماء إلى المصنع وسَمِعوا عن السيارة الجديدة.

٤ كلّ صباح تَجلِس المديرة على مكتبها وتَكتُب خطابات.

٥ كلّ يوم يَأكُل الرِجال سمكاً في المطعم، وبعد ذلك يَشرَبون زجاجات كولا.

٦ منذ يومَين جلَسَت وزيرة التعليم مع المدرّسات.

٧ لا يَعرِف الوزراء الشارع ولا يَسمَعون من الشّعب.

٨ ماذا فَعَلَت الملكة يوم الثلاثاء الماضي ومتى رَجَعَت إلى القصر؟

Exercise 11

	Health	Education	Industry
went to a small school outside the city		✔	
went to a cement factory			✔
travelled by train		✔	
usually has lunch on the balcony	✔		
drank tea			✔
listened to the teachers		✔	
usually plays tennis every Thursday			✔
ate lunch in a cafeteria	✔		
put on a yellow plastic hat			✔
went to a distant town	✔		
usually writes letters on the computer		✔	

Exercise 12

يوم الخميس الماضي لَمْ يذهب *(didn't go)* وزير الصحّة إلى الوزارة بالسيّارة، ولكنّه رَكِبَ *(rode)* الأوتوبيس وذهب *(went)* إلى مستشفى صغير في مدينة بَعيدة. عادةً يجلس *(sits)* الوزير مع زوجته في الشُّرفة ويأكل *(eats)* الغداء في الشمس كلّ يوم خميس، ولكن يوم الخميس الماضي أكل *(ate)* الغداء مع الممرّضات والممرّضين في كافيتريا المستشفى.

ذهبَت *(went)* وزيرة التعليم بالقطار إلى مدرسة صغيرة خارِج المدينة يوم الخميس الماضي. لَمْ تكتب *(didn't write)* الوزيرة خطابات على الكمبيوتر في مكتبها، بَلْ سمعَت *(heard/listened)* من المدرّسين والمدرّسات عن حَياتهم وعَمَلهم.

ويوم الخميس الماضي أيضاً لبس *(put on/wore)* وزير الصناعة قبّعة بلاستيكية صفراء وذهب *(went)* إلى مصنع أسمَنت مع العُمّال والمهندسين في أوتوبيس المصنع. عادةً يلعب *(plays)* الوزير التِّنِس كلّ يوم خميس ولكن يوم الخميس الماضي لَمْ يلعب *(didn't play)* التنس، بَلْ جلس *(sat)* مع العمّال في المصنع وشرب *(drank)* الشاي مَعَهُم.

Exercise 13

1 he rode the bus; **2** a distant town; **3** the female and male nurses; **4** outside the town; **5** but rather she heard; **6** about their life and their work; **7** a cement factory; **8** with the workers; **9** a yellow plastic hat; **10** he didn't play tennis

Unit 19

Exercise 1

١ مارس — شهر مارس بعد فبراير وقبل أبريل.

٢ يونيو — شهر يونيو بعد مايو وقبل يوليو.

٣ سبتمبر — شهر سبتمبر بعد أغسطس وقبل أكتوبر.

٤ أغسطس — شهر أغسطس بعد يوليو وقبل سبتمبر.

٥ يناير — شهر يناير بعد ديسمبر وقبل فبراير.

٦ مايو — شهر مايو بعد أبريل وقبل يونيو.

٧ أكتوبر — شهر أكتوبر بعد سبتمبر وقبل نوفمبر.

٨ أبريل — شهر أبريل بعد مارس وقبل مايو.

Exercise 2
Try to check your sentences with an Arabic-speaker.

Exercise 3

غَداً، فبراير ٢٣، سيحضُر الوزير اجتماعاً مع رئيس الوزراء الساعة الحادية عشرة صباحاً. وبعد ذلك سيَستَقبِل أُستاذة من كلّية الطبّ في مكتبه الساعة الخامسة إلا ربعاً.

Exercise 4
Try to check your diary entries and descriptions with an Arabic-speaker.

Exercise 5
Try to check your presentation with an Arabic-speaker or post it in an online language-learning forum for comment.

Exercise 6

Meaning	*Present*	*Past*	*Form*	*Root*
to heat	يُسَخِّن	سَخَّن	II	سخن
to meet	يُقابِل	قابَل	III	قبل
to teach	يُدَرِّس	دَرَّس	II	درس
to clean	يُنَظِّف	نَظَّف	II	نظف
to try	يُحاوِل	حاوَل	III	حول
to use	يَستَخدِم	اِستَخدَم	X	خدم
to mend/fix	يُصَلِّح	صَلَّح	II	صلح
to enquire	يَستَعلِم	اِستَعلَم	X	علم

Exercise 7

	الشهر
الدراسة في المدرسة	مايو
الامتحانات	يونيو
بيت الجدّ والجدّة	يوليو
لبنان	أغسطس
الدراسة في الجامعة	سبتمبر

Exercise 8

I met Zeinah in the library two weeks ago and I asked her about her plans for the future.
Zeinah said: 'I will study in school until [the month of] May. The month of June is the month of exams. And in the summer I will be busy. In [the month of] July I will travel to the house of my grandfather and my grandmother in the countryside. Then I'll fly to Beirut in August in order to visit my friend in Lebanon. I'll return in September to begin the studies in university.'
I asked her, 'Do you know in which university you'll study?'
Zeinah said, 'Actually I don't know now, but I will know in the last week of August. The university will send an official letter. I hope that the letter is from the University of Oxford or Cambridge!'

Exercise 9

ستَدرس في المدرسة حتّى شهر مايو. شهر يونيو هو شهر الاِمتِحانات. في الصيف ستَكون زينة مَشغولة. في شهر يوليو، ستُسافِر إلى بيت جدّها وجدّتها في الريف، ثمّ ستَطير إلى بيروت في شهر أغسطس لِتَزور صديقتها في لبنان. ستَرجع في سبتمبر لِتَبدأ الدراسة في الجامعة.

Unit 20

Exercise 1

	Arabic film	American film	French film
Thursday showing times	1:30 PM		3:00 PM
Friday showing times	1:30 PM	9:00 PM	6:00 PM
Saturday showing times	4:45 PM		

Exercise 2

١ الساعة الثانية ظهرًا، يوم يناير ١٤

٢ الساعة السادسة والنصف صباحًا، يوم أكتوبر ٢٤

٣ الساعة الثامنة مساءً، يوم يوليو ١٠

٤ الساعة الخامسة إلا ربعًا، يوم ديسمبر ١٥

٥ الساعة السابعة والثلث صباحًا، يوم مارس ٦

٦ الساعة الحادية عشرة إلا خمس دقائق صباحًا، يوم أبريل ١١

Exercise 3

Future	Present	Past	Subject	Meaning
سَأَذْهَب	أَذْهَب	ذَهَبْتُ	أنا	to go
سَتَشْرَب	تَشْرَب	شَرِبَتْ	هي	to drink
سَتُفَضِّل	تُفَضِّل	فَضَّلْتَ	أنتَ	to prefer
سَيَحْضُر	يَحْضُر	حَضَرَ	هو	to attend
سيَقولون	يَقولون	قالوا	هم	to say
سَتَأْخُذين	تَأْخُذين	أَخَذْتِ	أنتِ	to take
سَنَسْتَعْلِم	نَسْتَعْلِم	اِسْتَعْلَمنا	نحن	to enquire
ستَزورون	تَزورون	زُرْتُمْ	أنتم	to visit
سَتُنَظِّف	تُنَظِّف	نَظَّفَتْ	هي	to clean
سَأَعْرِف	أَعْرِف	عَرَفْتُ	أنا	to know
سَيَجْري	يَجْري	جَرَى	هو	to run
سنُسافِر	نُسافِر	سافَرْنا	نحن	to travel
سَيَسْتَخْدِمون	يَسْتَخْدِمون	اِسْتَخْدَموا	هم	to use
ستَرْجِعين	تَرْجِعين	رَجَعْتِ	أنتِ	to return
سَأَلْعَب	أَلْعَب	لَعِبْتُ	أنا	to play
سَتُقابِل	تُقابِل	قابَلْتَ	أنتَ	to meet

Exercise 4

March	France/Belgium
April	Germany
May	England
June	America
July	America
August	Canada
September	Mexico

Exercise 5

Try to check your comparisons with an Arabic-speaker or post them in an online language-learning forum for comment.

Exercise 6

١ كلّ يوم يَحضُر الوزير اجتماعاً.

٢ كلّ يوم تَذهَب زينب إلى البنك.

٣ غداً سَنَزور المتحف في وسط المدينة.

٤ أمس نَظَّفْتُ المطبخ بعد الإفطار.

٥ يوم الخميس القادِم سَيأْخُذون القطار إلى المدرسة.

٦ السبت الماضي ذَهَبَ الأصدقاء إلى المدينة وشَرِبوا القهوة.

٧ السنة الماضي سافَرْنا إلى الريف ولكنّنا لم نَركَب/ما رَكِبْنا الخيل.

٨ كلّ أسبوع يَسْتَقبِل الأمير رئيس الوزراء.

٩ الصيف القادم سَنُسافِر إلى لبنان.

١٠ لم يَلْعَبوا/ما لَعِبوا كُرة الريشة في النادي أمس.

Exercise 7

These are model answers: yours may vary slightly.

١ صلّحتُ المائدة المكسورة.

٢ لم أغسِل/ما غَسَلتُ قميص أحمد. سَأغسِلهُ غداً.

٣ كَتَبتُ خطاباً لأمّي.

٤ لم ألعَب/ما لَعِبتُ التنس في النادي. سألعَب غداً.

٥ لم أحضُر/ما حَضَرتُ الاِجتِماع في البنك. سأحضُرهُ غداً.

٦ طَبَختُ العشاء.

٧ غَسَلتُ الأطباق.

٨ لم أخرُج/ما خَرَجتُ مع الكلب إلى النهر. سأخرُج مَعَهُ غداً.

٩ لم أذهَب/ما ذَهَبتُ إلى السوق. سأذهَب غداً.

١٠ زُرْتُ جدّتي.

English–Arabic glossary

The following glossary contains the key words presented in *Mastering Arabic 1*. The glossary is presented in English alphabetical order.

- The meanings given are as used in this book. There may be alternative English or Arabic meanings. For these, you will need to use a dictionary.
- Plurals are given in brackets after the singular.
- The ending ـات (-āt) in brackets after a singular noun means that the word can be made plural using the sound feminine; the ending ـون/ـين (-ūn/-īn) means that the word can be made plural using the sound masculine (see page 88 to remind yourself of these two plurals).
- Verbs are followed by *(v.)* after the English. (If a word is not followed by *(v.)*, you can presume that it is *not* a verb.) Both the past and present tenses are given in Arabic.

web

Go to the website to download further notes to help you use Arabic dictionaries and online translation sites.

A

about *(a subject, etc.)*	عَنْ
above	فَوْقَ
accountant	مُحاسِب (ون/ين)
actor	مُمَثِّل (ون/ين)
actress	مُمَثِّلة (ات)
actually	في الحَقيقة
address	عُنْوان (عَناوين)
advertising agency	وَكالة الإعْلان
aeroplane	طائِرة (ات)
Africa	أفْريقيا
after	بَعْدَ
after that	بَعْدَ ذلِك
afternoon	بَعْدَ الظُّهْر
agency	وَكالة (ات)
agent	وَكيل (وُكَلاء)
ago *(… ago)*	مُنْذُ …
all	كُلّ
all right!	حَسَناً!
almonds	لَوْز
ambassador	سَفير (سُفَراء)
America	أمْريكا
American	أمْريكيّ (ون/ين)
and	وَ
and so	فَـ
apartment	شَقّة (شُقَق)
apples	تُفّاح
April	أَبْريل

Arab/Arabic *(adj.)*	عَرَبيّ (عَرَب)
Arabic *(language)*	العَرَبيّة
artefact	تُحْفة (تُحَف)
as well	كَذلِك
ask *(v.)*	سَأَل / يَسْأَل
Asia	آسْيا
at *(also used for possession)*	عِنْدَ
attempt *(v.)*	حَاوَل / يُحاوِل
attend *(v.)*	حَضَر / يَحضُر
August	أغُسطُس

B

badminton	كُرة الريشة
bag *(handbag, case, etc.)*	حَقيبة (حَقائِب)
bag *(plastic, paper, etc.)*	كِيس (أكْياس)
baker	خَبّاز (ون/ين)
bakery	مَخْبَز (مَخابِز)
balcony	شُرْفة (شُرَف)
ball	كُرَة (ات)
balloon	بالون (ات)
bananas	مَوْز
bank	بَنْك (بُنوك)
basket	سَلّة (سِلال)
be *(v.)*	كان / يكون
beautiful	جَميل
bed	سَرير (أَسِرَّة)
before	قَبْلَ
before that	قَبْلَ ذلِك

begin *(v.)*	بَدَأ / يَبْدأ
beginning	بِداية (ات)
below	تَحْتَ
beside	بِجانِب
best/better	أَفْضَل
best wishes *(close of letter, etc.)*	مَعَ تَحِيَّاتي
between	بَيْنَ
bicycle	دَرَّاجة (ات)
big	كَبير
bill	حِساب
birthday	عيد ميلاد (أَعْياد ميلاد)
biscuits	بَسكَويت
black *(masc./fem.)*	أَسْوَد / سَوْداء
blog	مُدَوَّنة (ات)
blue *(masc./fem.)*	أَزْرَق / زَرْقاء
boat	مَرْكَب (مَراكِب)
book	كِتاب (كُتُب)
book *(v.)*	حَجَزَ / يَحْجِز
bookshop	مَكتَبة (ات)
bottle	زُجاجة (ات)
box	عُلْبة (عُلَب)
boy	وَلَد (أَوْلاد)
bread	خُبْز
breakfast	إفْطار
broken	مَكْسور
brother	أَخ (إخوَة)
building *(structure)*	بِناء (أَبْنِية)

burger	بورجَر
bus	باص (ات) / أُتوبيس (ات)
busy	مَشْغول
but	لكِن

C

cabin *(on boat)*	قَمْرة (ات)
cabinet *(government)*	مَجْلِس (مَجالِس) الوُزَراء
cake	كَعْك
call *(v.)*	دَعا / يَدعو
camel	جَمَل (جِمال)
can *(possible)*	مُمكِن
candle	شَمعة (شُموع)
capital *(city)*	عاصِمة (عَواصِم)
car	سَيّارة (ات)
carpenter	نَجّار (ون/ين)
carry *(v.)*	حَمَل / يَحمِل
carton	عُلْبة (عُلَب)
certainly!	حاضِر!
chair	كُرْسيّ (كَراسي)
chairman	رَئيس (رُؤَساء)
chairmanship	رِئاسة (ات)
cheap	رَخيص
cheese	جُبْنة
chef	طَبّاخ (ون/ين)
chemistry	الكيمْياء
chicken	دَجاجة (دَجاج)
China	الصّين

Chinese	صينيّ (ون/ين)
chips *(fries)*	بَطاطِس مُحَمَّرَة
cinema	سينِما (ات)
city	مَدينة (مُدُن)
class *(lesson)*	دَرْس (دُروس)
clean *(v.)*	نَظَّف / يُنَظِّف
clear *(sky, water, etc.)*	صَافٍ
clock	ساعة (ات)
cloud	غَيْم (غُيوم)
cloudy	غَائِم
club *(sports, etc.)*	نادٍ (نَوادٍ)
coffee	قَهْوَة
coffee beans	بُنّ
cola	كولا
cold	بارِد
colleague	زَميل (زُمَلاء)
colour	لَوْن (أَلْوان)
company	شَرِكة (ات)
complain	شَكا / يَشْكو
concerning	عَنْ
condition	حال (أَحوال)
conference	مُؤْتَمَر (ات)
continent	قَارة (ات)
cook *(person)*	طَبَّاخ (ون/ين)
cook *(v.)*	طَبَخ / يَطْبُخ
copper	نُحاس
cotton	قُطْن

country	دَوْلة (دُوَل)
countryside	ريف (أَرْياف)
course *(of a meal)*	طَبَق (أطْباق)
court *(tennis, etc.)*	مَلْعَب (مَلاعِب)
couscous	كُسْكُس
cup	فِنْجان (فَناجين)
cupboard	خَزانة (ات)

D

daughter	اِبْنة (بَنات)؛ بِنْت (بَنات)
day	يَوْم (أَيَّام)
day after tomorrow	بَعْدَ غَد
day before yesterday	أَوَّل أَمْس
dear *(opening of letter) (masc./fem.)*	عَزيزي / عَزيزَتي
December	ديسَمبِر
degree *(temperature, etc.)*	دَرَجة (ات)
delicious	شَهيّ؛ لَذيذ
deputy	نائِب (نُوَّاب)
desert	صَحْراء
desk	مَكْتَب (مَكاتِب)
desserts	حَلَوِيّات
different	مُخْتَلِف
Dinar	دينار (دَنانير)
dinner	عَشاء
Dirham	دِرْهَم (دَراهِم)
do *(v.)*	فَعَل / يَفْعَل
doctor	طَبيب (أَطِبّاء)
dog	كَلْب (كِلاب)

donkey	حِمار (حَمير)
door	بـاب (أبْواب)
drawing	رَسْم (رُسوم)
drink *(v.)*	شَرِب / يَشْرَب
drum	طَبْلـة (طُبول)

E

east	شَرْق
eat *(v.)*	أَكَل / يَـأكُل
economy	اِقْتِصاد
education	تَـعْليم
eggs	بَيْض
Egypt	مِصْر
Egyptian	مِصْريّ (ون/ين)
eight	ثَمانِية
eighteen	ثَمانِية عَشَر
eighty	ثَمانِين
eleven	أَحَد عَشَر
embassy	سِفارة (ات)
emir	أَمير (أُمَراء)
emirate	إمارة (ات)
engineer	مُهَنْدِس (ون/ين)
engineering	الـهَنْدَسة
England	إنْجِلترا
English *(adj.)*	إنجِليزيّ (إنجِليز)
English *(language)*	الإنـجِليزيّة
enjoyable	مُمْتِع
enquire	اِسْتَعْلَم / يَسْتَعْلِم

entrance	مَدْخَل (مَداخِل)
evening	مَساء
every	كُلّ
every day	كُلّ يَوْم
exam	اِمْتِحان (ات)
exhibit *(v.)*	عَرَض / يَعْرِض
exhibition	مَعْرَض (مَعارِض)
exit	مَخْرَج (مَخارِج)
exit *(v.)*	خَرَج / يَخْرُج

F

face	وَجْه (وُجوه)
factory	مَصْنَع (مَصانِع)
faculty *(university)*	كُلِّية (ات)
fantastic	رائِع
fast	سَريع
father	أَب (آباء)
February	فَبراير
field	حَقْل (حُقول)
fifteen	خَمْسة عَشَر
fifty	خَمْسين
figs	تين
film	فيلْم (أفلام)
finally	أَخيراً
find *(v.)*	وَجَد / يَجِد
first	أَوَّل
firstly	أَوَّلاً
fish	سَمَك

five	خَمْسة
flag	عَلَم (أَعْلام)
flies	ذُباب
fly *(v.)*	طَار / يَطير
for	لِـ...
forty	أَرْبَعين
four	أَرْبَعة
fourteen	أَرْبَعة عَشَر
France	فَرَنْسا
French	فَرَنْسيّ (ون/ين)
Friday	يَوم الجُمعة
fried	مَقْليّ
friend	صَاحِب (أَصْحاب)؛ صَديق (أَصْدِقاء)
from	مِنْ
fruit	فَواكِه
future	مُسْتَقْبَل

G

game	لُعْبة (لُعَب)
geography	الجُغْرافيا
German	أَلْماني
Germany	أَلْمانيا
girl	بِنْت (بَنات)
give me	أَعْطِني
glass *(material)*	زُجاج
glass *(tumbler)*	كوب (أَكْواب)
go *(v.)*	ذَهَب / يَذْهَب
go back *(v.)*	رَجَع / يَرْجَع؛ عاد / يَعود

go out *(v.)*	خَرَج / يَخرُج
gold	ذَهَب
good evening	مَساء الخَيْر
good evening *(reply)*	مَساء النُّور
good morning	صَباح الخَيْر
good morning *(reply)*	صَباح النُّور
goodbye	مَعَ السَّلامة
grandfather *(plural also = ancestors)*	جَدّ (أجْداد)
grandmother	جَدّة (ات)
great!	رائِع!
green *(masc./fem.)*	أخْضَر / خَضْراء
greeting	تَحِيَّة (ات)
grilled	مَشْويّ
grocer	بَقّال (ون/ين)

H

half	نِصْف
hat	قُبَّعة (ات)
have	عِندَ / لِـ / مَعَ
he	هُوَ
head *(of organisation, etc.)*	رَئيس (رُؤَساء)
health	صِحَّة
hear *(v.)*	سَمِع / يَسْمَع
heart	قَلْب (قلوب)
heat	حَرارة
heat *(v.)*	سَخَّن / يُسَخِّن
heavy	ثَقيل
hello	أَهْلاً

help	مُساعَدة (ات)
helper	مُساعِد (ون/ين)
hen	دَجاجة (دَجاج)
her	...ـــها
here you are *(masc./fem./plural)*	تَفَضَّل / تَفَضَّلي / تَفَضَّلوا
his	...ـــهُ
history	تاريخ
hold *(a meeting, etc.) (v.)*	عَقَد / يَعْقِد
holiday	عُطْلة (عُطَل)
hope *(v.)*	أَمَل / يَأْمَل
hospital	مُسْتَشْفى (مُسْتَشْفيات)
hot	حارّ
hotel	فُنْدُق (فَنادِق)
hour	ساعة (ات)
house	بَيْت (بُيوت)
how?	كَيْفَ؟
how are you?	كَيْفَ الحال؟/كَيْفَ حالك؟
how many?	كَم؟
how much?	بِكَم؟
hundred	مائة (مئات)
husband	زَوْج (أَزْواج)

I

I	أَنا
I'd like...	أُريد...
ice-cream	آيس كريم
important	هامّ
in	في

in front of	أَمام
in the middle of	في وَسَط
increase *(v.)*	زاد / يَزيد
industry	صِناعة (ات)
inexpensive	رَخيص
investigation	تَحقيق (ات)
invite *(v.)*	دَعا / يَدعو
Iraq	العِراق
Iraqi	عِراقيّ (ون/ين)
it *(masc.)*	هُوَ
it *(fem.)*	هِيَ
Italian	اِيطاليّ (ون/ين)
Italy	اِيطاليا

J

January	يَناير
Japan	اليابان
Japanese	يابانيّ (ون/ين)
job *(work)*	عَمَل (أَعْمال)
Jordan	الأُرْدُنّ
Jordanian	أُرْدُنّيّ (ون/ين)
juice	عَصير (عَصائِر)
July	يوليو
June	يونيو

K

key	مِفْتاح (مَفاتيح)
kilo	كيلو
king	مَلِك (مُلوك)

	kitchen	مَطْبَخ (مَطابِخ)
	know *(v.)*	عَرَف / يَعْرِف
L	language	لُغة (ات)
	last *(final)*	آخِر
	laundry/launderette	مَغْسَلة (مَغاسِل)
	law *(academic study)*	الحُقوق
	lead *(v.)*	قاد / يَقود
	leader	زَعيم (زُعَماء)
	leadership	زَعامة (ات)
	leather	جِلْد
	Lebanese	لُبْناني (ون/ين)
	Lebanon	لُبْنان
	lecture	مُحاضَرة (ات)
	left *(direction)*	يَسار
	lesson	دَرْس (دُروس)
	letter *(mail)*	خِطاب (ات)
	library	مَكتَبة (ات)
	Libya	ليبْيا
	Libyan	ليبْيّ (ون/ين)
	life	حَياة
	light *(weight)*	خَفيف
	like *(v.)*	أَحَبّ / يُحِبّ
	like *(I'd like)*	أُريد
	live *(v.)*	سَكَن / يَسْكُن
	long	طَويل
	lunch	غَداء

M

macaroni	مَكَرونة
madam	مَدام
man	رَجُل (رِجال)
manager	مُدير (مُدَراء)
mangoes	مَنجة
many	كَثير
March	مارِس
market	سوق (أسواق)
masterpiece	تُحفْة (تُحَف)
matches	كَبْريت
mathematics	الرياضِيّات
May	مايو
me	...ني
meat	لَحْم
medicine *(study)*	الطِّبّ
meet *(v.)*	قابَل / يُقابِل
meeting	اِجْتِمَاع (ات)
mend *(v.)*	صَلَّح / يُصلِّح
middle	وَسَط
Middle East	الشَّرق الأوْسَط
mild	مُعْتَدِل
milk	حَليب
million	مَلْيون (ملايين)
minister	وَزير (وُزَراء)
ministry	وِزارَة (ات)
minute *(time)*	دَقيقة (دَقائِق)
moderate	مُعْتَدِل

	monastery	دَيْر (أدْيِرة)
	Monday	يَوم الاِثْنَين
	month	شَهْر (شُهور)
	more/most	أَكْثَر
	morning	صَباح
	mosque	مَسْجِد (مَساجِد)
	mother	أُمّ (أُمَّهات)
	mountain	جَبَل (جِبال)
	museum	مَتْحَف (مَتاحِف)
	music	موسيقى
	my	...ـي
N	name	اِسْم (أَسْماء)
	nation	دَولة (دُوَل)
	nationality	جِنْسيَّة (ات)
	necklace	قِلادة (قَلائِد)
	new	جَديد
	newspaper	جَريدَة (جَرائِد)
	nine	تِسْعة
	nineteen	تِسْعة عَشَر
	ninety	تِسْعين
	no	لا
	noon	ظُهْر
	north	شَمال
	November	نُوفَمبِر
	now	اَلآن
	number *(numeral)*	رَقْم (أَرْقام)
	nurse	مُمَرِّضة (ات)

O

October	أُكْتوبَر
official *(adjective)*	رَسْميّ
office	مَكْتَب (مَكاتِب)
oil	زَيت (زُيوت)
old *(of objects)*	قَديم
old *(of people)*	كَبير السِّن
Oman	عُمان
Omani	عُمانيّ (ون/ين)
on	عَلَى
on the left of	عَلَى يَسار
on the right of	عَلَى يَمين
one	واحِد
onions	بَصَل
open *(v.)*	فَتَح / يَفْتَح
oranges	بُرْتُقال
our	...ـنا
outside (of)	خارِج

P

packet	عُلْبة (عُلَب)
palace	قَصْر (قُصور)
palm tree	نَخْلة (نَخْل)
party *(celebration)*	حَفْلة (ات)
past *(the past)*	الماضي
pen	قَلَم (أقْلام)
people *(the people; the populace)*	شَعْب (شُعوب)
period *(of time)*	فَتْرة (فَتَرات)
photographer	مُصَوِّر (ون/ين)

picture/photograph	صورة (صُوَر)
piece	قِطْعة (قِطَع)
pigeons	حَمام
pitch *(football, etc.)*	مَلْعَب (مَلاعِب)
pizza	بيتزا
plan	خِطّة (خِطَط)
plane	طائِرة (ات)
plastic	بلاستيك
plate	طَبَق (أطْباق)
play *(v.)*	لَعِب / يَلعَب
playing field	مَلْعَب (مَلاعِب)
please *(masc./fem.)*	مِن فَضْلَك / مِن فَضلِك
poor	فَقير (فُقَراء)
potatoes	بَطاطِس
Pound *(money)*	جُنَيه (ات)
prefer *(v.)*	فَضَّل / يُفَضِّل
prepare *(v.)*	جَهَّز / يُجَهِّز
presidency	رِئاسة
president	رَئيس (رُؤَساء)
price	سِعْر (أَسْعار)
prince	أَمير (أُمَراء)
princess	أَميرة (ات)
private	خاصّ
profession	مِهْنة (مِهَن)
professor	أُسْتاذ (أساتِذة)
pupil *(school)*	تِلميذ (تَلامِذة؛ تَلاميذ)
put on *(clothes, etc.) (v.)*	لَبِس / يَلْبَس

Q

quarter	رُبْع (أَرباع)

R

rain	مَطَر (أَمْطار)
rainy	مُمْطِر
rather *(but rather)*	بَلْ
receive *(guests, etc.) (v.)*	اِسْتَقْبَل / يَسْتَقبِل
red *(masc./fem.)*	أَحْمَر / حَمْراء
religious education	التَّربية الدينيّة
restaurant	مَطْعَم (مَطاعِم)
return *(v.)*	رَجَع / يَرجِع؛ عاد / يَعود
rice	أَرُز
rich	غَنيّ
ride/take transport *(v.)*	رَكِب / يَرْكَب
riding *(horses)*	رُكوب (الخَيْل)
right *(direction)*	يَمين
ring	خاتِم (خَواتِم)
river	نَهْر (أَنْهار)
River Nile	نَهْر النيل
Riyal	رِيال (ات)
roasted *(in the oven)*	في الفُرْن
robbery	سَرِقة (ات)
room	غُرْفة (غُرَف)
rose	وَرْدَة (وَرْد)
royal	مَلَكيّ
run *(v.)*	جَرَى/يَجْري
Russia	روسيا
Russian	روسيّ (روس)

S

salad	سَلَطة (ات)
sandals	صَندَل (صَنادِل)
sandwich	سَنْدويتش (ات)
Saturday	يوم السَّبْت
Saudi *(country)*	السَّعوديّة
Saudi *(nationality)*	سَعوديّ (ون/ين)
say *(v.)*	قال / يَقول
science	عِلْم (عُلوم)
school	مَدْرَسة (مَدارِس)
sea	بَحْر (بِحار)
second *(adj.)*	ثاني
sell *(v.)*	باع / يَبيع
September	سِبتَمبِر
service	خِدْمة (ات)
service *(at your service)*	تَحْت أَمْرَك
seven	سَبْعة
seventeen	سَبْعة عَشَر
seventy	سَبْعين
shampoo	شَامبو
shape	شَكْل (أشْكال)
she	هِيَ
sheikh	شَيْخ (شُيوخ)
shirt	قَميص (قُمْصان)
short	قَصير
shorts	شورت (ات)
show *(v.)*	عَرَض / يَعْرِض
silk	حَرير

silver	فِضّة
since *('since 2013', etc.)*	مُنْذُ
sir	سَيِّدي
sister	أُخْت (أَخَوات)
sit down *(v.)*	جلَس / يَجلِس
sitting room	غُرفة الجُلوس
six	سِتّة
sixteen	سِتّة عَشَر
sixty	سِتّين
sky	سَماء (سَمَوات)
sleep *(v.)*	نام / يَنام
small	صَغير
so	فَـ...
soap	صابون
son	اِبْن (أبْناء)
south	جَنوب
Spain	أَسْبانيا
Spanish	أَسْبانيّ (ون/ين)
sport	رِياضة (ات)
state *(condition)*	حال (أحْوال)
state *(country)*	دَوْلة (دُوَل)
stay *(in hotel, etc.) (v.)*	نَزَل / يَنْزِل
street	شارِع (شَوارِع)
strong *(bodily strength)*	قَوِيّ
strong *(emphatic)*	شَديد
student	طالِب (طَلَبة؛ طُلاب)
study *(v.)*	دَرَس / يَدْرُس

Sudan	السودان
Sudanese	سودانيّ (ون/ين)
sugar	سُكَّر
sun	شَمْس
Sunday	يوم الأحَد
sunny	مُشْمِس
sunrise	شُروق الشَّمْس
supper	عَشاء
sweet	حُلْو
swimming pool	مَسْبَح (مَسابِح)
sword	سَيف (سُيوف)
Syria	سوريا
Syrian	سوريّ (ون/ين)

T

table	مائِدة (مَوائِد)
take *(v.)*	أَخَذ / يَأْخُذ
tall	طَويل
tea	شاي
teacher	مُدَرِّس (ون/ين)
telephone	تليفون (ات)
television	تليفِزيون (ات)
temperature	دَرَجة الحَرارة
ten	عَشَرة
tennis	تَنِس
tent	خَيْمة (خِيام)
thank you	شُكْراً
theft	سَرِقة (ات)

their *(masc.)*	...ـهُمْ
their *(fem.)*	...ـهُنَّ
then	ثُمَّ
there is/there are	هُناكَ
there is not/there are not	لَيْسَ هُناكَ
these *(people)*	هؤُلاءِ
these *(non-humans)*	هذِهِ
they *(masc.)*	هُمْ
they *(fem.)*	هُنَّ
they *(non-humans)*	هِيَ
thief	لِصّ (لُصوص)
third *(a third)*	ثُلْث (أَثْلاث)
thirteen	ثَلاثة عَشَر
thirty	ثَلاثَين
this *(masc.)*	هذا
this *(fem.)*	هذِهِ
three	ثَلاثة
throw *(v.)*	رَمَى / يَرمي
Thursday	يوم الخَميس
time	وَقْت (أَوقات)
tin *(of beans, etc.)*	عُلبة (عُلَب)
to/for *(in order to/for you, etc.)*	لِـ...
to *(towards)*	إلَى
today	اليَوْم
tomatoes	طَماطِم
tomorrow	غَداً
toothpaste	مَعْجون الأسنان

total	مَجْموع
towards	إلى
tower	بُرْج (أَبْراج)
town	مَدينة (مُدُن)
toy	لُعْبة (لُعَب)
train	قِطار (ات)
travel	سافَر / يُسافِر
tree	شَجَرة (شَجَر)
trip *(journey)*	رِحْلة (ات)
trousers	سِرْوال (سَراويل)
truth	حَقيقة (حَقائِق)
try *(attempt) (v.)*	حاوَل / يُحاوِل
try *(sample) (v.)*	جَرَّب / يُجَرِّب
tube	أُنبوبة (أنابيب)
Tuesday	يوم الثُلاثاء
twelve	اِثنا عَشَر
twenty	عِشْرين
two	اِثْنان

U

ugly	قَبيح
united	مُتَّحِد
United Arab Emirates (UAE)	الإمارات العَرَبيّة المُتَّحِدة
university	جامِعة (ات)
until	حَتّى
use *(v.)*	اِسْتَخْدَم / يَسْتَخْدِم
user	مُسْتَخْدِم (ون/ين)
usually	عادةً

V

vegetables	خَضْرَوات
visit *(n.)*	زِيارة (ات)
visit *(v.)*	زار / يَزور

W

waiter	جَرسون
wake up *(v.)*	صَحَى / يَصْحو
walk *(v.)*	مَشى / يَمْشي
wash *(v.)*	غَسَل / يَغْسِل
washing powder	مَسْحوق الغَسيل
watch *(wrist) (n.)*	سَاعة (ات)
watch *(witness/see) (v.)*	شاهَد / يُشاهِد
water	مَاء
watermelons	بَطِّيخ
we	نَحْنُ
weak	ضَعيف
wear *(v.)*	لَبِس / يَلبَس
weather	طَقْس
website	مَوْقِع (مَواقِع)
Wednesday	يَوْم الأَرْبِعاء
week	أُسبوع (أَسابيع)
west	غَرْب
what *(+ noun)*?	ما؟
what *(+ verb)*?	ماذا؟
what's your name?	ما اِسْمك؟
when?	مَتَى؟
where?	أَيْنَ؟
which?	أَيّ؟

	white *(masc./fem.)*	أَبيَض / بَيضاء
	whole/unbroken	سَليم
	why?	لِماذا؟
	wife	زَوْجة (ات)
	wind *(fem.)*	ريح (رِياح)
	window	شُبّاك (شَبابيك)
	with	مَعَ، بِـ...
	wood	خَشَب
	work *(n.)*	عَمَل (أَعْمال)
	work *(v.)*	عَمِل / يَعْمَل
	worker	عامِل (عُمّال)
	world (*the World*)	العالَم
	write *(v.)*	كَتَب / يَكتُب
Y	year	سَنة (سَنوات / سِنون)؛ عام (أعْوام)
	yellow *(masc./fem.)*	أصْفَر / صَفْراء
	Yemen	اليَمَن
	Yemeni	يَمَنيّ (ون/ين)
	yes	نَعَم
	yesterday	أَمْس
	you *(masc./fem./plural)*	أَنْتَ / أَنْتِ / أَنْتُمْ
	young	صَغير السِنّ
	your *(masc./fem./plural)*	...ـكَ / ...ـكِ / ...ـكُمْ
Z	zero	صِفْر

Index

The following index contains the key Arabic themes, vocabulary sets, structures and grammar in *Mastering Arabic 1*, referenced by page number. You can use the index to revisit information for reference at any point in your studies.

web

Go to the website to download a learning and teaching grid showing the coverage of key topics across the *Mastering Arabic* series.